Report Writing for Police and Correctional Officers

Report Writing for Police and Correctional Officers

By Bruce L. Berg, Gregory Gibbs, and Michael E. Miller

McGraw Hill

Connect
Learn
Succeed™

REPORT WRITING FOR POLICE AND CORRECTIONAL OFFICERS

Published by McGraw-Hill, a business unit of The McGraw-Hill Companies, Inc.,
1221 Avenue of the Americas, New York, NY 10020. Copyright © 2013 by The
McGraw-Hill Companies, Inc. All rights reserved. Printed in the United States of
America. No part of this publication may be reproduced or distributed in any form
or by any means, or stored in a database or retrieval system, without the prior written
consent of The McGraw-Hill Companies, Inc., including, but not limited to, in any
network or other electronic storage or transmission, or broadcast for distance learning.

Some ancillaries, including electronic and print components, may not be available
to customers outside the United States.

♻ This book is printed on recycled, acid-free paper containing 10% postconsumer
waste.

1 2 3 4 5 6 7 8 9 0 QDB/QDB 1 0 9 8 7 6 5 4 3 2

ISBN 978-0-07-81114-64
MHID 0-07-81114-63

Vice President & Editor-in-Chief: *Michael Ryan*
Vice President of Specialized Publishing: *Janice M. Roerig-Blong*
Sponsoring Editor: *Jessica Cannavo*
Marketing Coordinator: *Angela FitzPatrick*
Lead Project Manager: *Jane Mohr*
Design Coordinator: *Margarite Reynolds*
Cover Designer: *Studio Montage, St. Louis, Missouri*
Cover Image: *Brand X Pictures*
Buyer: *Susan K. Culbertson*
Media Project Manager: *Sridevi Palani*
Compositor: *Laserwords Private Limited*
Typeface: *10/12 Sabon LT Std Roman*
Printer: *Quad/Graphics*

All credits appearing on page or at the end of the book are considered to be an
extension of the copyright page.

Library of Congress Cataloging-in-Publication Data
Berg, Bruce L. (Bruce Lawrence), 1954–
    Report writing for police and correctional officers / by Bruce L. Berg,
        Gregory Gibbs and Michael E. Miller.
        p. cm.
    ISBN 978-0-07-811146-4 (alk. paper)
    1. Police reports. 2. Report writing. 3. Criminal investigation. I. Gibbs, Gregory.
II. Miller, Michael E. III. Title.
    HV7936.R53B47 2013
    808.06'6363—dc23
                                                    2011036295

www.mhhe.com

Dedication

To Jill
To Kris
Gregg Gibbs

To Betty and Shea
Mike Miller

Bruce L. Berg received his PhD in sociology from Syracuse University. Dr. Berg served as an assistant professor at Florida State University in the School of Criminology (currently known as the College of Criminology and Criminal Justice); he later joined the faculty in the Department of Sociology at the University of Massachusetts, Harbor Campus, as a visiting assistant professor. Dr. Berg assisted in the development of a new PhD program housed in the Department of Criminology at Indiana University of Pennsylvania. In 1998 he began teaching in the Department of Criminal Justice at California State University, Long Beach, where he served as a full professor and graduate advisor to the department's Accelerated Masters Program. Previously, Dr. Berg served as the department's chair and graduate advisor and as the director of Interdisciplinary Studies for the university. He published five textbook titles, including three on police topics, and nearly four dozen referred articles and an assortment of invited essays and encyclopedia entries in the areas of policing, qualitative research, juvenile delinquency, and women in policing and corrections.

Sadly, Dr. Berg passed away before this project could be completed. His family and friends, as well as students, past, present, and future, will sorely miss his wisdom, insight, and humor.

Gregg Gibbs received a bachelor of science in law and a juris doctorate from Western State University, College of Law. He is an active member of the California Bar Association and handles cases in civil law. Gibbs has been teaching classes at California State University, Long Beach, since 2001. He teaches in the areas of policing, criminal law, search and seizure, the adjudication process, and substance abuse. Gibbs has been a member of the Irvine (California) Police Department for thirty-two years, including more than thirteen years as a sergeant working various assignments. He worked nearly every assignment in the department from traffic investigation and enforcement to field training officer and FTO program manager. Gibbs also has experience as a narcotics investigator specializing in financial investigations. As a member of the State of California Commission on Peace Officer's Standards and Training Ad Hoc Committee on Field Training, he assisted in the development of statewide standards for training new officers. Gibbs is also a team leader on the department's SWAT.

Michael E. Miller received his PhD in public affairs from the University of Central Florida, with a concentration in criminal justice. He holds master's and bachelor of arts degrees in public administration. Miller is currently an assistant professor in the School of Legal Studies at South College in Knoxville, Tennessee, where he teaches criminal justice courses. Previously he taught criminal justice and sociology courses as an adjunct instructor at the University of Central Florida. In November 2007 Miller retired from the Orange County Sheriff's Office in Orlando, Florida, after twenty-five years of service, holding the rank of captain. During his career he worked in Uniformed Patrol, Special Investigations (Narcotics), and Criminal Investigations. He held leadership and management positions as patrol supervisor, Narcotics Unit sergeant, Special Investigations Division lieutenant, Uniformed Patrol Sector commander, and Criminal Investigations Division major case commander. Miller is a 1999 graduate of the Southern Police Institute's (SPI) Administrative Officers' Course at the University of Louisville.

INTRODUCTION

One of the most important, yet often ignored, aspects of police and correctional work is report writing. A well-written report can assist a prosecutor in obtaining a conviction, whereas a poorly written report can be used by the defense to suggest sloppy police work or confused thinking on the part of an arresting or investigative officer. Such tactics cause juries to contemplate whether an officer who is careless in his or her writing might also be careless in other aspects of police work. Similarly, liability issues can soar when a correctional officer drafts an unreadable or grammatically flawed report.

Police and correctional work requires a considerable amount of writing—something television programs seldom clearly illustrate during their faced-paced shootouts and police chase scenes, or when depicting prison galleries with tiers of screaming and/or fighting inmates. Once the smoke clears, the screeching tires are silent, and the inmates are settled, officers involved in such activities in the real world are challenged with the task of writing up these incidents. Whether an officer is working on patrol, participating in an investigation, or working in a corrections facility, he or she must write reports daily. These reports will be used, sometimes for years, during the course of a criminal investigation, prosecution, and incarceration of a suspect and/or felon. The reports will be read by supervisors, police administrators, prosecutors, defense counsel, judges, jurors, wardens, and more and more frequently the media. Consequently, police report writing must be clear and concise and contain a description of the necessary elements of the crime to permit a prosecutor to convince a judge or jury that the accused did in fact commit the crime. Correctional reports must similarly offer clear and concise writing to ensure that proper services are obtained and unnecessary liabilities are not incurred. While these qualities are present in all good police reports, the excellent report helps the prosecutor describe the scene and the state of mind of the individuals involved in an incident.

The authors of *Report Writing for Police and Correctional Officers* each possess extensive experience from law enforcement, criminal law, and academia. Their combined work experience provides a more integrated and multidisciplinary approach to learning and applying the fundamentals of police and correctional report writing. The practical examples in this book originate from the real-world experiences of the authors in patrol operations and criminal investigations. The mechanics and fundamentals of English and grammar are drawn from many years of experience as published authors and scholars.

This book offers potential and in-service officers an opportunity to strengthen their writing ability by providing a brief introduction to the necessary aspects of the written English language as well as specific police- and correctional-related report writing skills. It begins with a general description of report writing and its importance to both police and correctional officers (Chapter 1), and proceeds to cover various important technical aspects of writing (parts of speech, Chapter 2; and grammar and mechanics of writing, Chapter 3). Next, the book examines necessary areas and issues associated specifically with police report writing (taking field notes, Chapter 4; writing a good narrative, Chapter 5; writing crime and incident reports, Chapter 6; writing arrest reports, Chapter 7; and writing search warrants, Chapter 8). The final chapter (Chapter 9) examines reports endemic to correctional officers and settings and expressly considers their importance and nature.

FEATURES OF THE BOOK

As indicated, *Report Writing for Police and Correctional Officers* includes nine chapters. Each chapter begins with a chapter outline of key topics, and an introduction. At the end of each chapter there is a summary on main ideas, a series of exercises related to the chapter, and a list of glossary terms used in that chapter. Glossary terms are indicated within the chapter by bold font and are defined at the end of the book. The exercises are carefully designed for hands-on student practice of concepts learning in each chapter. The book includes perforated pages to permit the exercises at the end of chapters to be torn out and turned in for review, and/or grading by the instructor.

Pedagogically, there are three types of exercises. First, we have written exercises that ask the student to identify writing mistakes as covered in the preceding chapter. Second, there are opportunities for students to complete specific types of reports discussed in a given chapter in response to a set of facts we have provided. Third, there are two types of practice exercises that ask the student to correct entries that were intentionally created with errors in them. These errors will involve grammar and/or mechanical elements. The second kind of exercise in this category involves inclusion of proper content elements. All of the exercises have instructor support material within the instructor's manual. The book ends with a list of references and an appendix that includes commonly misspelled homophones, commonly misspelled words used in reports, and commonly misused homonyms.

SUPPLEMENTS

Please visit the book specific website at http://www.mhhe.com/bergrw1e. The password-protected instructor site contains an Instructor's Manual, Test Bank, and chapter PowerPoints.

COURSE

Any number of schools could use this book as an essential supplement. It is appropriate for use in courses at junior or community colleges, technical colleges, online colleges, four-year colleges, and university settings with departments of administration of justice, criminal justice, and/or criminology. Many of these programs include a course on police writing, writing for criminal justice practitioners, or similarly titled classes. Some schools offer classes in basic police and/or correctional officer writing, skills for professional development, police report writing, or similarly worded course titles.

acknowledgments

The authors would like to gratefully acknowledge the significant contributions of the following individuals and reviewers who assisted in the development of this book. This work could not have been completed without their diligence and commitment to the writing and editing process. The quality of the book is a direct result of their efforts.

Joanne Anzenberger, *Housatonic Community College*

Patricia Brown, *Eagle Gate College*

David Houston, *South College*

Kevin Dooley, *Central New Mexico Community College*

Steven Lee Martin, *Des Moines Area Community College*

Luke J. Tillman, *Southwestern Illinois College*

1

Police Reports and Their Purpose

INTRODUCTION

This book is intended to provide basic report writing skills for the inexperienced and experienced police and correctional officer, as well as for students interested in becoming police or correctional officers. The effect from a poorly written report can be as disastrous as arriving too late at the scene of a shooting, only to find wounded or dead victims. In other words, a bad report can injure or kill an investigation as quickly as a bullet can injure or kill a victim. While most of our examples and language are directed to *officers,* students should still think about and use the tips and rules offered to improve their writing while in school as well as once they are on the job. We begin by discussing why effective police and correctional reports are necessary.

THE NEED FOR EFFECTIVE POLICE AND CORRECTIONAL REPORTS

One of the most important, yet often ignored aspects of police and correctional work is report writing. Television shows—a major influence on many people's decisions about joining the police or corrections—place little or no emphasis on the kinds of writing or the amount of writing necessary in police and correctional work daily. Nonetheless, a well-written report can assist a prosecutor in obtaining a conviction whereas a poorly written report can be used by the defense to suggest sloppy police work, or confused thinking on the part of an arresting or investigative officer. Such tactics cause juries to start thinking about whether an officer who is careless in his or her writing might also be careless in other aspects of police work. Similarly, liability issues can soar when a correctional officer drafts an unreadable or grammatically flawed report on some fight or other incident occurring in the jail or prison.

Ironically, when you think about the requisite skills needed to be a good police officer or to perform the job well, you seldom think about skills associated with writing. Rather, you most likely think of defensive tactics, upper-body strength, decision-making skills, proficiency with firearms, and perhaps several other special-ized tasks. Yet, the ability to prepare high-quality police reports is likely not to even be on the list. When you consider the requisite skills for correctional work, you may be at an even greater disadvantage because little information about exactly what cor-rectional officers do has trickled down to the general public. What is known is more likely directed toward custodial activities such as escorting prisoners from one side of a correctional facility to another, or breaking up fights and riots. To be sure, little information is known by the general public concerning the kinds or amounts of writing that is endemic to correctional officers.

The truth of the matter is that police and correctional work requires a con-siderable amount of writing—something television programs seldom clearly illus-trate during their faced-paced shootouts and police chase scenes, or when depicting prison galleries with tiers of screaming and/or fighting inmates. Once the smoke clears, the screeching tires are silent, and the inmates are settled, officers involved in such activities in the real world will be set with the task of writing up these incidents. Whether in patrol, investigations, or custody, officers write reports every day and these reports will be used, sometimes for years, during the course of a criminal investigation, prosecution, and incarceration of a suspect and/or felon. These reports will be read by supervisors, police and correctional administrators, prosecutors, defense counsels, judges, jurors, wardens, and more and more frequently the media. Police reports must be written clearly and concisely and contain a description of the necessary elements of the crime to permit a prosecutor to convince a judge or jury that the accused did in fact commit the crime. Correctional reports must similarly offer clear and concise writing to ensure that proper services are obtained, criminal elements are included, and unnecessary liabilities are not incurred.

Unfortunately, a good deal of law enforcement and correctional officer writing is cluttered with unnecessary verbiage, overly formal language, unclear and imprecise reporting that lacks necessary description of the **corpus delicti** (body or elements of the crime) of the incident being reported, mistakes, jargon, and inconsistencies. Part of the problem may be that there is a kind of culture of police and correctional writing that has been longstanding in most police communities and correctional institutions, and which seems to be perpetuated during the field training process (Rutledge, 2000). This custom of writing instructs young, inexperienced officers to use too many words and to write like a bad B-movie script with improper sentence construction and frequently is redundant and drafted in passive voice. The real problem with this old and traditional custom of police and correctional writing style is that it is almost like teaching officers a second language, when they already know English and could be writing using standard conventions of grammar, syntax, active voice construction, and most of all, proper spelling.

To best understand the importance of the written report, consider the importance of writing as a means of communicating and maintaining records. Police and correctional writing is not designed to entertain, or even be terribly creative, but rather to communicate necessary pieces of information that may be important later during a secondary investigation, or if the case goes to court, during prosecution. Wallace and Roberson (2004, p. 3) suggested that *writing* is a method of recording and communicating ideas through a system of visual marks. While this definition may seem simplistic, it is actually quite complex.

Let's consider it. The first part involves the recording of ideas in a systematic manner that is shared by others so that it may be communicated and understood. The notion that it is *recorded* suggests that it is a more lasting or permanent conveyance of ideas than through spoken language; thus, writing permits review, consideration, revision, and even forecasting of ideas to other situations. Finally, the concept of a system of visual marks indicates that there is a specific manner in which these symbols of shared meanings must be ordered if they are to be meaningful to others. In other words, they must be legible and placed in an accurate order, and the correct symbols must be used if they are to provide the intended shared meanings. *Twin talk,* or the secret language between some twins, occurs among about 40 percent of identical twins (Astington & Baird, 2005). Frequently, these twins develop various gestures, nicknames, abbreviations, and terminology that they use only with one another; other people, even other family members, are at a loss about what is being said. Such a communication system is simply unworkable for police and correctional officers. Thus, even when other police or correctional officers may be able to read and understand the reports of colleagues, the prose must be similarly understandable to many other types of people.

Another definition of writing, more specific to police reports, can be found in the work of Frazee and Davis (2004) who wrote, "Traditionally, a report meant a 'police report' or narrative you have to write after completing an investigation. But, actually, reports take many different forms. A report is defined as the following: any documentation recorded on a departmental form, or other approved medium (computer disks), and maintained as a permanent record" (p. 86). In short, these documents involve a kind of technical writing, and not a secret communication, or a creative piece of literature.

Police and correctional officers' reports should be understood as a category of technical writing, and as indicated earlier, the business of technical writing is quite a bit different than usual essay and creative types of writing taught in high schools and colleges. It is not, however, constructed in a foreign language and should be guided by the same structural and grammatical rules as any other standard written English format. Police and correctional reports provide a means for maintaining official records of events and incidents, including those actions that officers may have done or may have been unable to do, or simply failed to do. Police and correctional reports are important documents and must be understood as representing official records or specific agencies.

RECORD-KEEPING SYSTEMS

Record-keeping systems are systems, processes, and technology used to capture and maintain official records in criminal justice agencies. You might reasonably ask why police agencies and correctional institutions need to keep official records. The obvious answers, of course, are that these reports document criminal or, in some cases, rule-violating incidents; or they may be used to maintain a record of investigative tasks as they are accomplished during that segment of the event; or they accurately record what transpired for certain other pertinent players in the game who, while not present, will need to know the facts of the incident (e.g., investigators, administrators, and prosecuting and defense attorneys).

However, there are a number of less obvious reasons to maintain accurate, well-written records. Among these are efforts on the part of agencies to support or defeat allegations of wrongdoing, or to provide necessary evidence of proper policy and procedures having been used to avoid liability lawsuits.

The Value of Reports

Reports provide the data needed to investigate and apprehend criminals and to solve crimes. In correctional settings, reports similarly allow for investigations of incidents and events that occur in the facility. Investigators and patrol officers frequently use reports to refresh their memory before testifying in court. Trials and court hearings may occur months or years after an incident or arrest. A well-written report can make an officer's testimony much more accurate and valuable. A poorly written or inaccurate report can create doubt in the mind of the jury as to the veracity or competence of the officer. A few minutes taken to write a complete and accurate investigative report can save an officer or investigator considerable embarrassment and ridicule later on the witness stand.

In some agencies, officers type their reports on typewriters or computers, and then file the paper versions. Others use computers to input their reports directly into the agency's information storage system and database, thereby maintaining an electronic record of the reports. Some police departments have taken to using a digital dictation system, in which officers use a telephone to reach a special digital computer processor that handles the officer's voice data like data keyed in from a computer (Associated Press, 2004; Manning, 2000). However the data are stored, the reports are a valuable asset to the department by performing the following functions:

- Provide a written record and a readily accessible memory bank of police and correctional facility business and information.
- Refresh an officer's memory regarding further investigation and administration.
- Provide a means of controlling communication throughout the police department or correctional institution and their associated agencies.
- Provide a database of information for solving similar crimes, perhaps committed by the same criminal or inmate.
- Furnish a base of accurate statistical information on which decisions about resource allocation and policy may be based.
- Aid in identifying criminal, problem, or behavioral patterns, which in turn allows the development of intervention plans.
- Aid in assessing the effectiveness of personnel distribution and analyzing overall agency operations.
- Assist in identifying unusual or periodic intra-agency problems.
- Assist in documenting needs for budget requests and justifications.
- Produce statistical information to be contributed it local, state, or FBI crime databases.
- Provide a vital tool for an agency in carrying out its varied objectives.
- Provide a source of accurate, detailed, and succinct information to prosecute a criminal or inmate where a law has been violated.

AN OVERVIEW OF BASIC WRITING ELEMENTS FOR REPORTS

A number of major issues will be discussed in greater detail throughout the chapters of this book. Among these are spelling and jargon use, verb tense, active and passive voice constructions, pronoun agreement, first- versus third-person writing, gender neutrality, excessive verbiage and legalese, and accuracy, conciseness, and clarity. To ensure that you fully appreciate and understand these basic issues, each is explained briefly in the following sections.

Spelling and Jargon Use

Whether you are a good speller or a mediocre one, it is a good idea to have a standard paperbound dictionary handy when writing reports. If you are not sure how something is spelled, it is unwise to guess and hope you have spelled it correctly. Look up the word and be sure it has been spelled correctly. When writing on a computer, most word processing programs will have a *spelling and grammar* check that will automatically underline a misspelled word, usually in red. If the spell check is unable to offer the correct spelling of your uniquely created spelling arrangement, do not leave it spelled incorrectly. Either look it up in a paperbound dictionary or choose a different word that you can spell correctly. Similarly, avoid using **jargon**; these are specialized terms with specific meanings associated with a particular occupation or profession. Granted, if you are a police officer using various terms associated with *cop speak,* other police officers will likely understand what you have written. However, as stated, many people—including non–police officers—are likely to read these reports and may or may not be able to understand the various elements of jargon. It is important to keep reports clearly written and understandable. The best way to ensure this is to write in active direct sentences omitting as much jargon as possible. For example, do not use penal or correctional codes and sections, unless they are specific to the crime(s) or incident listed in the report; and define what these codes are in that report at least the first time the code is used. When slang or jargon is used, it should be only when the subject of the report has used these terms, and you are quoting directly.

Verb Tense

Before even discussing verb tense, let's define what a verb is. Most grammar books will tell you that a verb is a word that shows some sort of action (*run, jump, hit, kick,* etc.) or suggests a state of being (*is, are, was ,were, am,* and so forth) (see, for example, Straus, 2008). In both police and correctional officer report writing, verbs are likely to be used with a good deal of regularity, so let's now consider **verb tense**. Three major tenses tend to be used in police and correctional report writing: present, past, and future. Present tense involves a construction describing a current event or occurrence:

> I am notifying my superior about the incident.

Past tense involves a construction describing something that has occurred already:

> I notified my superior about the incident.

Future tense involves a construction where something is described as occurring later or at some time in the future:

> I will notify my superior later today.

Active and Passive Voice Constructions

Active voice allows the reader to understand who did what to whom. In other words, when the subject of a sentence is in action (acts or performs some activity) the verb is in active voice. When the subject of the sentence is the recipient of some action, the verb is in the **passive voice**.

> Officer Billington used his handcuffs to restrain the violent inmate.
> [active voice]

> Acting violently, the inmate was restrained with handcuffs.
> [passive voice]

The first case tells us who did what action to whom, namely, Officer Billington's action of handcuffing the inmate. In the second sentence, however, we know only what happened to the inmate—that he was handcuffed—but not who handcuffed him. It is best to write reports in active voice because such sentences tend to be clear and concise and provide correct and accurate information.

Pronoun Agreement

Pronouns are words that are used to take the place of, or to refer back to, nouns or some other pronoun. The pronoun used should agree with the noun it is being used to replace, called **pronoun agreement**. Pronouns permit us to speak about people, places, and things without unnecessary repetition.

> Officer Johnson arrived at an active crime scene and drew Officer Johnson's gun.

The awkwardness of this sentence should be obvious as you read the sentence; if you recite the sentence aloud, however, it will likely also sound odd or awkward. A more effective version of this sentence would state it as:

> Officer Johnson arrived at an active crime scene and drew <u>his</u> gun.

It is also important that the reader be able to discern to whom the pronoun is referring. Frequently, people misuse pronouns (or overuse them) creating awkwardness and confusion in the sentence. For example,

> Officer Johnson and the suspect both had weapons drawn; <u>he</u> then fired <u>his</u> weapon.

The obvious confusion here is who shot whom? A more effective version of this sentence would inform the reader exactly who did the shooting:

> Officer Johnson and the suspect both had weapons drawn; Johnson then fired his weapon.

The use of pronouns in report writing will be examined in greater detail in Chapter 2.

First- versus Third-Person Writing

Many police departments and correctional agencies have traditionally instructed their new officers to draft reports using **third person** (referring to the point of view of the noun—discussed more fully in Chapter 2). This may have involved expressions such as *this officer, the undersigned officer, this writer,* or even *the responding officer.* The basic logic underlying these efforts was the belief that such a writing style would offer a greater amount of objectivity to the report, thereby creating a more professional type of technical writing. Unfortunately, objectivity is achieved not through third-person-oriented writing, but through accurate factual report writing, with the omission of personal opinions and inappropriate types of statements or epitaphs. As we will reiterate in Chapter 2, police and correctional officers must take ownership of their statements by using the **first person** in their reports—a style of writing where the writer uses *I* to describe what he or she observed, did, or said, and what was told to him or her by others.

> <u>The undersigned officer</u> arrived at the scene in time to see both inmates being pulled apart by other officers. [third person]
>
> <u>I</u> arrived at the scene in time to see both inmates being pulled apart by other officers. [first person]

Gender Neutrality

Gender neutrality refers to language that neither stereotypes either sex nor appears to be referring to only one sex when that is not the writer's intention. Before the major gender-neutral writing waves of the early 1980s, most writers, and certainly most reports written by police and correctional agencies, used *he* and *him* as universal terms that applied both to males and females. It was simply an accepted writing convention of the times. Today, most writers both inside and outside policing and correctional agencies find the use of specifically gendered statements unacceptable. Most of the one-time gender-specific terms have been replaced by gender-neutral ones. For instance, police*man* is replaced by *police officer*; mail*man*, by *postal carrier* or *postal worker*. Accurate gender neutrality can be accomplished by using the proper pronoun for each specific sex when the gender of the individual is known and relevant in the writing. For instance,

> The witness, Janet Margolis, checked <u>her</u> apartment for missing items while Officer Bartlett completed <u>his</u> burglary report in the living room.

If both males and females are involved in the action or activity being described in the sentence, use a plural gender-neutral pronoun to account for both.

> Each officer should check <u>his</u> flashlight to be sure it is functioning properly. [gender-specific pronoun]

> Officers should check <u>their</u> flashlights to be sure they are functioning properly. [plural gender-neutral pronoun]

It is important to recognize, however, that you cannot use plural pronouns such as *their* in sentences where the subject is singular.

Excessive Verbiage and Legalese

When writing in passive voice, it is easy to use too many words or write in a confused or verbose manner, termed **excessive verbiage**. This tends to create confused writing and indirect statements rather than crisp, direct, active voice sentences. Perhaps the individual acquired the writing style during a creative writing class in high school or college, thinking that adding excessive amounts of superfluous verbiage makes the writing more artistic, dramatic, or lyrical. Police or correctional report writing does not need to be artistic, dramatic, or lyrical. These are official documents of events that should be maintained by the agency and should be written as clearly, objectively, and accurately as possible. These reports should be detailed, but only insofar as this detail is relevant to describing necessary events, people, and elements of a crime or incident.

Another problem related to words used in the report is the use of **legalese** (legal-sounding or associated terms). Many agencies encourage the convention of using legalese in their efforts to sound both objective and professional. Unfortunately, these efforts often result in the writing sounding unnatural, mechanical, and difficult to understand. Here are examples of clear writing and legalese:

> The suspect entered the house by breaking the window and unlatching the lock. [clear writing]

> The perpetrator used stealth to gain entry to the edifice, deploying an implement to break the glass, thereby permitting the unlatching of the lock. [legalese]

While this last sentence may *sound* more officious and legalistic, it is simply too wordy and indirect a construction.

Accuracy and Factual Statements

Police and correctional reports should include clearly worded, accurate facts about what is going on, who is present, and what was observed. Anything beyond these factual statements, such as inferences, supposition, and personal opinions, should be kept separate or labeled to avoid confusion by a reader. Subjective summaries and conclusions should be avoided. Instead, the report should describe the actual behavior, movement, or action that might allow the reader to conclude it was a furtive gesture.

> The suspect made a furtive gesture. [subjective]
>
> The suspect moved his hand to the inside of his jacket, suggesting he might have a weapon concealed there. [factual]

Reports should also always contain statements about where information has been derived, and from whom.

Conciseness and Clarity

Conciseness is related to an economy of words used in the report. As suggested previously, reports should not be verbose in their construction. Be mindful about writing long, unwieldy and run-on sentences that are not only grammatically inaccurate but also very hard to follow. On the other hand, do not write in such an abbreviated or stilted fashion that sentences do not provide sufficient information to accurately convey the facts, or the necessary elements of a crime or incident. The better the writing, the clearer the information will be conveyed. Clarity, then, has to do with clear, concisely created sentences. Many of the issues discussed earlier will reappear in greater detail during discussions on these and related issues in later chapters of this book.

Reading and Writing Go Hand in Hand

Two things go hand in hand when it comes to good writing—reading and practice writing. It is likely somewhere along the line a teacher may have mentioned this to you, but it is just as likely that you dismissed the notion as quickly as you heard it. You should not do so. The more you read, the better your writing becomes. Although not always immediately recognizable, reading does improve a person's writing in several ways. First, the more you read, the more words, terms, and phrases you learn. This expands your vocabulary and ability to choose better and more precise words when writing reports. Second, the more you read, the more you are able to recognize and unconsciously absorb and learn different writing structures. This allows you to quickly recognize when a sentence has been constructed incorrectly, or to create more complex sentences accurately and with proper grammar. Even short bouts of regular reading, say 15 or 20 minutes a day, can have a beneficial effect on your writing over time; and it doesn't matter if the reading is novels or police technical manuals. The important thing is to read!

Similarly, writing is like any other skill: It requires practice. No one wakes up one morning and suddenly discovers he or she is a brilliant writer. Writing takes practice. The more you write, rewrite, and edit your writing, the better a writer you will become. Do not leave writing assignments for the last minute; this will result in your turning in inadequate first drafts with many flaws. Rather, leave sufficient time to write a draft, edit it, and perhaps rewrite it. Always proofread your reports, and never rely solely on a computer's grammar and spelling check tool. There is no shortcut to a real physical proofreading of your work. As you begin to write and edit your work more regularly, you will see how quickly your writing can improve. When you are a good writer, writing reports stops being a chore and becomes a simple exercise.

TYPES OF REPORTS

Every police agency uses a wide variety of forms and types of reports. Each report type is designed to meet the unique requirements and mission of each agency. Some state highway patrol agencies, which focus primarily on traffic enforcement, may use report forms that are primarily suited for traffic crash and traffic homicide investigations. Other state law enforcement agencies primarily provide advanced investigative and technical support to local police and sheriff's departments. These agencies typically use reports designed to document findings in criminal or administrative investigations. This variety of forms is needed because each agency investigates different types of incidents and conducts a range of specific types of investigations.

Most local police departments, state and county correctional agencies, and sheriff's offices use a variety of reports to document the types of investigations conducted by their officers and investigators. The layout of most criminal justice and correctional report forms follows a standard format. Each agency designs the placement of information on its report forms to meet its unique administrative needs or requirements. Despite the differences in appearance, essentially all report forms are designed for the same basic purpose: to provide a template for officers to record statistical data to document the people, places, and things related to an incident. They also allow the officer to write clear, concise, and accurate accounts of the investigations and actions in an organized and logical way. Within the grouping of types of reports there are several different styles of reports. Each form is used for a specific purpose by officers and investigators. It is important to understand the differences and similarities between each style.

Incident or Complaint Reports

The **incident or complaint report** is the standard report used by most police and correctional agencies in the criminal justice field. An example of an incident or complaint report is shown in Figure 1-1. It is the preliminary report used to document the full range of criminal and administrative incidents that warrant the attention of police and correctional officers. For police officers this includes everything from homicide investigations to misdemeanor thefts. Correctional officers use incident reports to document criminal acts committed within jails and prisons or violations of institutional rules.

Incident or complaint reports usually have a standard front section or cover sheet that captures the basic information about a given incident or investigation (i.e., dates, times, crime type, agency case number, and location of incident). They should also contain essential information on the people involved in the investigation including names, identifiers, addresses, and contact information of victims,

figure 1-1 Incident/Complaint Report

MISDEMEANOR and/or MISCELLANEOUS REPORT

ORIGINAL

CRIME OR INCIDENT: __647g PC PROWLER__   FILE NO.: __07-234__

STATION: __Central__   DATE RECEIVED: __05/22/07__   TIME: __2105__   RECEIVED BY: __Sgt. J.R. Brown__

LAST   FIRST   MIDDLE
INFORMANT'S NAME: __BRONSON, Helen   Marie (Ms.)__   TELEPHONE: __555-4256__   E-MAIL: __Brony@aol.com__

STREET   CITY   ZIP
ADDRESS: __567 Maple St., Apt. "C"   Chico, California   95926__

LAST   FIRST   MIDDLE
VICTIM'S NAME: __Same as above__   TELEPHONE: _____   E-MAIL: _____
(IF DIFFERENT
FROM INFORMANT)
ADDRESS: _____ __Same as above__

LOCATION: __567 Maple St., Apt. "C"__   DATE OCCURRED: __05/22/07__   TIME: __1950__

SUSPECT __Unknown Suspect__

ADDRESS_____ TELEPHONE_____

	SEX	RACE	AGE	HEIGHT	WEIGHT	HAIR	EYES	DIST. MARKS
DESCRIPTION	M	W	17-19	5'10"	150-170	Blond	Unk	High cheek bones, scar over left eye

OTHER DESCRIPTION __Long Blond Hair, shoulder length, parted in center; small round silver rimmed__
__glasses; Brown leather jacket; blue jeans; Dk. blue sneakers__

VEHICLE __(NONE SEEN)_____ LICENSE NO._____

DETAILS OF CRIME OR INCIDENT:

Dispatched by radio at 2105 hours 05/22/07 to contact female victim of a Peeping Tom, at Apt. "C", 567 Maple St. Suspect was scared away. Last observed fleeing north on Maple St.

Apt. located mid-block on W side of Maple; 3-story white stucco; Caucasian middle-class neighborhood. Apt. set back 30' W of sidewalk line.   A 6' wooden fence borders property on both sides and rear. Victim, W/F, age 42, resides on first floor.

Victim states that she was sitting alone in her living room, which fronts on Maple St., watching TV at 7:50 p.m. 05/22/07, when she heard a noise outside ground floor window on E side of her apartment. Victim states that she looked out the side window but saw no one. She states that 10 minutes later she again heard noises outside the same window, and moved to draw the shade. On approaching the window, victim observed the young man described above, peering into her window. She states the suspect immediately fled, once he realized he had been seen; suspect ran north on Maple St.

Victim states that she resides alone and has been bothered on three previous occasions by a suspect of similar appearance and description. Bronson mentioned that due to the poor lighting outside her house, and because the lights were on inside, the description of the suspect may not be entirely accurate.

Several overlapping footprints were noted outside victim's front window; one clear shoeprint located; cast made. Neighbors were contacted and interviewed—no one heard or saw possible intruder; no further description provided.

Follow-up investigation to be conducted.

INVESTIGATING OFFICERS __Wilson #34/Brown #18__   SUPERVISOR __Sgt. O'Malley__ reporters, witnesses, suspects, and assisting officers. Internal agency information such as the investigating officer's name, rank, badge or identification numbers, and unit assignment should also be completed in this section. Space should also be provided to route the report to the appropriate areas within the agency for additional investigation, for criminal prosecution, or for final disposition. The format of this first page is typically fill-in-the-blank or open block style.

The cover sheet section of the incident or complaint report provides facts relevant to the investigation (e.g., *who* was involved, *what* is his or her role in the investigation, *where* did the incident take place, and *when* did the incident occur). This page provides an organized listing of essential statistical information about the case to establish a basis for the reader to understand the narrative summary or synopsis to follow. Formatting the report in this way contributes to a better quality investigative report. Not cluttering the narrative portion of the report with the statistical and demographic information produces a much clearer and more understandable narrative.

The next page or section of the complaint or incident report usually provides an open block section for the officer to write a summary or synopsis of the investigation. This portion of the report should provide the *how* and *why* elements of the incident or investigation, if known. It is the most critical section part of the report and should not be rushed or left incomplete. Adequate time taken here will produce a much better work product and a more successful prosecution or resolution to the case later. This portion of the report is where the observations and actions of the investigator take shape and meaning. A well-written narrative provides the reader with the actions of the officer or investigator, a detailed account of the crime scene, the testimony of witnesses, and descriptions of the evidence. The narrative summarizes the officer's actions and observations chronologically and guides the reader through the facts of the investigation to a logical conclusion or finding.

The incident or complaint report is the mainstay of most police agencies. Almost any incident involving a criminal act will be initially documented on this type of report format.
Source: Brand X Pictures

Supplemental Reports

Most criminal investigations or incidents involve multiple officers and investigators who each contribute to the investigation at different times. Investigative reports typically evolve as the case develops, with new facts and details being added over time. Because each patrol officer or investigator has a unique role in the investigation, he or she documents individual observations and actions separately. Ultimately these **supplemental reports** become the official record of the case and are used in future criminal proceedings or follow-up investigations. Figure 1-2 provides an example of a supplemental report. Investigators must update case files with supplemental information at each stage of the investigation. Supplemental reports are designed to allow for additional information to be added to an incident report from each participating officer. They can also be used by the original investigating officer to add additional information or findings developed after the incident report has been submitted.

Each agency has its own distinct design for supplemental reports. However, some common characteristics are found in most report formats. Supplemental reports typically contain areas to provide basic information that links them to the original incident or complaint report. Fill-in-the-blank or open block style areas are usually provided on the top of the form for the date of the original report, agency case number, location of incident, and any additional victim or witness information to be included. The supplemental reporting officer's name, rank, and agency information is then listed in the appropriate location on the form. The remainder of the form is left for a narrative or summary information. Fill-in-the-blank, open block style, or check boxes for routing and disposition information are also included on the form.

Arrest Reports

Arrest reports are another type of report used primarily by law enforcement officers. Figure 1-3 shows an example of an arrest report. These reports share many of the same formatting characteristics as incident or complaint reports but are specifically used to document facts and evidence to support probable cause when a suspect is arrested. Arrest reports provide areas where specific criminal charges can be listed and the associated criminal statute or ordinance numbers documented. This information is used by jail personnel to make bond or release disposition decisions. The importance of accuracy in listing the appropriate charges and statutes cannot be overstated. Placing the incorrect charge or statute number on an arrest report can potentially jeopardize the prosecution of the case. Arresting officers should always verify the accuracy of this information.

Officers frequently condense arrest reports to just the basic information detailing the elements of the crime and to establish probable cause for the arrest. Their feeling is that only the basic facts are needed for initial review by judges and prosecutors. A complete and detailed account of the incident is then documented in the complaint or incident report. This can be problematic if the writer is not careful to select all of the necessary information for review by the judge or prosecutor who will make a probable cause determination. If relevant details are omitted for the sake of brevity or to save time, the arrest could be invalidated and the suspect released. The best course of action is always to write reports as thoroughly and completely as possible. In this way nothing is left to chance and all of the relevant facts and findings are presented.

figure 1-2 Supplemental Report

Robbery		**69.CASE NO.** 07-313
Jackson Police Department		

70.CODE SECTION 459 PC	**71. CRIME** Burglary	**72. CLASSIFICATION** Commercial Jewelry Store	
73.VICTIM'S LAST NAME, FIRST, MIDDLE (FIRM IF BUS.) Sparkle's Jewelry Store		**74. ADDRESS** 246 Barnard St RESIDENCE [ ] BUSINESS [X]	**75. PHONE** 555-1505

<u>FOLLOW-UP REPORT</u>

On 07/15/07, 1030 hours, WALTER J. SAUGER, Mgr., Fidelity Loan Co., 208 S. Spring Street, contacted the station and advised Officer TUSCILLO that an unknown individual had tried to pawn a lady's W/G diamond ring, set with a 1/2 karat diamond in a basket setting, engraved "J.A.". SAUGER stated that he did not like the looks of the suspect and refused to take the item. The unknown person left the store and walked south on Spring St., according to SAUGER. Suspect is described as M/W/A, 35–38 yrs, 5'7–9", 160–170, wearing dark trousers, a faded blue shirt with white square buttons; dk. brn. hair, neck length; and dk. sunglasses.

Since the above jewelry fit the description of some of the property taken in the burglary of the SPARKLE'S JEWELRY STORE on 07/13/07, reporting officer proceeded to S. Spring Street, where an individual similar to the person described by SAUGER was observed walking south on the east side of Spring St. Suspect was placed under arrest by Officer TUSCILLO at 1040 hours. At that time Officer TUSCILLO informed the suspect that he had the right to remain silent and that any statement he might make could be taken down and used against him in a court of law. He was also advised that he had the right to an attorney of his own choice and to have an attorney present during questioning; that if he so desired and could not afford an attorney, one would be appointed for him without charge. At that time suspect stated that he understood his rights, but was willing to make a statement.

A search of the suspect discovered several articles of jewelry similar to the items taken in the SPARKLE store burglary as well as an eight-inch screwdriver. The screwdriver tip appeared similar to the tool impression left on the window ledge of the victim jewelry store.

Suspect was identified as HARRY AMES, 406 Maple St., San Francisco, California 94118, and claimed he had just been released from Soledad Prison on 07/10/07, where he had served four years for burglary. He was booked at Central Jail on suspicion of Burglary, Booking #6345K.

BENJAMIN SCHWARTZ, owner of Sparkle's Jewelry Store, identified the three rings and a lady's Bulova watch recovered during the search of AMES, all part of the stolen jewelry taken in instant case on 07/13/07.

(Include in report)
<u>SUSPECT</u>:   (description)
<u>PROPERTY</u>:   (list of items, description, value)
<u>ARREST REPORT</u>:   (attach copy of arrest report)

REPORTING OFFICERS Tuscillo, Michele #436	**RECORDING OFFICER** Tuscillo	**TYPED BY** mmk	**DATE AND TIME** 07/15/07 1030	**ROUTED BY** Miller

FURTHER ACTION [X] YES [ ] NO	**COPIES TO** [X] DETECTIVE [ ] JUVENILE [X] DIST. ATTNY [ ] SQ./P.D.	[X] C11 [ ] PATROL [ ] OTHER___ [ ] OTHER___		
			REVIEWED BY George Aplin, Capt.	**DATE** 07/15/07

figure 1-3 Arrest Report

Arrest Report
Irvine Police Department

CA0303600   **Arrestee #_____**   **DR #**

INVOLV. CODES:	ARR – ARRESTEE	DATE	TIME	LOCATION		
(BOXES 1 & 39)	DET – DETAINED					
	MHD – MENTAL HEALTH					

1. INV CODE	2. NAME (LAST) (FIRST) (MIDDLE)	3. SEX M ☐ F ☐	4. RACE W B H C J F I P O A U	5. DOB	6. AGE

7. ALIAS, SCARS, MARKS, TATTOOS, NICKNAMES	7A. G.E.T. ☐ Y ☐ N

8. HT.	9. WT.	10. HAIR	11. EYES	12. OLN	13. OLS ☐ CA	14. POB	15. SOCIAL SEC. #	16. CII #

17. BOOKING #	DATE	TIME	18. ADDRESS	19. CITY	20. STATE	21. ZIP

22. RESIDENCE PHONE ( )	23. OCCUPATION	24. EMPLOYER/ADDRESS (SCHOOL IF JUVENILE)	25. BUSINESS PHONE ( )

26. CODE SECTION / DESCRIPTION

OF WARRANTS ATTACHED ☐

27. PARENT/GUARDIAN NOTIFIED (LAST) (FIRST) (MIDDLE) (IF JUVENILE) ☐	28. DOB	29. PHONE # ( )	30. NOTIFIED BY	31. DATE/TIME

32. ARRESTEE'S VEHICLE DESCRIPTION	VYR	VMA	VMO	VST	COLOR(S)	33. IDENTIFYING FEATURES OF VEHICLE

34. DISPOSITION OF VEHICLE
☐ IMPOUNDED   ☐ LEFT AT SCENE   ☐ OTHER

35. ARRESTEE STATUS (ADULT) ☐ OCJ ☐ BAIL ☐ 849 ☐ PROMISE TO APPEAR ☐ RELEASED TO_____	36. ARRESTEE'S STATUS (JUVENILE) ☐ OCJH ☐ RELEASED TO PARENTS ☐ RECOMMEND CSP ☐ REFER TO PROB ☐ OTHER_____	37. MIRANDA YES ☐ NO ☐ DATE: BY: TIME:	38. INVOKED? ☐

Arrestee #_____

39. INV CODE	40. NAME (LAST) (FIRST) (MIDDLE)	41. SEX M ☐ F ☐	42. RACE W B H C J F I P O A U	43. DOB	44. AGE

45. ALIAS, SCARS, MARKS, TATTOOS, NICKNAMES	45A. G.E.T. ☐ Y ☐ N

46. HT.	47. WT.	48. HAIR	49. EYES	50. OLN	51. OLS ☐ CA	52. POB	53. SOCIAL SEC. #	54. CII #

55. BOOKING #	DATE	TIME	56. ADDRESS	57. CITY	58. STATE	59. ZIP

60. RESIDENCE PHONE ( )	61. OCCUPATION	62. EMPLOYER/ADDRESS (SCHOOL IF JUVENILE)	63. BUSINESS PHONE ( )

64. CODE SECTION / DESCRIPTION

OF WARRANTS ATTACHED ☐

65. PARENT/GUARDIAN NOTIFIED (LAST) (FIRST) (MIDDLE) (IF JUVENILE) ☐	66. DOB	67. PHONE # ( )	68. NOTIFIED BY	69. DATE/TIME

70. ARRESTEE'S VEHICLE DESCRIPTION	VYR	VMA	VMO	VST	COLOR(S)	71. IDENTIFYING FEATURES OF VEHICLE

72. DISPOSITION OF VEHICLE
☐ IMPOUNDED   ☐ LEFT AT SCENE   ☐ OTHER

73. ARRESTEE STATUS (ADULT) ☐ OCJ ☐ BAIL ☐ 849 ☐ PROMISE TO APPEAR ☐ RELEASED TO_____	74. ARRESTEE'S STATUS (JUVENILE) ☐ OCJH ☐ RELEASED TO PARENTS ☐ RECOMMEND CSP ☐ REFER TO PROB ☐ OTHER_____	75. MIRANDA YES ☐ NO ☐ DATE: BY: TIME:	76. INVOKED? ☐

Some agencies combine incident reports with arrest reports to eliminate redundancy and save the writer time. Others might mandate that officers complete both incident and arrest reports separately for each incident. Whatever the individual agency procedures, the same report writing fundamentals that apply to investigative reports also apply to arrest reports. Each arrest report must be well written, concise, and clear. It must contain all of the necessary elements and facts to validate the arrest. The primary difference between arrest and incident reports is that arrest reports *are going* to be scrutinized by prosecutors and judges specifically to determine if probable cause existed to justify the arrest, whereas many incident reports do not result in a criminal prosecution. The civil liability for making an unlawful arrest is frequently based solely on the quality of the arrest report. Officers who *fail* to accurately and completely document their actions and observations put themselves and their agency at risk of being found liable for civil damages. The best protection is a complete and thorough investigation that is well documented.

The importance of writing quality reports and narratives cannot be overstated. Officers are frequently assessed and evaluated solely on the basis of their writing ability. Promotions, transfers, and professional reputations often are based on the opinions of superiors and decision makers who may read an incident or supplemental report. An officer never knows who ultimately will read or review his or her work product. An investigative report can find its way into courtrooms, executive offices, and frequently onto the front page of newspapers. A well-written and complete investigative summary demonstrates competence and diligence and is the hallmark of a professional officer. A poorly written or incomplete report could permanently damage an officer's or criminal justice agency's reputation.

TECHNOLOGY AND POLICE REPORTS

The advent and proliferation of computers has changed forever how businesses and governments operate. The speed at which computers can process, organize, store, and transmit data has revolutionized the day-to-day practices of even the most basic private and public functions. Most facets of the criminal justice system have been similarly transformed and improved.

A wide variety of crime-solving technologies has emerged from this period of technological development and innovation. Some of the more significant achievements include automated fingerprint identification systems, DNA databases, crime mapping software, expanded access to criminal records, and the wireless transmission of crime data. These innovations have greatly improved the crime-solving capability of today's law enforcement officer (Foster, 2005). An equally important area of these technological innovations is the increased use of computers to write, store, and transmit incident and arrest reports. According to a 2003 Department of Justice, Bureau of Justice Statistics report, the number of police and sheriff's departments that use paper reports as the primary means to transmit criminal incident field data to central information systems has decreased from approximately 87 percent in 1997 to 58 percent in 2003. During these same time periods, the use of computer and data devices for recording and transmitting field data increased from 9 to 38 percent in local police departments and from 7 to 33 percent in sheriff's offices. These numbers illustrate how technology is influencing report writing and police data management capabilities.

The use of mobile computers for law enforcement dates back to the 1970s with the first deployments of **mobile data terminals (MDTs)** and **computer-aided dispatch (CAD)** systems (Brewer, 2007). MDTs were "dumb" terminals, with keyboards and screens, that allowed officers to receive calls for service information from computers housed at a central headquarters. MDTs have no actual computing power but allow officers to access various driver's license, motor vehicle, and wanted person's records in the field. CAD systems incorporate software that assists in the management and dispatching of police calls for service (Foster, 2005). These systems allow information related to calls for service to be transmitted directly to the MDT in the officer's vehicle.

The size and portability of modern computers has made them a mainstay in most police agencies. A full range of law enforcement practices has been adapted to incorporate the use of personal computers and **personal digital assistants (PDAs)**. Most police agencies now equip their officers with **mobile data computers (MDCs)**. The MDC is a microcomputer, usually a laptop computer, that is installed in the officer's vehicle. These computers allow the officer to access various databases to query driver's license, vehicle registration records, and wanted person's information. Some more advanced systems also have the capability for the officers to view photographs, mug shots, and fingerprints in the field (Foster, 2005).

Many new devices and products have emerged that can assist officers in inputting and formatting reports. The laptop personal computer is probably the best-known technology used by officers to format and record reports. Other smaller devices, such as PDAs, provide the portability that allows officers to use them while working in assignments using motorcycles or bicycles or on horseback. Detectives and crime scene investigators use PDAs at remote crime scenes where a laptop might not be practical (Brewer, 2007). These devices provide the durability and capability for officers to access and input information while in the field to assist in investigations and information gathering (Geohegan, 2009). This information can then be transmitted wirelessly to other users.

As computer technology continues to evolve, the trend is toward smaller, faster, and more powerful machines that have greater capability and flexibility in field use. These laptop computers and PDAs have transformed the way officers organize and input written incident and arrest reports. The concept of creating a technological environment where the officer has all of the equipment needed to complete reports in the field has been referred to as the *mobile office* (Foster, 2005). A mobile office typically consists of a laptop computer, mobile radio, and wireless capability to transmit information. According to Foster, "It has been estimated that mobile office concept can reduce the time a police officer spends in the station on paperwork by 37 percent" (2005, p. 169).

Using Technology for Police Report Writing

A significant portion of officers' time is spent writing reports. It is estimated that up to 20 percent of a front-line officer's time is spent completing reports (Brewer, 2007). A wide variety of technology currently exists that allows officers to complete reports electronically. This technology ranges in sophistication from software that allows officers to input data and reports into report form templates that is then printed in paper format, to extensive computer systems that capture, store, and relay data electronically to various locations and users.

Automated Report Writing Systems.   Many agencies use **automated field reporting systems (AFRSs)** to allow officers in the field to input incident and crime data. These systems reduce the time required to complete incident reports and improve the quality of data collected in the reports. This allows officers to use MDCs to complete incident reports in the field without leaving their assigned areas (Groff & McEwen, 2008). CAD information can be automatically populated onto an electronic report form on the officer's MDC when a call is dispatched. This ensures the accurate transfer of the information and reduces redundant data entry for the officer (Gavigan, 2008).

These report writing software systems allow officers to input information into reports and conduct data queries of agency records to complete the necessary information. Once the report has been completed it can be electronically transmitted to supervisors for review. Once approved, the supervisor can then route the report to the appropriate sections of the agency (e.g., records, court liaison, investigations).

Records Management Systems.   Many police agencies use a **records management system (RMS)** to automate the processes of data entry, storage, retrieval, and sharing of information about persons, vehicles, wanted persons, and other records (Groff & McEwen, 2008). More advanced jurisdictions use an integrated system or criminal justice information system, which allows the report to be routed electronically to other outside agencies (e.g., the prosecutor's office, the jail, or court systems) (Foster, 2005). These systems automate and streamline the report writing process and allow for a more efficient dissemination of information to various users and criminal justice stakeholders.

These integrated report writing and records management systems represent the state of the art in law enforcement information management systems (Gavigan, 2008). The technology needed to support these integrated systems can be very sophisticated. They rely on multiple components all working in combination to be effective. Not all criminal justice agencies use these more advanced systems. The cost of hardware and software to support these systems can make them prohibitive for smaller or budget-constrained agencies.

Report Writing Software   Some police and correctional agencies use laptop or desktop computers only as word processors to assist officers in completing incident or arrest reports. This use of technology greatly increases the speed at which officers can complete investigations, and improves the appearance and organization of reports. A wide variety of report formats can be developed using word processing software such as WordPerfect or Microsoft Word. These **report writing software** programs allow the officer to input information and narrative summaries into a standard template or format. Different templates can be created for a variety of incident types. These templates typically use a combination of the fill-in-the-blank, open box type, or check the box formats to enter data. Some templates can incorporate pull-down menus to assist the officer in making a selection from a group of choices. Many of these report templates use a tabbed or window design to allow the writer to navigate from one area of the report to another and input information into the correct section. These sections are typically related to persons, vehicles, evidence, or other property associated with the investigation. The tabbed or windows design allows for more space to document and describe these items, and produces a more complete but less cluttered final report. A free-form narrative section is provided to allow for a detailed written synopsis of the investigation or incident.

Report writing software products typically provide spelling and grammar checks that can aid the writer in the proper formation and editing of reports. Once all of the information is entered and formatted, the completed report can be saved onto a storage device or printed as hard copy. It can then be disseminated as needed to supervisors for approval or other components of the system. The main advantage that these systems share is that they allow the writer to save and revise drafts and versions of a report for later editing and correction.

Other Police Report Writing Technologies

Most of the traditional word processing products used in personal computers use a keyboard as the point of data entry. Many agencies have sought out solutions that can speed up report writing without sacrificing the quality of the report. Dictation is another faster way to enter data into a report. This method has been in use for some time in law enforcement, but recent advancements have changed the way it can be used to write reports. The advancements in smaller digital recorders have made them very practical for officers and investigators to record narratives and interviews for transcription to reports or witness statements. The recording quality of these devices makes them much more effective than older analog tape recorders for capturing and dictating information (Dees, 1999).

Some agencies have implemented automated dictation reporting systems for report writing. These systems provide the officer with a mechanism to call into a computer via telephone and dictate the report. The system is equipped with software that converts voice to transcribed text. Other systems use transcription specialists who manually enter the report data into the system as the officer dictates the report to them. These systems save the officer time that would be spent writing, but require a significant amount of logistical support to operate efficiently. They also require the officer to review the completed report once it is transcribed, checking for accuracy and completeness and making corrections. As digital recording technology has improved and the cost of these systems has decreased, more agencies have sought out this solution as a time-saving measure for officers (Dees, 1999).

Several emerging technologies have been developed to allow more flexibility in getting data into a report form. These technologies allow the officer to electronically "write" with a stylus or smart pen onto a computer touch screen or prepared surface. The device then transforms the script into text. Others use an **intuitive pen** which captures the data as the officer writes on any surface and then downloads the data into the computer via a docking station (Dees, 2005). These systems transfer the data electronically into a format that can be recognized by the computer and convert it to text. This allows the writer to use freehand writing to input the data. The method allows officers to capture and record information with greater speed and ease (Simon, 2005).

Another technology that has greatly influenced how officers investigate crimes and identify suspects is the use of video evidence. The proliferation of video monitoring systems in businesses and public areas has provided police agencies with valuable evidence of criminal activity and has helped identify and prosecute offenders. In-car video systems in patrol cars have been used in law enforcement since the 1970s for traffic enforcement, but the advances in this technology and the value to agencies for public integrity issues have greatly increased their use in recent years. Officers must be trained to accurately and completely transfer the actions from video into the narrative body of their reports. The reality of using this evidence is

Computer technology has greatly enhanced the report writing capability of police officers.
Source: © Mikael Karlsson

that a picture is worth a thousand words; however, the officer must document the actions occurring on the video images for them to be used in court. If the officer's account of the video evidence differs from what appears in the video, the evidence may be deemed worthless or the officer's testimony may be discredited.

All of these technologies are designed to increase an officer's capability to complete well-written and thorough reports in a timely manner. They each have distinct advantages and limitations, but all rely on a well-trained and capable officer who is able to capture ideas and information and relate them in a meaningful way. No technology can take the place of a human being inputting the data or writing the narratives.

chapter summary

1. One of the most important aspects of police and correctional work is report writing. Unfortunately, most television shows and movies about law enforcement provide little or no emphasis on the kinds of writing or the amount of writing necessary in police and correctional work. Good writing is an essential skill for any law enforcement professional to master and continually improve on.

2. A well-written report can assist a prosecutor in obtaining a conviction, while a poorly written report can be used by the defense to suggest sloppy police work, or confused thinking on the part of an arresting or investigating officer.

3. Police and correctional writing is not designed to entertain, or even be terribly creative, but rather to communicate necessary pieces of information that may be important later during a secondary investigation—or if the case goes to court, during prosecution.

4. Police and correctional reports document criminal or, in some cases, rule-violating incidents. They may be used to maintain a record of investigative tasks as they are accomplished during that segment of the event, and to accurately record what transpired for other pertinent criminal justice partners who need to know the facts of the incident.

5. Proper spelling is an important part of report writing. Misspelled words can make an otherwise well-written report look unprofessional or incomplete. The use of police jargon in a report is another way to reduce the value of a report. Jargon can confuse the non–police officer reading the report and make the report difficult to follow or understand.

6. Three major tenses tend to be used in police and correctional report writing: present, past, and future. Present tense involves a construction describing a current event or occurrence. Past tense involves a construction describing something that has occurred already. Future tense involves a construction where something is described as occurring later or at some time in the future.

7. Writing in an active voice allows the reader to understand who did what to whom. In other words, when the subject of a sentence is in action (acts or performs some activity), the verb is in active voice. When the subject of the sentence is the recipient of some action, the verb is in the passive voice.

8. Pronouns are words that are used to take the place of, or to refer back to, nouns or some other pronoun. Pronouns permit us to speak about people, places, and things without unnecessary repetition.

9. Gender neutrality refers to language that neither stereotypes either sex nor appears to be referring to only one sex when that is not the writer's intention. Officers should use gender-neutral writing in their reports to avoid stereotyping subjects or influencing the meaning or tone of their words.

10. More is not necessarily better in police report writing. Police writing should be clear and concise. Adding unnecessary words or legal terminology only bores or confuses the reader. Effective writers stick to the facts and include only details or information that add clarity and value to the report.

11. Police and correctional agencies use a wide variety of reports depending on the nature of their work. These include incident or complaint, supplemental, and arrest reports. Each agency modifies these reports to meet its individual needs and purpose.

12. The advent and proliferation of computers has changed how police agencies operate and capture information. Today, laptop computers are standard issue for most law enforcement agencies. They are used to complete reports and transmit data to records management systems that then transfer information to other criminal justice partners electronically.

Exercises: Writing a Good Narrative

WRITING AN ARREST REPORT

INSTRUCTIONS: Draft a narrative report using the following facts:

Case number:	2009-20345
Date and time of incident:	October 23, 2009, 1400 hours
Nature of incident:	Theft
Location:	Save-a-lot Grocery, 456 W. Main Street, Anytown, MN
Reporter:	Joe Sanderson, White/Male, DOB: 09-22-56, home address: 1235 47th Street, Anytown, MN
Witness #1:	Mary Franks, White/Female, DOB: 12-23-82, home address: 4322 Duncan Place, Anytown, MN
Witness #2:	Marcus Henry, Black/Male, DOB: 10-03-92, home address: 6601 Masters Avenue, Apartment 33B, Anytown, MN
Suspect:	Barbara Mills Jones, White/Female, 01-20-84, home address: 33 Whisper Hills Place, Apartment 5A, Anytown, MN
Evidence:	1 six-pack of 12-oz cans of Budweiser beer, valued at $7.36, 3 packages of sirloin steaks valued at $26.98

Facts of the incident:

Mr. Sanderson, who is the store manager, was told by one of his employees, Mary Franks, that she saw a woman stuffing packages of meat inside a baby carriage. Another employee, Marcus Henry, watched the woman walk out of the store, pushing the baby carriage without paying for the meat. Mr. Sanderson ran out into the parking lot and stopped the woman. He recovered three packages of meat and a six-pack of beer from the baby carriage.

When you arrive at 1415, Ms. Jones and Mr. Sanderson are in the manager's office. Ms. Jones is sobbing and visibly upset. She admits to stealing the meat and beer because she says that her husband left her and she has nothing to eat. She has a seven-month-old baby, Margaret Jones, DOB 03-15-09, in the baby carriage.

Mr. Sanderson, Mr. Henry, and Ms. Franks provide you with written statements of what they saw. Mr. Sanderson indicates that the store policy is to prosecute all shoplifters. You arrest Ms. Jones and drive her to the Anytown Municipal Jail. Child welfare advocates are notified and take custody of Margaret Jones. The meat and beer are inventoried, photographed, and released back to Sanderson.

WRITING AN INCIDENT REPORT

INSTRUCTIONS: Draft a narrative report using the following facts:

Case number:	CI 2009-49991
Date and time of incident:	October 25, 2009, 1730 hours
Nature of incident:	Inmate stabbing
Location:	Middleburg Correctional Facility, Hallway between Building 2A and the Mess Hall
Reporting officer:	C/O David Morris
Victim:	Marcus Davidson #99872
Witness #1:	Sergeant Mary Faulkner
Witness #2:	C/O John Brown
Witness #3:	Inmate Curtis Smith #34790
Witness #4:	Inmate Brandon Fields #56912
Suspect:	Inmate Darius Prentice #44551
Evidence:	4-inch homemade metal shank knife wrapped with tape
Injuries:	2-inch stab wound to the lower left back

Facts of the incident:

Several inmates from Building 2A were being escorted back to their cell block from the Mess Hall by C/O Brown, Sgt. Faulk, and C/O Morris. Inmate Davidson was walking between inmates (Smith and Fields) in a single-file line. They passed another group of inmates heading into the Mess Hall. Inmate Prentice was walking in the hallway toward the Mess Hall when he lunged at Davidson and stabbed him in the lower back with a small knife. Inmates Smith and Fields restrained Prentice until Faulkner and Brown could take him into custody. The knife was recovered by C/O Morris, who also responded to the scene. Davidson was taken to the infirmary with a non-life-threatening wound. Prentice was placed in lockdown pending further investigation.

exercise 3

WRITING A COMPLAINT REPORT

INSTRUCTIONS: Draft a narrative report using the following facts:

Case number:	2009-20677
Date and time of incident:	October 25, 2009, 1830 hours
Nature of incident:	Residential burglary
Location:	344 Marshal Street, Anytown MN
Reporter:	Barry Myers, White/Male, DOB: 04-12-53, home address: 344 Marshal Street, Anytown, MN
Witness:	Mildred Pierce, White/Female, DOB: 02-23-42, home address: 342 Marshal Street, Anytown, MN
Suspect:	Unknown at this time
Evidence:	Concrete block, possible blood evidence

Facts of the incident:

You respond to a residence at 344 Marshal Street. The homeowner, Mr. Barry Myers, meets you at the curb and advises that his house has been broken into today. He estimates sometime between 8:30 a.m. when he left for work and 6:00 p.m. when he arrived home.

Mr. Myers walks you to the back of his home and shows you a bedroom window that has been broken and is pushed open. When you look through the window you see broken glass inside the room and what appears to be a piece of concrete block on the floor. Mr. Myers says that he had some lose blocks sitting next to the house from a building project he was finishing.

You search the interior of the house and find that several rooms have been ransacked and the contents of drawers and cabinets have been strewn throughout the home. At the bedroom windowsill, where the window was broken, you see drops of what appear to be blood on the inside of the sill and on the carpet below.

Mr. Myers advises that he has no idea what exactly has been taken and will have to do an inventory of his belongings to find out. Mr. Myers says that his neighbor Mrs. Pierce is a retiree who stays home during the day. She might have seen or heard something.

Mrs. Pierce says that she saw an old beatup brown work truck parked in Mr. Myers's driveway at around 11:00 this morning. Two men were driving the truck and they stayed at Myers house for about 15 to 20 minutes. She thought they were a lawn service since they were walking all around the house.

exercise 4

WRITING A SUPPLEMENTAL REPORT

INSTRUCTIONS: Draft a narrative supplemental report using the following facts:

Case number:	2009-20677
Date and time of incident:	October 26, 2009, 1730 hours
Nature of incident:	Follow to residential burglary
Location:	344 Marshal Street, Anytown, MN
Reporter:	Barry Myers, White/Male, DOB: 04-12-53, home address: 344 Marshal Street, Anytown, MN
Witness:	Fred Johnson, White/Male, DOB: 05-23-62, home address: 346 Marshal Street, Anytown, MN

Stolen property:

1 Remington, .30-06 rifle, serial #R124392, value $600.00

1 Glock , 9 mm, semiautomatic pistol, serial #B234678, value $500

1 Dell laptop computer, serial #D33457HVC25790, value $1,200

$230 in cash

You are called back to the scene of the prior burglary by Mr. Myers. He has completed a detailed inventory of his belongings and provides you with the descriptions of the stolen items. He has also located another witness, Mr. Johnson, who came home for lunch at around 11:15 a.m. and saw a brown landscaping truck parked in his neighbor's driveway. He was suspicious so he wrote down on a piece of paper the name of the landscaping company visible on the side of the truck.

glossary terms

2

Good Writing Means Writing Well: Understanding the Parts of Speech

INTRODUCTION

This chapter examines the parts of speech that compose the prose you will be using to write reports. This is often the scariest part of writing: writing with proper grammar and syntax. Sometimes when students hear terms such as *noun, pronoun, verb, adjective, preposition, conjunction, interjection, adverb,* and *homophone,* confusion sets in. But in truth, most of you probably already know more than you realize, and you are really skilled at using the parts of speech. However, reviewing the terms and seeing how they work in reports will make your writing more effective. For example, let's consider the noun. In elementary school some teacher certainly introduced you to the *noun.* It is likely he or she told you "nouns represent people, places, or things," and indeed this is an accurate way of thinking about nouns. Nouns also include actions, qualities, and beliefs. All of this will be better explained as this chapter unfolds.

Let's now consider the noun's assistant—the pronoun. Correctly using nouns and pronouns in an incident is essential. The question may be, however, what *point of view* were you using when you wrote these nouns and pronouns? The point of view of a piece of writing is the perspective from which that writing is written: first person (*I* or *we*), second person (*you*), or third person (*he/she/it/one* or *they* or some other neutral noun or pronoun). Table 2-1 shows both common personal pronouns and their possessive forms.

When one of the authors of this book first began policing back in the 1980s, most police reports were written in what can be described as *third person,* or *third-person omnipotent.* Technically, third person involves the writer of a narrative avoiding the use of the pronoun I or we. Rather, the writer used terms like *the author,* the *writer,* or in the case of these early police reports, *the responding officer* frequently written as R/O. Under these circumstances officers would write sentences such as this:

> R/O arrived at the scene and observed two male suspects running North, down Oak, away from the victim who was lying on the ground in front of the ATM located at the corner of Maple and Oak.

table 2-1 Common Personal Pronouns and Their Possessive Forms

Point of View	Singular	Plural	Police Use
First person	I, me (my, mine)	we, us (our, ours)	**Singular (Plural)**
Second person	you (your, yours)	you (your, yours)	I, me (my, mine)
Third person	he, him (his)	them, they (their, theirs)	you (your, yours)
	she, her (her, hers)		
	it (its)		Officer (Officers)
			Suspect (Suspects)
			Victim (Victims)
			Witnesses (Witnesses)

Similarly, others in the narrative report were described in the third-person pronouns such as *the suspect, the witness, the victim,* and so forth. In some cases, departments preferred the use of the officer's name:

> <u>Officer Johnson</u> arrived at the scene and observed two male suspects running North, down Oak, away from the victim. . . .

But this always seemed a little stilted since Officer Johnson was the author of the report, and would be signing it at the bottom. Today, most police departments prefer the use of first-person singular when writing in the voice of the police officer. Thus, if Officer Johnson was writing today, she would write:

> <u>I</u> arrived at the scene and observed two male suspects running North, down Oak, away from the victim. . . .

Similarly, suspects, witnesses, and victims have begun to be listed by their pronouns and proper nouns (their specific names) when that information is known. While suspects may not be known in all cases, frequently this information will be obtained when interviewing the victim and/or a witness. Thus, when the writing the narrative, an officer might write something such as:

> Victim Ronald Miller identified the suspects as Earl Martin and Franklyn Burton. Suspects Martin and Burton were described as. . . .

The definitions for the various points of view a writer may use are discussed in the following sections.

First Person

When writing the narrative portion of a police or correctional report, you should use *first-person* narration. You are the *I* who describes what you observed, did, or said, and what was told to you by others. When referring to other people in the narrative, use their proper names (nouns). You should also note that incident reports must be consistently written in past tense, not present tense.

Second Person

The *second-person* point of view, which emphasizes the reader, works well for giving advice or explaining how to do something. Second-person point of view works well in certain literary devices and types of writing but is seldom used in police or correctional reports. It may be used in offering directions or in rule books, textbooks, and some other forms of correctional writing.

Third Person

At one time writing in *third person* was the standard practice in police and correctional reports. When using third-person narration, you use either proper names (nouns) or pronouns such as *he*, *she*, and *they* when referring to people in the narrative. Biographical narratives (writings about other people's lives) and expository writings generally are written in the third person.

NOUNS

One of the questions many officers frequently have is whether or not to capitalize the first letter of a **noun**. The technical distinction here is usually referred to as *proper nouns*, which refer to particular people, places, things, or ideas, versus *common nouns*, which refer to everyday names of people, places, things, or ideas (Fawcett, 2004). Proper nouns are capitalized, as in the cases of *Mr. Johnson, Dr. Deeds, England, October, and Chief Markson.* Common nouns may be illustrated by the terms *month, officer, art, anger,* and *age.* Officers may commonly encounter other types of nouns, including *concrete nouns, abstract nouns, and compound nouns.* Concrete nouns refer to things that can be seen felt, smelled, or heard. Examples of concrete nouns are *water, dirt, gas, pepper, books, guns, knives,* and *cuffs.* Abstract nouns describe qualities, concepts, and beliefs; for instance, *courage, hunger, liberty, detention,* and *custody.* Compound nouns comprise more than a single word, yet represent only a single noun; for instance, *Orange County, traffic stop sign, half moon,* and *detention cell.* In some cases, compound nouns are a combination of two or more small words to form a single word, such as *tooth* and paste to form *toothpaste.*

In addition to standard rules of grammar related to nouns, many police departments require that officers use all capital letters when writing names of individuals used in the narrative of incident reports (these names are proper nouns). Some departments use this device to make it easier to locate names when reviewing reports.

So, what is the actual purpose of a noun? Basically, nouns serve as the subject of a sentence, or as some sort of complement (direct or indirect object of a *verb* or a *preposition*). These other structural terms related to the sentence will be more fully explained later in this book. For now, let's consider pronouns.

PRONOUNS

Pronouns are words that can be used to replace a noun or another pronoun (Fawcett, 2004). Okay, again many of you may recall that fourth-grade (compound noun) teacher who told you that *"pronouns* take the place of a noun." That probably makes a little more sense now that you understand what a noun actually is. But what exactly does it mean when a word *takes the place of* a noun? Let's consider the following paragraph written with only nouns:

> I entered the premises at 1427 Hillsdale Street and found Officers Murphy and Constence speaking with the victim Ms. Hillary Ferguson. Ms. Ferguson stated that her daughter Jessica Ferguson and Jessica Ferguson's friend from school Madelaine Katz were on their way to the home of Ms. Hillary Ferguson when confronted by the suspect Martin Podster. Officer Murphy questioned Jessica Ferguson and asked if Ms. Hillary Ferguson knew Jessica Ferguson would be walking home with Madelaine Katz.

Many readers will read this passage and know there is some problem with the way it has been written. What might this problem be? It is using only proper nouns rather than proper nouns and pronouns. Let's consider how this paragraph might be rewritten:

I entered the premises at 1427 Hillsdale Street and found Officers Murphy and Constence speaking with the victim Ms. Hillary Ferguson. Ms. Ferguson stated that her daughter Jessica Ferguson and her daughter's friend from school Madelaine Katz were on their way to Jessica's home when confronted by the suspect Martin Podster. Officer Murphy questioned Jessica Ferguson and asked if her mother knew she would be walking home with Madelaine Katz.

As you reread the passage with the pronouns added it is likely that uneasy feeling you had when reading the first version is gone. As in the case of the nouns, there are several different types of pronouns, including *personal pronouns, possessive pronouns, demonstrative pronouns, relative pronouns, reflexive pronouns, interrogative pronouns*, and *indefinite pronouns*. Let's consider these various pronouns.

Personal Pronouns

Personal pronouns represent people or things: *I, me, you, he, him, she, her, it, we, us, they, them.*

> Officer Thomson [proper noun] came to see him [personal pronoun] about a stolen car.

Possessive Pronouns

Possessive pronouns indicate possession or ownership: *mine, yours, hers, his, theirs, ours, its.*

> Sergeant Davidson [proper noun] uses his [possessive pronoun] pen to write the report about the fight.

Demonstrative Pronouns

Demonstrative pronouns demonstrate or indicate a particular person or thing: *this, that, these, those.*

> That [demonstrative pronoun] gun is his [possessive pronoun] service weapon.

Relative Pronouns

Relative pronouns are words that relate one part of the sentence to another, or refer to some other element of the sentence: *who, whom, which, that, whose.*

> The witness whose [relative pronoun] home the officers entered was sitting on the couch. [Notice how the word *whose* refers to the word *witness*.]
>
> The knife [common noun] was dripping with blood, but officers could not determine whose [relative pronoun] weapon it was.

Reflexive Pronouns

Reflexive pronouns, also referred to as intensive pronouns, reflect or refer to someone or something else in the sentence in a kind of possessive manner: *myself, yourself, himself, herself, itself, ourselves, yourselves, themselves.*

An <u>officer</u> [common noun] must ask <u>himself</u> [reflexive pronoun] whether or not shooting a <u>suspect</u> [common noun] is the proper course of action.

The correctional <u>officer</u> [compound noun] thought to <u>himself</u> [reflexive pronoun] how evasive the <u>inmate</u> [common noun] had been when questioned about the theft.

Interrogative Pronouns

Interrogative pronouns ask a question or interrogate in the course of the sentence: *who, whom, which, whose, what.*

<u>Officer Billiet</u> [proper noun] could not determine <u>what</u> [interrogative pronoun] the <u>suspect</u> [common noun] was trying to tell <u>him</u> [personal pronoun].

Indefinite Pronouns

Indefinite pronouns include *all, another, any, anybody, anyone, both, each, either, everybody, everyone, everything, few, many, most, much, neither, no one, nobody, none, nothing, one, other, others, several, some somebody, someone,* and *something.* Indefinite pronouns are sometimes confused with adjectives because the writer mistakenly thinks these words are modifying a noun or pronoun—which is, in fact, the job of the adjective. Let's consider adjectives.

ADJECTIVES

As suggested earlier, **adjectives** are words that modify or describe a noun or pronoun (Fawcett, 2004).

The <u>witness</u> [noun] identified the <u>tall</u> [adjective] <u>suspect</u> [common noun].

Certain words such as *a, an,* and the are a special category of adjective called *articles.* The words *a* and *an* are referred to as indefinite articles because they do not indicate anyone or anything in particular—no *specific* noun or pronoun: *a gun, an* amulet. The word *the* is called a definite article because it names someone or something specific: *the* gun, *the* amulet.

<u>Officer Billet</u> [proper noun] found <u>a</u> [indefinite article] <u>fingerprint</u> [common noun] on <u>the</u> [definite article] beer <u>bottle</u> [common noun].

<u>Officer Billet</u> [proper noun] found a fingerprint on <u>a</u> [indefinite article] beer bottle.

He noticed that <u>the</u> [definite article] fingerprint on <u>the</u> [definite article] bottle was bloody.

<u>Officer Billet</u> [proper noun] found <u>the</u> [definite article] <u>gun</u> [proper noun].

Adjectives describe or indicate amounts, or limit size or quantity of a noun or pronoun. In some cases, adjectives show relative comparisons between elements in a sentence; for instance: *big, bigger, biggest; good, better, best; fast, faster, fastest; tall, taller, tallest; slow, slower, slowest.*

The <u>officers</u> [common noun] captured two <u>suspects</u> [common noun] because <u>their</u> [possessive pronoun] <u>cruiser</u> [common noun] was <u>faster</u> [adjective] than the <u>suspect's car</u> [compound noun].

VERBS

Verbs are the most essential words in a sentence. Some verbs indicate elements of action and may actually be called *action verbs*. These are the most common verbs used in writing and speaking; they are usually pretty easy to identify in a sentence. There are four basic parts of verb forms: present, past, past participle, and present participle (Fawcett, 2004). The present form of a verb is considered the common form; for instance: *run, jump, punch, kick*, and *hammer*. The past and past participle actually look the same, as in the case of *ran, jumped, punched, kicked*, and *hammered*. The present participle usually is formed by addinging to the present tense (sometimes called the present infinitive), as in *runn<u>ing</u>, jump<u>ing</u>, punch<u>ing</u>, kick<u>ing</u>*, and *hammer<u>ing</u>*.

> The [article] <u>suspect</u> [noun] <u>ran</u> [verb] down the alley.
>
> The [article] suspect [noun] was kicking [adjective] the arresting officer [compound noun].

In addition to action verbs, there are *verbs of being*. Verbs of being include words such as *was, is, am, were*, or similar forms of being.

> <u>Officers</u> [common noun] <u>were</u> [helping verb] <u>looking</u> [verb] for a [article] <u>suspect</u> [common noun].
>
> <u>The</u> [article] <u>district attorney</u> [common noun] <u>asked</u> [past-tense verb] <u>the</u> [article] <u>officer</u> [common noun] where <u>she</u> [pronoun] <u>was</u> [verb of being] when <u>she</u> [pronoun] made <u>the</u> [article] <u>arrest</u> [noun].

There are two main types of verbs: action verbs and linking verbs. Action verbs are words such as *ran, played*, or *kicked*. Some verbs serve the function of linking in a sentence. These words include *appear, feel, look, remain, smell, stay, become, grow, prove, seem, sound, taste*. The biggest confusion is that these verbs sometimes act as action verbs, while at other times they serve as linking or helping verbs. The basic test is whether you can substitute a form of being (*am, is, was*, and so on) and allow the sentence to make sense. If it does, the verb is a linking verb.

> The coffee <u>tasted</u> too bitter for the officer to digest.
>
> TEST: The coffee is (<u>was</u>) too bitter for the officer to digest. [This sentence works and *taste* is a linking verb.]

What about the following:

> The officer <u>tasted</u> the bitter coffee.
>
> TEST: The officer is (<u>was</u>) the bitter coffee. [Hey, that doesn't work because *taste* is not a linking verb in this sentence.]

ADVERBS

Certain words modify or change a verb or an adjective; these are known as **adverbs** (Fawcett, 2004). In fact, adverbs may also modify other adverbs. Adverbs typically describe the following sorts of things:

- Where something is: *there, here, outside, inside, nearby, far away, under, above.*
- When something occurs: *now, then, later, immediately, yesterday, tomorrow, the next day.*
- How something occurs: *quickly, slowly, stupidly, happily, effortlessly.*
- How often something occurs, or its duration: *often, seldom, frequently, once, twice, never, always.*
- How much of something (the extent of something): *hardly, extremely, minimally, greatly, more, less, too, excessively.*

> Yesterday, [adverb] Officer Jones [proper noun] apprehended [action verb] two suspects [common noun].

In the preceding example, *yesterday* modifies the verb *apprehended*. In effect, the word *yesterday* describes *when* the action of apprehending the suspects occurred.

Many adverbs also may be formed by simply adding an *–ly* to the adjective; so when you see a word ending in an *–ly*, usually it is an adverb. Table 2-2 shows a series of common adjectives and their adverb forms.

Some adverbs do not work with the *–ly* convention. For example, the word *fast* cannot be changed to an adverb by adding *–ly*; there simply is no word *fastly*. So, an example of this might be as follows:

> The police cruiser moved fast, but was no match for how fast the suspect's car was moving. [Notice that the suspect's car does not move *fastly*; there is no such word as *fastly*.]

table 2-2 Adjectives to Adverbs

Adjectives	Adverbs
bad	badly
quick	quickly
awful	awfully
kind	kindly
quite	quietly
happy	happily
shy	shyly
pensive	pensively
cold	coldly
neat	neatly
keen	keenly
coarse	coarsely

The correctional officer chased the inmate down the gallery; the chase lasted a <u>long</u> time, but not as <u>long</u> as the chase last week. [Again, there is no such word as *longly*, so the adverb remains *long*.]

Many students, police, and correctional officers love a special form of adverb known as a **conjunctive adverb**. Conjunctive adverbs join independent clauses together to form a single sentence; they are sometimes referred to as transitional words and phrases. These words should not be overused. Table 2-3 lists some common conjunctive adverbs.

Because conjunctive adverbs are not true conjunctions, a semicolon and a comma are required when connecting two independent clauses or conjunctive adverbs. Conjunctive adverbs, other than *so* or *otherwise*, require a semicolon preceding them and a comma following them.

Conjunctive adverbs are used to join short sentences (complete clauses) together to form more complex thoughts; however, you must punctuate correctly: (Hey, did you notice the use of the conjunctive adverb *however* in the last sentence?)

1   Each clause on either side of the conjunctive adverb must be a complete thought.

2   A semicolon (;) must be placed in front of the conjunctive adverb and a comma (,) immediately following it.

3   The two clauses are closely related thoughts or ideas.

4   You have used the correct conjunctive adverb.

As indicated, a conjunctive adverb connects two ideas (independent clauses). If the words listed in Table 2-3 interrupt a thought, they are not conjunctive adverbs and are not punctuated as such. Similarly, you cannot simply connect two independent thoughts to form a single compound sentence. For example:

The correctional officer examined the inmate's clothes; <u>accordingly,</u> he left for lunch.

After reading the previous example, hopefully you are scratching your head and thinking, "Huh? I don't follow what the first clause has to do with the second one." Because the two clauses in the example are unrelated, the use of a conjunctive adverb (*accordingly*) is incorrect.

Here is a good example:

The correctional officer examined the inmate's clothes; <u>consequently,</u> he discovered the illegal contraband.

table 2-3 Common Conjunctive Adverbs

accordingly	for example	in particular	now
afterward	furthermore	instead	otherwise
again	generally	likewise	similarly
also	hence	meanwhile	so
besides	however	moreover	still
beyond	in addition	nevertheless	then
consequently	incidentally	next	therefore
finally	indeed	nonetheless	thus

Comparisons with Adjectives and Adverbs

Sometimes you may want to make a comparison between things, or indicate how one thing might measure up to another. You may want to indicate that one suspect is *taller* than another, or *heavier* than your partner, or *older* than the witness. In writing this in a report, you would use one of three possible degrees of adjectives and adverbs: a positive degree, a comparative degree, and a superlative degree.

- A *positive degree* makes a simple statement about a person, place, or thing.

  The correctional officer is very <u>tall</u>. [positive degree adjective]

- A *comparative degree* compares two, and only two, people, places, or things.

  The correctional officer was <u>taller</u> [comparative adjective] than his sergeant by five inches.

- A *superlative degree* compares more than two people, places, or things.

  The correctional officer is the <u>tallest</u> [superlative degree adjective] man in the facility.

Table 2-4 shows a table of different degrees of adverbs and adjectives.

A quick look at Table 2-4 reveals that you can change an adjective or adverb from its positive degree to its comparative degree by adding an *–er or –ier*. Similarly, you can move the adjective or adverb from comparative degree to superlative by adding an *–est* or *–iest* to the positive degree form. Occasionally, you will have an adjective or adverb that requires the addition of the word *more* or *most* to move the degrees from positive to comparative and then to superlative. Consider these examples:

  The captain of the guards is a <u>capable</u> [positive degree adjective] man.

  The warden is <u>more capable</u> [comparative degree adjective] than the captain of the guards.

  The superintendent is the <u>most capable</u> [superlative degree adjective] of all the personnel.

The test here is largely one *by ear* and is similar to adding *–ly* to a verb to make it an adverb. In other words, if you were to restate one of the previous examples

table 2-4 Adjective and Adverb Degrees

Positive	Comparative	Superlative
dirty	dirtier	dirtiest
old	older	oldest
deep	deeper	deepest
big	bigger	biggest
smart	smarter	smartest

and substitute the positive degree changed with an *–er* or *–ier*, it would not sound correct.

> The warden is <u>more capabler</u> than the captain of the guards.

To be sure, *capabler* is not a word, and it simply sounds incorrect in the sentence. Some adjectives will not follow these basic rules of degree and are considered *irregular*; the word itself actually changes as you move from the positive degree to the comparative and/or the superlative. Consider these irregular examples:

> The probationary officer writes reports <u>well</u>, but his training officer writes better; their sergeant, however, writes <u>best</u>.

> The correctional officer searches cells <u>badly</u>. His trainee actually does a <u>worse</u> job at searching, and the recruit demonstrates the <u>worst</u> skill at searches.

> Corporal Johnson is a <u>good</u> marksperson. Sergeant Morley is a <u>better</u> shot, but Lieutenant Brown is the <u>best</u> marksperson.

> I have too <u>much</u> paperwork to finish in one day. You have even more paperwork to finish. Officer Jackson has the <u>most</u> paperwork to finish.

Looking back at the last few pages, it is clear that there are a lot of rules associated with comparisons. Certainly this can make things a bit confusing. One rule of thumb is to try to keep adjectives and adverbs of comparison as simple as possible, and to read them aloud to *hear* how the sentence sounds. For example, read each of the following sentences aloud and see if you can hear the difference between the correct and clear form, and the awkward and incorrect form.

> The box on the table was <u>less big</u> than the one on the floor. [awkward]
> The box on the table was <u>smaller</u> than the one on the floor. [clear]

> The officer lifting weights was <u>more strong</u> than the other officer. [awkward]
> The officer lifting weights was <u>stronger</u> than the other officer. [clear]

> The officer felt <u>less powerless</u> when he drew his gun. [awkward]
> The officer felt <u>more powerful</u> when he drew his gun. [clear]

It is also important to be careful about where you place an adverb. Incorrect placement can make the sentence mean something completely different from what you intended. Consider these examples of proper and improperly placed adverbs.

> I had only been eating for ten minutes when the call came in to respond to a robbery in progress. [weak and improper placement]

This sentence actually says this: I had only been eating [I hadn't been sitting in a car, or running or dancing—only eating] for ten minutes when the call came in to respond to a robbery in progress.

> I had been eating for <u>only</u> ten minutes when the call came in to respond to a robbery in progress. [stronger and proper placement]

PREPOSITIONS

Prepositions connect nouns or pronouns, which are called the objects of the preposition. The preposition and its object form a prepositional phrase. Grammar books usually define prepositions as words that connect or link nouns and pronouns to some other word in the sentence (Fawcett, 2004).

> The officer <u>threw</u> the gun <u>in</u> the air.
>
> The officer <u>dropped</u> the gun <u>on</u> the ground.
>
> The officer <u>threw</u> the gun <u>under</u> the car.
>
> The officer shot the gun <u>at</u> the firing range.
>
> The officer dropped the gun <u>near</u> the suspect.

The underlined words link the two nouns, creating some sort of relationship between the words. These linking words are called *prepositions*. Table 2-5 provides a list of common prepositions.

So, how do you remember what a preposition is? One suggestion is to think about the word *position* which conveniently appears in the word *preposition*. A preposition frequently indicates the position of something: in, outside, under, over, in front of, and so forth. It is also important to remember something else that your fourth-grade teacher probably told you: You should never end a sentence with a preposition. Unlike with certain forms of adverbs and adjectives, where written sentences when read aloud frequently do not sound right to our ears, prepositions at the end of a sentence sometimes do. This is because in colloquial spoken English

table 2-5 Common Prepositions

about	below	except	near	throughout
above	beneath	excluding	next to	till
according to	beside	following	of	to
across	besides	for	off	toward
after	between	from	on	under
against	beyond	in	on account of	underneath
along	but	in addition to	onto	until
among	by	include	out	up
around	by way of	including	out of	upon
as	concerning	in front of	outside	with
at	considering	in place of	over	within
because of	down	in regard to	past	without
before	during	inside	since	
behind		instead of	through	
		into		
		like		

(regular conversational English), people regularly end sentences with a preposition. Consider for the following sentences:

<u>With</u> whom was the correctional officer speaking? [correct]

Who was the correctional officer speaking <u>with</u>? [incorrect]

If we read or speak these two sentences, many people will not notice that the second version is in error. In fact, many people reading that second example may find it hard to accept that this is not correct, because it is exactly how they speak (and likely write as well). These days, grammarians are saying that ending a sentence with a preposition is not always bad. Sir Winston Churchill was quoted as saying, "ending a sentence with a preposition is something with which I will not put up." Churchill was mocking fussy grammarians who say you should never end a sentence with a preposition. Let your conscience be your guide and strive for well-written and easily understood sentences.

CONJUNCTIONS

In addition to prepositions, another word that links or conjoins words in a sentence is a **conjunction**. Thus the role of a conjunction is to connect words with other words, clauses, and ideas. There are three major categories of conjunctions: coordinating, correlative, and subordinating.

Coordinating Conjunctions

Coordinating conjunctions include words such as *for, and, nor, but, or, yet, so*. These words can be used to connect two independent clauses (Glenn & Gray, 2007). An independent clause is a complete thought. Typically, the conjunction is placed between the two clauses, preceded by a comma. Many grammar books recommend remembering coordinating conjunctions by thinking about the acronym FANBOYS (for, and, nor, but, or, yet, so).

The inmate was angry, <u>but</u> he did not hit the other man.

The officer was hungry, <u>so</u> he decided to eat his lunch.

Correlative Conjunctions

Correlative conjunctions cannot work alone, but instead operate in pairs. These pairs appear in two places in a sentence and include *both/and, either/or, neither/nor, not only/also, not only/but also*, and *whether/or*.

Did anyone see <u>whether</u> the suspect <u>or</u> his accomplice had a weapon?

<u>Neither</u> the officer <u>nor</u> his partner could keep up the foot pursuit for more than four blocks.

Subordinating Conjunctions

Subordinating conjunctions are used to join a subordinating clause with a main clause. A subordinating clause depends on the rest of the sentence for its meaning.

table 2-6 Common Subordinating Conjunctions		
after	even though	so long as
although	how	so that
as	if	than
as if	inasmuch as	that
as in	in order that	through
as long as	in that	till
as much as	least	unless
as soon as	now that	until
assuming that	once	when
because	provided that	whenever
before	since	whether
even if		while

It does not express a complete thought, so it does not stand alone. It must always be attached to a main clause that completes the meaning. Table 2-6 provides a list of some of the most common subordinating conjunctions.

You may have noticed that the word as is written in italics. That is to remember to mention a problem many people have when deciding whether to use the words *as* or *like*. (Hey, did you catch the use of the correlative conjunctions in that last sentence?) Traditionally, the word *like* is a preposition, and it should be followed by an object to create what is called a prepositional phrase. As is a conjunction, and it should be followed by a clause containing a subject and a verb.

> The inmate runs like a deer does. [incorrect—it is not necessary to repeat the verb *does*]
>
> The inmate runs like a deer. [correct]
>
> The inmate runs as a deer does. [correct—*as* is followed by a clause]

In standard English, the word *like* is never used with clauses.

INTERJECTIONS

You may have noticed that periodically we pose questions about whether you caught some example of one of the grammatical rules described in this chapter. We frequently begin such questions with the term *hey*. Beginning a sentence with *hey, gads, oops, well, whoa, wow, yikes, ouch*, and similar words indicating some sort of emotion are called **interjections**. Interjections can either stand alone, or be included as part of a sentence.

When an interjection is used as part of a sentence, it does not have any grammatical relation to the other words in that sentence. In other words, you can remove the interjection and the meaning of the sentence will remain unchanged (Glenn & Gray, 2007). Assuming the sentence had been grammatically correct with the interjection, it will remain grammatically correct if you remove it. In common writing, when an interjection is used to express strong emotions or surprise and it stands alone, you should use an exclamation point (!) after the interjection: *Wow! Is that really what you think?* If you are employing milder terms in the middle of a sentence, you should use a comma after the interjections: *Darn! that shoelace keeps coming undone.* Interjections are not typically used in police or correctional reports, unless the officer is quoting a suspect, witness, or victim. In these reports, for example, an officer may write the exclamation of some profanity uttered by an inmate, suspect, victim, or witness verbatim, and in this case it may well be an interjection.

HOMOPHONES

Homophones are words that sound alike but have different meanings and spellings (Glenn & Gray, 2007). Words such as *to, too,* and *two* have very different spellings and meanings and are commonly misused. Some of these words will sound alike, such as *sole/soul, break/brake, dear/deer,* and *ensure/insure.* Others may sound similar but have different meanings, such as *believe/belief, marry/merry, desert/ dessert, accept/except, council/counsel.* Improper use of words may confuse the reader or can convey the wrong meaning of a sentence. It may also lead the reader to believe that the writer is incompetent or that the report was hastily written. Effective writers choose their words carefully and ensure that they are using the appropriate words and spelling.

If you are uncertain about the correct meaning of a word, consult a dictionary before you use it in a sentence. Most word processing software programs with spell checkers will not always detect the improper use of these words. Remember that the quality of your written work reflects directly on you and that even small mistakes in grammar can tarnish an otherwise well-written report. The appendix provides a listing of the most frequently confused homophones.

chapter summary

1. Nouns are the people, places, things, and ideas that make up a written narrative. Knowing when and how to properly integrate nouns in a sentence makes for a richer and more accurate written report.

2. Pronouns take the place of a noun in a sentence. They allow the writer to use words such as *I, me, her, him,* or *them* in place of a noun. In this way the narrative is easier to read and not so redundant. Several different types of pronouns are used to take the place of a noun.

3. Adjectives are words that modify or describe a noun or pronoun. They allow a writer to describe, indicate amounts, or limit the size or quantity of a noun or pronoun.

4. Verbs are the most essential words in a sentence. They indicate the elements of action or help link a sentence together.

5. Adverbs are words that describe a verb or an adjective. Adverbs typically describe how, when, where, how much, or how many in a sentence.

6. A preposition is a word that connects or links a noun and a pronoun to some other word in a sentence. They establish a relationship between these words.

7. Conjunctions are words used to link or conjoin words in a sentence. Their role is to connect words with other words, clauses, and ideas.

8. Interjections are words that can either stand alone, or be included as part of a sentence. When an interjection is used as part of a sentence, it does not have any grammatical relation to the other words in that sentence. They are most often used to show or indicate emotion.

9. Homophones are words that sound alike but have different meanings and spellings. If you are uncertain about the correct meaning of a word, consult a dictionary before you use it in a sentence.

Exercises—Using the Parts of Speech

USING NOUNS CORRECTLY

INSTRUCTIONS: In each sentence, cross out the noun used incorrectly and write the correct noun in the space provided.

1. The police chief had very strong opinions about the roles of men and woman in police work.

   _____

2. Younger officers often mimic the conduct of their peer in dealing with combative suspects.

   _____

3. The suspect gained entry in the residence and took a set of rare coin.

   _____

4. The narcotics agent detailed the activity of multiple suspect at the residence under suspicion for manufacturing methamphetamine.

   _____

5. Research on child abuse indicates that either parent might be capable of abusing their child.

   _____

6. When parents do not use the proper child safety seats when driving they risk the life of their children.

   _____

7. Talking during a public meeting is disrespectful of other who may be trying to listen to the speakers.

   _____

8. The witness indicated that one of the girl was seen leaving the scene of the robbery.

   _____

9. The attorney stated that he was acting on behalf of his clients, Mr. Smith, when he made the motion during the trial.

   _____

10. Police officers are one of the few persons in the criminal justice system who can detain suspects.

    _____

exercise 1

exercise 2

USING PRONOUNS CORRECTLY

INSTRUCTIONS: In each sentence, circle the correct pronoun.

1. Officer Manning placed the suspect in the backseat of (his / their) patrol car.

2. The suspects ran from the scene and left contraband in the backseat of (his / their) car.

3. Mary told the officer that her driver's license was located in (their / her) purse.

4. Each police agency has (its / their) own distinct style.

5. The sheriff's office honored (its / the) senior officers with plaques signifying years of service to the agency.

exercise 3

WRITING CLEARLY

INSTRUCTIONS: Rewrite each sentence correctly in the space provided. (Answers may vary.)

1. On the radio they advised that the road was closed.

_____

_____

2. Officer Melton told the suspect that he should not have lied about his identity.

_____

_____

3. In the city of Fairfield they arrest litterers.

_____

_____

4. On the news, it said that the suspects were seen driving a blue-colored sedan.

_____

_____

5. Sergeant Smith is an excellent typist, yet he has never had a lesson in it.

_____

_____

USING ADJECTIVES AND ADVERBS CORRECTLY

INSTRUCTIONS: In each sentence, circle the correct adverb or adjective.

1. Have you ever seen (real / really) marijuana?
2. Try to approach the suspects (quietly / quiet).
3. The smell from the decomposing body was (awful / awfully).
4. The officer (gladly / glad) gave the citizen directions to the courthouse.
5. Officer Brown, a (high / highly) skilled marksperson, was able to shoot a perfect score at the firing range.
6. The officer (carefully / care) approached the door to the suspect's residence.
7. Detective Green smelled an (unusual / unusually) odor coming from the garage.
8. Recruit Barnes performed (poor / poorly) on his timed run for the police academy.
9. The weapon used by the robbery suspect (actual / actually) turned out to be a pellet gun.
10. The witness (hastily / hasty) wrote a statement as to what she had seen.

exercise 4

USING PREPOSITIONS CORRECTLY

INSTRUCTIONS: In each sentence, circle the correct preposition.

1. The suspect was found hiding (in / on) the bedroom.
2. After the crash the suspect's vehicle came to rest (in / on) Chesterfield Street.
3. The child was struck by a vehicle after he ran (in / on) the street.
4. (In / On) July, the state issued new restrictions for underaged drivers.
5. (On / In) Sunday, the victim discovered that his house had been burglarized.
6. That mess (in / on) your locker must be cleaned up.
7. The town of Myrtle Beach is located between Charleston and Wilmington, North Carolina, (on / in) the coast of South Carolina.
8. Mr. Johnson also owns several businesses (in / on) Santa Barbara.
9. Mrs. Mason placed several items (on / in) the table in front of the witness.
10. Officer Patton stepped (in / on) the bridge before jumping into the water below.

exercise 5

exercise 6

USING HOMOPHONES CORRECTLY

INSTRUCTIONS: In each sentence, circle the correct homophone.

1. The driver stated that he engaged the emergency (break / brake) before his vehicle struck the tree.

2. The state trooper's patrol car was struck as he pulled through the (break / brake) in the highway median.

3. During the investigation blood stains were discovered on the (sole / soul) of the suspect's shoe.

4. During the interview the suspect invoked his right to speak with his legal (council / counsel).

5. The city ordinance banning alcohol on the beach was voted in by the city (council / counsel).

6. The victim states that she told the suspect that she could not (accept / except) a ride in his car.

7. The crime scene technician collected everything in the bedroom (accept / except) the carpet on the floor.

8. Sergeant Grant told Officer Smith to thoroughly search the suspect before he was transported to the booking facility to (ensure / insure) that he had no weapons or contraband on his person.

9. Detective Barnes stated that the suspect would be arrested to (assure / ensure) the victim that justice would be served and she would have her day in court.

10. The condemned prisoner ordered chocolate cake for (desert / dessert).

glossary terms

3

The Mechanics of Writing

INTRODUCTION

This chapter discusses some of the technical mechanics associated with writing in general, and report writing in particular. These include issues of spelling, agreement of gender and number, and common punctuation (periods, commas, semicolons, colons, quotation marks, italics, and apostrophes). In addition, this chapter examines what a sentence is and how and when to start new paragraphs.

Many writers tend to focus more heavily on sentence structure and word usage and may neglect the technical mechanics of writing. This can be a serious error. The mechanics of writing are in many ways the nuts and bolts of a written work. When these elements are incorrectly used, a report or narrative may contain incorrect information or confuse the reader. A misspelled word, an improperly abbreviated term, or incorrect punctuation can not only make the report look sloppy but also may cause the reader to misunderstand or misinterpret the intended meaning. Learning the proper mechanics of writing will produce a better report which is a positive reflection on the author.

WORDS COMMONLY MISSPELLED IN POLICE REPORTS

As implied in Chapter 1, there is no substitution for a good dictionary or thesaurus and you should never do any writing without having one available. Spelling errors in police reports can create comical sentences that amuse supervisors when they review the report. These same supervisors may take a dim view of having to ask you repeatedly to rewrite your reports. Perhaps more significantly, spelling errors can also create problems for a prosecutor if these errors create inaccurate descriptions or details of a crime, or are used to suggest that such careless mistakes are indicative of the caliber of the investigative work done by the officer or agency issuing the report. For example, spelling a suspect or defendant's name incorrectly, or spelling it several ways in the same report, does not convey the impression of an efficient agency. Certain words have been used so commonly in policing and corrections that officers should blush with embarrassment when they are misspelled.

Spelling errors can sometimes arise because the writer simply has made a typographical error (hit the wrong key on the keyboard); other errors may derive from actually not knowing how to spell a word. But there are also times when spelling errors involve the use of the wrong word because a *homonym* has been erroneously selected rather than the correct word. A **homonym** is a word that is identical in form with another word, either in sound (as a homophone) or in spelling (as a homograph) or in both, but differs from it in meaning (Glenn & Gray, 2007).

There are seven <u>days</u> in a week.
The officer felt like he was in a <u>daze</u> after being struck on the head.

The correctional officer <u>led</u> (guided) the new inmate through the gallery to his cell.
Inmate Johnson struck inmate Oxford with a <u>lead</u> (metal) pipe.

When police and correctional officers write reports, it is very important that the proper word is used. Using the wrong homophone may be funny to the reader, but it is also an indication of inaccurate writing that could go badly if brought up in court by a defense attorney during a criminal trial. It suggests a level of carelessness that a defense attorney may be able to suggest extends to other areas of the officer's work. For example, writing up a narrative about a fight in a prison yard could include the following incorrect homophone:

> I witnessed inmate Johnson punching inmate Borden with his <u>bear</u> hands. When questioned, inmate Johnson explained he <u>boar</u> a grudge against inmate Borden because of a bad wine deal from the previous week.

Okay, so let's consider what is actually written here. This passage says that inmate Johnson has hands consisting of a furry animal, a *bear,* which he used to hit inmate Borden—funny, perhaps, but inaccurate. Perhaps even more comical, the next sentence suggests that inmate Johnson held some sort of male wild pig (a *boar*) against inmate Borden. Clearly, it is very important to be mindful about the use of homophones when writing reports. The appendix includes a list of many of the most commonly misused homophones; it would be wise to learn these and know the difference between each word. It also contains a list of commonly misused homonyms.

Knowing the proper word to use in the case of homonyms can cut down on overall writing time and make it less stressful to write reports. In addition to knowing which similar-sounding word is the correct word to use, a number of words used in police and correctional reports are frequently misspelled. There are no quick and easy tricks to better spelling other than learning to correctly spell the words. The appendix provides a list of many of the words that tend to be misspelled in many forms of writing, including police and correctional reports.

AGREEMENT OF GENDER AND NUMBER

Agreement of words in a sentence typically refers to nouns and pronouns. **Gender agreement** has traditionally been thought of as being fairly simple and of little importance. Modern English typically has nouns that are neutral in form, although some are specifically masculine or feminine, and in such cases there is a basic rule to follow with regard to pronouns: The pronouns should agree with the preceding noun (the antecedent noun). Thus, the basic rule is to make pronouns specify the gender of the preceding noun, which generally is also the subject of the sentence. In other words, if a sentence is talking about a female (the noun specifically refers to a female), the pronoun should indicate this gender. Assume, for example, that in the following sentence Officer Johnson is a woman:

> Officer Johnson drew <u>her</u> service revolver and pointed it at the suspect.

On the other hand, had Officer Johnson been a male, the sentence would have indicated the following:

> Officer Johnson drew <u>his</u> service revolver and pointed it at the suspect.

Indefinite pronouns—that is, pronouns that do not specify or permit the writer to know the gender of the noun—present a slight problem. The problem is that indefinite pronouns often refer to both sexes, masculine and feminine. When you say *Everybody ran to the center of the room*, the indefinite pronoun *everybody* includes individuals of both genders, masculine and feminine. When the indefinite pronoun is the antecedent of another pronoun, the general convention today is to use both masculine and feminine pronouns (the phrase *his or her*) in place of the indefinite pronoun to remain gender neutral. In the sentence *Everyone reached for <u>his or her</u> service revolver at the same time*, the indefinite pronoun *everyone* is the antecedent of the phrase *his or her*. While this form tends to sound a little awkward, it avoids the criticism of being gender biased in your writing.

When a sentence does show that the indefinite pronoun refers to members of only one gender, the pronoun that refers to that gender should be used; for example: *Everyone attending the ladies auxiliary received <u>her</u> certificate of attendance on the second Tuesday of the month*. In this last sentence, it seems pretty likely that each of the people being referred to by the word *everyone* is a woman, and the pronoun *her* can be used correctly. So the basic rule is, in cases where it is unclear whether the antecedent is masculine or feminine, use the pronoun phrase *his or her*; in situations where it is known or can be determined, use the appropriate pronoun gender.

Someone left <u>his</u> fingerprints on the window pane.

Everyone has the ability to protect <u>his or her</u> home from burglars.

Indefinite pronouns can also present a problem with regard to **number agreement**. Some indefinite pronouns are always singular while others are always plural; and some may be either singular or plural. Let's consider these various types of pronouns.

Pronouns That Are Always Singular

The following pronouns are examples of those that are always singular. A pronoun that is used in place of one of these indefinite pronouns, then, must also be singular.

another	neither
anybody	nobody
anyone	no one
each	one
either	other
everybody	somebody
everyone	someone

It is interesting to note that among indefinite pronouns *another, anyone, anybody, each, everyone, everybody, someone, somebody, no one*, and *nobody* are always singular. This is sometimes confusing to writers who may think that *everyone* and particularly *everybody* seem to be referring to more than one person. The same is true of the words *either* and *neither*, which are also always singular, yet it would seem appealing to think of them as plural since they seem to be referring to more than one. Let's take a look at a series of examples that show proper agreement between pronoun and antecedent when this antecedent is singular.

<u>Neither</u> of the inmates had <u>his</u> call-out sheet. [not *their*]

If <u>anyone</u> wants a sheet of paper, <u>he</u> can obtain one from the sergeant. [not *they*]

<u>One</u> can have extra time in the yard if <u>he</u> can state a good reason. [not *they*]

<u>Someone</u> left <u>his</u> baton in <u>his</u> locker. [not *their*]

Pronouns That Are Always Plural

Some pronouns are always plural. A pronoun that is used in place of one of these must also be plural. Let's take a look at some common **plural pronouns**:

both

few

many

others

several

Again, it is interesting to note that the phrase *many a one* would be included on the list of **singular pronouns**, whereas *many*, when appearing by itself, is on the plural list. When singular expressions such as *a man, a one, a person*, and so forth are added to *many*, the pronoun becomes singular, not plural.

<u>Several</u> officers found <u>their</u> patrol cars unlocked. [*several*—plural]

Only a <u>few</u> deputies would sacrifice <u>their</u> lives in the line of duty. [*few*—plural]

<u>Many</u> inmates brought <u>their</u> lunches on the road with them. [*many*—plural]

<u>Others</u> found <u>their</u> keys in the drawer. [*others*—plural]

Pronouns That Are Singular or Plural

The pronouns *all, any, some,* and *none* may be used as either singular or plural words, depending on the meaning of the full sentence. When these pronouns refer to *number*, they are generally regarded as plural pronouns. On the other hand, when these terms refer to *quantity* or to a *mass*, they are generally regarded as singular.

The pronoun *none* is singular when it is clear that it refers to *no one*, or *not one*. Unfortunately, it is frequently difficult to discern the number of this pronoun since there are sentences where it may carry a plural idea. The basic rule is that when you want to express the notion of singularity, then use *no one*, or *not one*. Let's take a look at a series of examples.

<u>Some</u> found <u>their</u> cruisers in total disarray. [*some*—plural]

<u>Some</u> of the rope powder has lost <u>its</u> flexibility. [*some*—singular]

<u>All</u> of the officers were waiting for <u>their</u> salary checks. [*all*—plural]

There is no blood on the knife. <u>All</u> of <u>it</u> has been washed clean. [*all*—singular]

Do <u>any</u> of the men have <u>their</u> badges on chains? [*any*—plural]

<u>None</u> have arrived for mess. [*none*—plural in use]

<u>None</u> of these is a typical example of a physical training course. [*none*—singular in use]

PUNCTUATION

Punctuation is quite literally the *rules of the game* in writing (Glenn & Gray, 2007). Once you learn these basic rules, writing becomes a fairly simple activity and does not need to be dreaded or put off. Punctuation is important in all writing, but you could argue it is particularly important in police and correctional reports. Poorly punctuated reports can cause confusion, be misleading, or may even be used to suggest the writer is careless not only in the written document but in the performance of his or her duties. This section will not extensively cover all the rules of punctuation, but will offer a basic coverage of many of the more common rules. One of the biggest problems that appears in many police and correctional reports is the overuse of punctuation, or perhaps more accurately, the erroneous overpunctuation of the document. Overpunctuation is often an indication that the writer does not understand how to punctuate sentences. In this sort of writing, it often appears as if the writer took a handful of punctuation marks and threw them at the page, with no real understanding of where they should be placed. A well-punctuated report can be a powerful tool and even influence a reader's understanding about the contents. Let's start with the period.

The Period

A complete sentence should end with a **period** (.), unless the sentence conveys a question, in which case a question mark (?) should be used to end the sentence. An important rule of thumb in writing any sentence is that it should contain only a single idea—one sentence, one idea. Another useful rule of thumb is that if the sentence runs five or more lines in length, it is likely more than a single idea. These long, unwieldy sentences tend to be written in passive voice, and this too can create confusion as a consequence of the indirect and convoluted structure of the sentence. Most sentences written in police and correctional reports should be direct, active voice, and end with a period.

Periods should also be used when using an abbreviation, but technically not when using an acronym. An acronym is a new word formed by using the capitalized first letters of a series of words, usually in a business or organization's name, and pronounced as this new word. For example, the World Health Organization is sometimes referred to as the acronym WHO, pronounced as if it were written "who." The Naval Criminal Investigation Service, on the other hand, should be abbreviated as N.C.I.S., since the letter combination forms a series of letters that cannot be pronounced and spoken as a word. Nonetheless, in the world of criminal justice, there are frequently times when this technical rule falls by the wayside, and abbreviations are written as if they are an acronym—as in the case of the FBI, which should be written F.B.I. but usually is not. Now you might argue that you can pronounce the series of letters in FBI as "fibby," but we'd argue that's a stretch. So, when writing police and correctional reports, you should be familiar with the standard convention of writing the abbreviations, acronyms, and pseudoacronyms of various agencies and organizations with which you regularly interface.

Occasionally you may see a series of three periods at the end of a sentence (...). These three periods are called an **ellipsis** and should be used to indicate an omission of quoted material (Glenn & Gray, 2007).

Jones stated: "I wasn't there until after 8:00 . . . I do recall, however, seeing three men follow me into the room about five minutes later."

In the preceding example, the information or details that Jones offered were not seen as pertinent to the notes the officer was recording, so they were omitted. Therefore, an ellipsis is used to indicate that more information may have existed but has not been shown. Let's take a look at a more complex punctuation mark, namely, the comma.

The Comma

Many people do not understand how to correctly use **commas** (,). They tend to place them in their writing as spaces for taking a breath and not because they belong there. The result is comma placement with little grammatical rhyme or reason. Proper use of commas occurs in seven different instances. These include commas for introductory elements, to separate items in a series, to separate modifiers, as interrupters, with coordinating conjunctions to separate independent clauses, to separate a dependent clause from an independent clause, and to separate elements shown in an address and elements of a report.

Commas for Introductory Elements This sort of comma use may introduce extra information for the reader, such as when, where, or why something may have occurred.

> On Saturdays, Officer Merchant has lunch at his usual 11:00 A.M.
>
> Today, the cruisers were all in working order.
>
> After work, most of the officers meet at Gillie's Bar and Grill for a beer.

Commas to Separate Items in a Series A series typically refers to the listing of three or more elements in succession. When this occurs, a comma should be used to separate each element.

> The contents of the inmate's cell were inventoried as one cot, one toilet, one sink, and one shelf.
>
> Officer Bardon examined the interior of the car and noted seeing two bullet cartridges, a knife with a six-inch blade, and a pair of brass knuckles, all lying on the back bench seat.

Commas to Separate Modifiers When you use two or more modifiers to modify the same word, a comma should be used to separate these modifiers. A good rule of thumb is to use the comma if you could alternatively place the word *and* between the modifiers.

> The tall, old man was the only witness to the crime.
>
> The victim had soiled himself and was wet, smelly, and embarrassed.
>
> Many people believe that inmates are stupid, belligerent, violent people.

Commas as Interrupters Commas may be used to set off material that adds information and is potentially relevant for the reader, even though it is not essential to the meaning of the sentence. When the information is essential to the meaning of the sentence, it should not be set off by commas. In other words, the clause *interrupts* the general flow of the sentence by interjecting additional information. A good rule of thumb is to read the sentence aloud without the additional information. If the sentence makes sense without it, then use the commas.

> My sergeant, who is also my cousin, never arrives late to work.

If you read this example aloud, and omit the phrase in between the commas, it reads *My sergeant never arrives late to work*. This is a solid sentence; it just doesn't tell you that the sergeant is the speaker's cousin—added information. Let's consider another example.

> Checking to see if your gun is loaded, is a good idea, for officer
> safety.

In this last example, if you read the sentence aloud and again omit the information in between the commas, it reads *Checking to see if your gun is loaded for officer safety*. This does not make sense; in fact, the omission actually tends to change the meaning of the sentence. Hence, you should not include the commas, and the sentence should appear as follows:

> Checking to see if your gun is loaded is a good idea for officer
> safety.

Commas with Coordinating Conjunctions (Using Commas between Independent Clauses)   Commas should be used along with a coordinating conjunction (*so, nor, but, or, yet, and, for*) to combine two completely independent clauses. Independent clauses are a series of words including a subject and a predicate that forms a complete thought. In other words, each clause could be a stand-alone sentence. If there is no coordinating conjunction used to join the clauses, then use of the comma is incorrect. In such cases, where a coordinating clause is absent, you should use a *semicolon* (discussed later).

> Officer Dwyer found the victim, but Officer Donald secured
> the area.

This example uses the comma correctly because there are two independent clauses separated by the coordinating conjunction followed by the comma.

> Officer Dwyer found the victim, Officer Donald secured the area.

This example is incorrect and is sometimes referred to as a *comma splice* because the two clauses have been linked together solely with the comma and no coordinating conjunction. This last sentence could have been written correctly if the writer had used a semicolon.

> Officer Dwyer found the victim; Officer Donald secured the area.

Commas to Separate a Dependent Clause Followed by an Independent Clause   When a sentence begins with a dependent clause followed by an independent clause, a comma should be placed after the dependent clause. If the sentence begins with an independent clause, you should not use a comma to separate these two clauses. A dependent clause does not stand alone as a sentence but depends on another clause to complete its meaning. For example, in the sentence *When I am* *hired by the Irvine Police Department, I will be very happy*, the first clause, *When I am hired by the Irvine Police Department*, does not by itself make much sense or form a complete sentence. When we add the second clause, *I will be happy*, the first clause (the dependent clause) now makes sense because of the added information of the second clause (the independent clause). Dependent clauses are also known as subordinate clauses. Consider the following examples of proper use of a comma when there is a dependent clause followed by an independent clause.

<u>When she saw the blood on her hands,</u> she realized she was in a lot of trouble.

    [dependent clause]   [independent clause]

<u>Before starting his cruiser,</u> Officer Jones always checked his shotgun and his radio.

    [dependent clause]   [independent clause]

As noted earlier in this section, when the independent clause comes first, you do not need to include the comma prior to the dependent clause.

She realized she was in a lot of trouble <u>when she saw the blood on her hands.</u>

    [independent clause]   [dependent clause]

Officer Jones always checked his shotgun and his radio <u>before he started his cruiser.</u>

    [independent clause]   [dependent clause]

Again, if you try reading these sentences aloud, you will notice that there is a smoother flow when reading the second set of examples (those with the independent clause first). Conversely, when you read the first version you tend to pause at the comma.

Commas to Separate Elements in a Report—Addresses, Dates, Names—and before Quotes   Commas are used when writing an address to set off towns, cities, and states, but are not used before writing a zip code.

Andres Johnson resides at 1482 Maple Street, Costa Mesa, CA 62014.

In dates, you use commas to separate the day of the week, the day of the month, and the year.

The traffic accident occurred on Tuesday, January 8, 2011.

Often, police and correctional reports use a numerical format that is not set off by commas, but rather by forward slashes or dashes.

01/08/09

01-08-09

A comma is also used when a proper name is used when the first and last names are inverted.

Bickerson, William.

Similarly, if a title follows a proper name, a comma is used.

> William Bickerson, Jr.
>
> William Bickerson, PhD

When writing reports, there may be occasions when you need to quote someone. If it is a short quote, it is considered part of the sentence and does not need to be set off by a comma.

> Officer Thomas interviewed the inmate who claimed "I didn't do anything."

On the other hand, if the quote is lengthy it will require being set off by a comma.

> Officer Thomas interviewed the inmate who claimed, "I didn't do anything; I was just sitting around minding my own business."

You may have noticed in this last example that a semicolon was used. Let's turn our attention to how and when to use semicolons.

The Semicolon

In most police and correctional reports, you should not need to use the **semicolon** (;) very often. Sentences should be short, direct, or active; consequently, these reports need not contain many complex sentences composed of multiple clauses connected by semicolons. As mentioned in the section on commas, the semicolon separates independent clauses when they are *not* joined by a comma and a coordinating conjunction, such as *so, nor, but, or, yet, and, for*. The semicolon is very useful when two independent clauses are closely related.

> Officer Johnson chased after the suspect; Officer Burton followed Johnson.
>
> The range officer demonstrated how to fire using a two-handed hold on the weapon; each recruit practiced shooting using the two-handed hold.

Be mindful, however, that using semicolons creates more complex sentences than are typically necessary in most police and correctional reports. Reports should state the facts of a case and include any relevant details. The result is that you should be writing fairly short, crisp, and direct sentences.

Semicolons are also used when separating long or possibly confusing items listed in a series, especially when these items already include commas.

> Each suspect was searched and found to be concealing the following items on their persons: Morris Brown, a knife and brass knuckles; Abraham Johnson, a knife and a 38-caliber short-nosed revolver; and Eric Munster, a 22-caliber pistol concealed in his belt buckle.

A semicolon may also be used when several sets of groups of items are listed in a series.

> Sergeant Jones was cataloging the SWAT team's supplies. He found there were five less-than-lethal shotguns and 100 rounds of bean pillows; three tack strips with repairable prongs and two with

nonrepairable prongs; four Tasers with attached (hard-wired) points and four with free-firing points.

Note that in the previous example, items that fit together logically were grouped together with independent clauses and separated by semicolons in a manner similar to how a comma might have been used to separate independent clauses.

The Colon

When you see a **colon** (:) in a document, it should give you the visual signal that *something is coming*, or *something will be following* (Glenn & Gray, 2007). Colons are a type of punctuation that is often misused. For example, headings in reports typically stand on their own on the line before the narrative or other written material they label; they do not require a colon after them. Nonetheless, many inexperienced writers place a colon after a stand-alone heading.

WITNESS STATEMENT [correct]
I was standing on the corner . . .

WITNESS STATEMENT: [incorrect]
I was standing on the corner . . .

The example illustrates what in writing is sometimes referred to as an "A heading." Most A headings are written in all capital letters and set in bold type. There simply is no reason to also include a colon in such a heading. If, however, you are not using the heading as a stand-alone heading on a separate line, but rather are using a "run-in" heading on the same line, it would be proper to use a colon because in this case the heading announces that something will immediately follow it.

WITNESS STATEMENT: I was standing on the corner . . .

Colons are also used as part of the standard format in most memorandums in businesses and in most police and correctional agencies. In this case, the headings on the memorandum (to whom it is addressed, from whom it has originated, the date, and an indication of the memorandum's subject) are all followed by a colon.

To:

From:

Date:

Subject:

Colons can be used inside a sentence to join together one complete sentence to another complete sentence. Frequently, a conjunction such as *and* or *but* preceded by a comma will suffice—or even a semicolon may work. But under certain circumstances, the colon is the best choice. In particular, when the second sentence explains the meaning of the first sentence, these two sentences may be joined by a colon.

> Officer Merton failed his test for sergeant for the third time: He just does not study enough before the exam.
>
> The recruit fired her weapon at the target and got a bull's-eye: The smoke hadn't settled when she realized it was not her target she had hit.

Whether or not to capitalize the first word following colons in a sentence is a bit confusing. APA style suggests that you capitalize the first word following a colon; however, style manuals vary. You should conform to your agency's general writing policy regarding whether to capitalize the first word after a colon.

Colons also may be used when for run-in lists, particularly when you use phrases such as *the following, as follows, these are, there are, these things.*

> The contents of the recovered purse included <u>the following</u>: one dark red lipstick; a change purse containing two quarters, two dimes, and one penny; a plastic bristle hair brush; a small packet of tissues; and a wallet containing five twenty-dollar bills, three five-dollar bills, and five singles.

In addition, a colon may be used when introducing a long quote. The rule here is fairly simple: If the quote is brief, introduce it with a comma; if the quote is long, introduce it with a colon.

> Officer Johnson noted what the witness said verbatim, "I ain't got nothing to say to you mother-fuckers!" [This brief quote requires only a comma.]

Officer Johnson noted what the witness said verbatim:

> I ain't got nothing to say to you mother-fuckers! Every time I do talk with the cops I get run in on some trumped-up bullshit charge, the cause of which I have to lose time at work and lose money. [This long quote requires a colon.]

You may have noticed in the last example, which was a direct quotation, that no quotation marks were used. Let's take a look at the rules pertaining to quotation marks.

Quotation Marks

You will see **quotation marks** in virtually all types of writing, and police and correctional reports are no different. Quotations are literal (verbatim) written repetitions of someone else's words. There are four basic uses for quotation marks (" "): to set off a direct quotation (quote), to set off certain types of writing, to indicate titles of published works in a reference list, and to draw attention to unusual use of a word. If you have graduated high school, the chances are pretty good that you've used quotation marks in each of these four major ways. Sadly, many of you have also misused or overused quotation marks, or used them erroneously in your writing. Let's review the proper use of quotation marks.

To Set Off a Direct Quote.   Whenever you write exactly what someone else has said or written, you are quoting directly. This requires placing quotation marks at the beginning of the passage (opening the quotation) and quotation marks at the conclusion of the passage being directly quoted (closing the quotation). Both opening and closing quotation marks must be present in a **direct quote**.

> The victim told me: "I was just standing at the corner waiting for my friend to pick me up, when that blue Ford came speeding by and two guys were shooting guns outt'a the windows."

If I were reading this in an officer's report, I would know that this was exactly what the victim had told the reporting officer; it is a direct quote. If the officer, however, had not used quotation marks, I would read the same passages thinking that the victim had said something along those lines but not necessarily exactly what I was reading. It is important, therefore, to differentiate between a direct quotation and an indirect or paraphrased statement. Quotation marks provide a visual signal of this distinction.

Quotation marks are also placed in front of and at the conclusion of each segment of a broken or interrupted quote.

> "I had to take a personal break," Officer Johnson stated, "then I returned to my original patrol."

> "I entered the premises with my gun drawn," explained Officer Rodriguez, "but once I saw it was a dog in the room, I holstered my gun."

Note that the period indicating the end of the sentence in quoted materials is placed inside the quotation mark, at the close of the quotation (see the previous examples).

Quoting Written or Literary Sources   Quotation marks are also used when citing material from written or literary sources. There are two styles of quotation of literary material, short quotes and long quotes. In short quotes, in addition to the quotation marks, you must indicate the source of the quoted materials exactly. This means the name of the author, the date of the publication from which this material was taken, and the page number on which this material appeared originally.

> According to Steinberg (2009), "when officers arrive at the scene of a crime, they must use extreme caution" (p. 23). [correct formatting]

> Information about police arrival is also common in the literature. For example, as Steinberg explains, "when officers arrive at the scene of a crime, they must use extreme caution" (Steinberg, 2009, p. 23). [correct formatting]

> Information about police arrival is also common in the literature. For example, as Steinberg explains, "when officers arrive at the scene of a crime, they must use extreme caution." (Steinberg, 2009, p. 23). [incorrect formatting with extra period inside quotation marks]

Each of the previous examples presents the same quoted material; however, each cites the material in slightly different ways. In the first example, the author and publication information is offered in the context of the sentence itself, and the quotation is concluded with a period. In the second example, the source information is placed parenthetically at the end of the quoted material. In the third example, the period is placed at the conclusion of the quotation, which is incorrect.

Long quotes, generally quotes of 40 or more words, are an exception to the quotation mark rule. When citing testimony or the transcription of an interview or interrogation, for example, set off (indent) text at both the left and right margins. Quotation marks are not needed to enclose the long quote, but double quotation marks are used for directly quoted material within the long quote. Frequently the long quote will be single-spaced, even when the line spacing in the surrounding text is double-spaced. However, this is not a grammatical rule but a choice of style. The citation for a long quote appears directly at the end of the quote as a parenthetical statement.

There are several purposes for vehicle accident reports available in the literature. For instance:

> Vehicle accident or collision reports, as they are referred to by some agencies, are an important source of information in a number of areas. First, in traffic fatalities, the collision report is part of a homicide investigation. As a result of such an investigation, a surviving driver may face aggravated vehicular homicide or vehicular homicide charges. Furthermore, the families of the victim deserve a thorough investigation of the victim's deaths. Second, information from collision reports can help courts assess liability in personal injury or property damage cases. Third, enactment of traffic and vehicle safety laws often result from information gathered from collision reports. (Berg, 2008, p. 198)

To Set Off Certain Types of Writing   If in the course of your report you mention certain types of other written works, such as the title of a short story or a poem, these should appear in your writing surrounded by quotation marks.

> Officer Meeker explained the concept of *sour grapes* to the juvenile by telling him the parable of the "Fox and the Grapes," from Aesop's Fables.
> Among her favorite poems was Ogden Nash's "Candy Is Dandy."

To Indicate Titles of Published Works in a Reference List   If you have cited a source for material quoted in your report, you need to indicate the full citation information of this reference somewhere in the document. This can be accomplished either at the bottom of the page (via a footnote) or in a separate listing of all references (via a reference list, or works cited list). In the latter case, the page should begin with an *A heading*, referred to earlier in this chapter, showing the title of the listing; for example, REFERENCES. The list of citations should be arranged alphabetically by the author's last name. A number of styles are used for referencing. The style used in this book is known as APA style, and is based on the *Publication Manual of the American Psychological Association* (2010). We will not extensively discuss citing variations for all of the different types of publications and media elements in this chapter. Here are some examples:

- **Newspaper:** Thomson, M. (2009, January 14). Two men rob local 7-eleven. *The Orange County Register*, pp. 5–6.

- **Magazine or journal:** Ward, S. M. (2011). Careers for correctional officers. *Journal of Corrections, 15*(1), 33–35.

- **Book:** Chandler, V. (2009). *Police agency ethics*. New York: McGraw-Hill.

- **Chapter or segment citation in anthology:** Pollock, J. M. (1997). Ethics and law enforcement. In Roger G. Dunham & Geoffrey P. Alpert (Eds.), *Critical issues in Policing: Contemporary readings* (3rd ed.). Prospect Heights, IL: Waveland Press.

To Draw Attention to an Unusual Use of a Term   Occasionally you may use a term or phrase in a nonstandard way or to convey a special sense. Quotation marks are used the first time the word or phrase is used. For instance, you might write: *The conman was a "master" of deception.* By placing *master* inside quote marks, you are conveying a kind of ironic note suggesting the conman was not really very good. Or you might write: *The officer "definitely" had a bad attitude about juvenile delinquents.* In this case, the effect is simply to draw attention to the word *definitely* or perhaps to emphasize the word. We suggest you avoid doing this. If you want to emphasize a word, or set it off from the others in the sentence, we recommend writing the word in italics, or with an underline. The next section focuses on the use of italics in writing.

Italics

In the past, when typewriters were the sole method used for preparing reports, it was difficult to emphasize words or phrases using italics. To draw attention you needed to either enclose the words or phrases in quotation marks or underline them. With today's technology, however, which offers the options of multiple fonts and styles it is possible to write words and phrases in **italics** to show emphasis. Let's consider the other general uses of italics.

In addition to using italics to emphasize specific words or phrases, italic type is used to indicate the titles of books, newspapers, journals, magazines, newsletters, and other publications.

> Captain Bertrum regularly reads *The Law Enforcement Bulletin* published by the FBI.
>
> Our department's Crime Intelligence Unit members regularly read the *L.A. Times* to see how the paper is reporting on crimes in their jurisdiction.

The title of movies, works of art, television and radio programs, and record albums are also italicized. Further, foreign language words, such as *ex post facto* or *modus operandi,* should be written in italics. A good rule of thumb to follow is to use italics when typing on a computer but to underline when writing by hand. It is also important to note that when using either italics or underlining for emphasis, you should not overdo it! If every other word is italicized or underlined, the emphasis is lost.

Another way to draw attention to a word or phrase is to type it in **boldface** type. Again, given the availability of computers, you are now able to change the typeface in a sentence to italics, boldface, or underlined. One of the common styles used in publishing is to print headings in boldface type; in addition, words that are defined in the line of text are often also printed in bold type. As with the the use of italics and underlining, boldface type should be used sparingly.

The Apostrophe

The **apostrophe** serves several important purposes when writing. Using it incorrectly or in the wrong places in a narrative will not only confuse the reader but also an change the meaning of a word or abbreviation. In this section we will discuss several instances when it is appropriate to use an apostrophe.

Singular Possessive   For the **singular possessive** case, an apostrophe is used to show possession or ownership.

> The <u>officer's</u> weapon was unloaded.

> The <u>suspect's</u> clothing was covered in blood.

The apostrophe is also used to show a relationship with someone else.

> My <u>mother's</u> brother is a supreme court justice.

> My <u>co-worker's</u> children do not live with him.

The apostrophe is used to show that someone has produced or created something. If the noun already ends in *s*, add an additional *s*.

> The <u>prosecutor's</u> case was well presented.

> <u>Officer Marks's</u> report was lacking in critical details.

Plural Possessive   For the **plural possessive** case, an apostrophe is used to show possession by more than one person.

> The <u>suspects'</u> masks were found after a search of their vehicle.

An apostrophe was used in the past to form the plurals of numbers and abbreviations. It is rarely used for this purpose today (Glenn & Gray, 2007, p. 221).

> These plurals are generally formed by simply adding *s*.

> 1980s

> Fours and fives

> DUIs

Contractions   A **contraction** is the shortened form of a word, syllable, or word group by omission of internal letters. An apostrophe is used to mark omissions in contractions, numbers, and words mimicking speech.

> You're [you are]

> Class of '09 [class of 2009]

> Y'all [you all]

SENTENCES

In this section we will discuss how to develop well-written sentences that convey ideas and actions in a clear and understandable way. A well-written narrative is nothing more than a series of well-constructed and thought-out sentences. A poorly written sentence can confuse the reader or potentially change the writer's intended meaning. Writers never know who will end up reading their work. Police reports often end up in courtrooms and newspapers, or discussed on the evening news. Poorly written sentences result in substandard and hard-to-understand reports. Attention to details and pride in authorship should always be the driving motivation for any writer.

One Idea, One Sentence

Each sentence should contain a subject and a verb and express a single thought. Inexperienced writers often get into trouble when they try to include too much information in one sentence or fail to accurately express a single thought. This results in a jumbled or crowded narrative that leaves the reader confused or frustrated. Effective writers should strive to complete each sentence as a single thought or idea. Putting sentences together into a well-constructed narrative makes for a quality document that is easy to read and understand.

> Officer Franks entered the residence and went into the bedroom and saw blood stains on the doorway and as he searched further discovered a body next to the bed. [incorrect]

> Officer Franks entered the residence and observed blood stains on the doorway leading into the bedroom. As he searched further, he discovered a body lying next to the bed. [correct]

In these examples the first sentence conveys two different ideas. The *first* idea is that the officer enters the residence and sees blood on a doorway before entering the bedroom. The *second* idea is that as he searches further he discovers a body lying next to the bed. If the writer combines these ideas into one sentence, this does not accurately describe the officer's actions. From the second example it is clear that one action led to another, which may be critical if this case gets to court. It may become vital to accurately describe the actions of the officer when entering the crime scene. A defense attorney might challenge the legality of the officer's actions and search if they are not completely and accurately documented in the police report. A poorly written sentence could produce doubt as to the true actions of the investigating officer. Often, it is these small details that become so vitally important when establishing probable cause for an arrest, supporting the legality of a search, or prosecuting a case. Remember, a well-written report will alleviate any doubt about what actions were taken and what observations were made.

Sentence Fragments and Correcting Them

A **sentence fragment** is nothing more than an incomplete sentence. A sentence should be able to stand on its own. To be complete, a sentence must contain a subject and a verb and convey a complete idea. When any of these elements is missing or the sentence is incomplete, it is considered a fragment. The following examples describe three types of common sentence fragments. They also demonstrate how to identify and correct these types of fragments.

1. Fragments begin with a verb ending in *–ing*.

    Running down the street. [fragment]

    The suspect was last seen running down the street. [corrected]

2. Relative clause fragments begin with *who, whose, which,* or *that.*

    Who came down the stairs when she heard a noise in the kitchen. [fragment]

    Mrs. Meyers came down the stairs when she heard a noise in the kitchen. [corrected]

3. A dependent clause fragment often begins with a subordinating conjunction such as *after, although, because, if,* or *when.*

    After his weapon was discovered. [fragment]

    The suspect confessed after his weapon was discovered. [corrected]

Sentence fragments can be corrected in two ways. First, they can be corrected by combining them with the preceding sentence by using proper punctuation, such as a comma or semicolon. Fragments can also be reconfigured into a complete sentence by rewriting them and adding the missing element. Sentence fragments should be avoided because they can confuse the reader and may change the idea or statement being conveyed.

The Run-On Sentence

A **run-on sentence** is a sentence that runs together two independent clauses without a conjunction or punctuation (Glenn & Gray, 2007). Inexperienced writers frequently incorporate run-on sentences in their writing. This often is the result of the writer hurrying to complete the work or attempting to cram too much information into a single sentence. A run-on sentence can confuse the reader by trying to combine two or more ideas or thoughts into a single sentence. The following examples illustrate how to identify run-on sentences and how to properly correct them.

> The victim Mrs. Smith is eighty years old she lives in the blue house on the corner. [run-on sentence]
> The victim, Mrs. Smith, who is eighty years old, lives in the blue house on the corner. [corrected]

> Officer Mills responded to the 7-11 convenience store and arrested the suspect who was caught stealing a six-pack of beer from the store by the manager. [run-on sentence]
> Officer Mills responded to the 7-11 convenience store. He arrested the suspect, who had been caught by the manager, for stealing a six-pack of beer from the store. [corrected]

> The witness Mr. Brown has poor eyesight he was wearing his glasses when he saw the suspect exit the victim's residence. [run-on sentence]
> The witness, Mr. Brown, has poor eyesight; however, he was wearing his glasses when he saw the suspect exit the victim's residence. [corrected]

Run-on sentences can be easily corrected by adding punctuation or using separate sentences for clearer meaning. By breaking up run-on sentences, the reader will not get lost in a sentence that is too long and that tries to convey too much information. Some writers may think that a long, complicated sentence sounds more important or shows more intelligence. The mark of a good writer, however, is the ability to convey ideas or information in a clear and understandable way. Clear, concise sentences can convey even very detailed or complex information in a meaningful way. Police and correctional reports typically contain a large amount of detailed and descriptive information on events and observations. It might be tempting to try to include all the details by writing long, complex sentences, but writing clear, concise sentences will convey this information much more effectively.

Subject Identification

Every complete sentence must contain two basic elements: a subject and a verb. The subject is the *who* or *what* word. The verb shows the action being performed or the state of being of the subject. The subject is the *who* or *what* that is performing the action or the *who* or *what* word to which a statement is made. When more than one person or thing performs the action in a sentence, it is called a compound subject. It is important to properly identify the subject in your sentences—**subject identification**. This makes your writing clearer and easier to understand. The subjects in these examples are identified by the underlining.

> <u>Officer Johnson</u> arrested the suspect in the parking lot.
>
> <u>Mrs. Broom</u> filed a report after she discovered her purse was missing.
>
> The blue <u>sedan</u> had fresh damage on the driver's side quarter panel.
>
> Her <u>grandfather and grandmother</u> lived in the house on the corner.
>
> <u>Running</u> causes my knees to ache.

Capitalization

In this section we will review when it is appropriate to capitalize a word. **Capitalization** is writing a word with its first letter in uppercase and the remaining letters in lowercase. Incorrect capitalization of words can confuse the reader or make a report look unprofessional or poorly written. The following is a list of when capitalization is required:

- The first word in a sentence.

  Officer Milton was patrolling Center Street when he encountered the suspect.

- A greeting or salutation.

  Dear Mr. Jones,

- Names, places, streets, buildings, titles, and family relationships when it substitutes for the person's proper name.

  David Smith

  New York City

  Main Street

  the Empire State Building

  Doctor Green

  Father, let's go; but, my father lives with me.

- Courts

  the Supreme Court

  the Fifth District Court of Appeals

- Nationalities, races, languages, religions, and political parties.

  American

  Asian male

  Chinese

  Methodist

  Democratic Party

- Brand names, registered trademarks.

    Microsoft

    Pepsi-Cola

- Titles of publications such as books, bulletins or journals, magazines, newspapers, poems, plays, and television and radio programs, as well as article titles and chapter titles and headings.

    Charlotte's Web

    The FBI Bulletin

    Time

    The New York Times

    "The Road Not Taken"

    Cats

    The Andy Griffith Show

    Prairie Home Companion

- Days, months, holidays, historical events, documents, and historical time periods.

    Monday

    February

    Christmas Day

    the Civil War

    the Declaration of Independence

    the Middle Ages

- Adjectives formed with proper nouns.

    black Labrador retriever

    Chinese restaurant

PARAGRAPHING

The building blocks for high-quality police reports or any written work are well-developed paragraphs. **Paragraphing** is a way of providing a framework for conveying information and ideas. If paragraphs are poorly designed or presented in an unorgaized way, the reader will be lost or confused. There are some very basic rules to follow when designing paragraphs.

Most paragraphs should have a **topic sentence.** This sentence states the main idea of the paragraph. The remaining sentences in the paragraph should build on the topic sentence in a logical and unified way. Frequently, the topic sentence is the first sentence in the paragraph, but it can appear anywhere in the paragraph. Every sentence in the paragraph should be clear and convey an idea related to the topic sentence. The reader should be able to easily follow the ideas being conveyed in these sentences.

Police reports are typically presented in a chronological order for clarity and to present facts in the order that they occurred or were discovered. This allows the police writer to naturally break up report writing into logical paragraphs based on when events occurred, or who was the object of the action being described (Berg, 2007).

As stated earlier, it is important for writers to ensure that each paragraph's ideas are clearly presented and properly developed so that one main idea is conveyed. Too many ideas or unrelated facts in a single paragraph can confuse the reader. Each paragraph should naturally and logically transition into the next paragraph. Conjunctions and transitional phrases can guide the reader from one paragraph to the next, such as *for example, however, moreover, subsequently,* and *accordingly.* These transitions tell the reader to get ready for additional ideas or information.

Good writers evaluate each paragraph as they edit their work: Does the paragraph convey a central idea or message? Does the topic sentence provide a clear idea? Do the supporting sentences in the paragraph add to that idea? Do the sentences flow in a logical order that can be easily followed? Do the paragraphs leading to and coming after this paragraph provide a logical flow of information?

ABBREVIATIONS

Abbreviations, shortened forms of a word or phrase, are an effective way to shorten the amount time it takes to record information. Using abbreviations or shorthand when taking notes at a crime scene or when summarizing information from a witness in the field can be useful. This allows the writer to capture information quickly but accurately for use later when more time is available to thoroughly spell out information and terminology. With the continually evolving use of texting shorthand on cell phones and PDAs (personal digital assistants) it might be tempting for more tech-savvy officers to use texting language in police reports. This practice should be avoided at all cost. Not everyone can interpret this language or slang, and it could easily cause confusion and misinformation in official reports—not to mention the fact that it is unprofessional. Remember, writers never know where their written work may end up or who might be reading it.

Every profession has a standard list of terms and phrases that are frequently abbreviated. These terms may be readily understood by people in the field; however, interpretation of these abbreviations can sometimes cause confusion. Similar abbreviations can have different meanings depending on how they are used. For example, *HRS* can be used to abbreviate Health and Rehabilitative Services or high rate of speed. One interpretation might be used in a child neglect case and the other for a traffic crash investigation. It is easy to see that the interpretation is completely different depending on the orientation or knowledge of the reader. For this reason abbreviations should be avoided in narrative reports (Berg, 2007).

chapter summary

1. The importance of correct spelling in reports cannot be overstated. Words that are misspelled can make an otherwise well-written report look shoddy and poorly done. Always consult a dictionary or thesaurus if you are unsure of the meaning or spelling of a word.

2. Sentences should be written using correct agreement of gender and number. This adds clarity to the report and assists the reader in following the flow of the narrative.

3. Using the correct punctuation and emphasis (periods, commas, semicolons, colons, quotation marks, italics and boldface, and apostrophes) in reports is extremely important. A good writer should have an understanding of the proper use of punctuation. Improper use can confuse the reader and make the report look unprofessional.

4. Quality reports are nothing more than a collection of well-constructed paragraphs and well-written sentences. Writing paragraphs that are thought out and that lead the reader to a logical conclusion are critical to quality report writing.

5   Knowing what constitutes a well-written sentence and how and when to start new paragraphs will contribute to a well-written report.

6. Abbreviations are an acceptable way to capture information for field notes when time is of the essence. However, in reports the use of abbreviations should be avoided. Although these terms may be readily understood by people in the criminal justice field, they can sometimes cause confusion.

Exercises—Practicing Writing Mechanics

USING HOMONYMS CORRECTLY

INSTRUCTIONS: In each sentence, circle the correct homonym. Note that some sentences require you to select two homonyms.

1. Officer Johnson put (forth / fourth) a great effort for the (sole / soul) purpose of catching the fleeing suspect.
2. Because of the (rain / reign) on the road, a car swerved ahead of him, and Officer Michaels had to cut across the (lane / lain).
3. The officers checked (they're / their) riot gear before entering the cell block. The weight of the gear made Officer Miller's shoulders (sore / soar).

CORRECTING MISSPELLED WORDS

INSTRUCTIONS: Write the correct spelling of each underlined word in the space provided.

1. The suspect was known by two other <u>alias</u>.

   _____

2. The sergeant instructed the recruits on not <u>hummiliating</u> a suspect.

   _____

3. The victim <u>identifed</u> the suspect from a six-pack of photos.

   _____

4. After being attacked, the woman screamed <u>hystericaly.</u>

   _____

5. The weapon was <u>noticable</u>, but concealed under the inmate's bunk.

   _____

6. Every time the officer spoke, she was <u>interruppted</u> by the suspect.

   _____

CHOOSING THE CORRECT INDEFINITE PRONOUN

INSTRUCTIONS: In each sentence, circle the correct indefinite pronoun(s).

1. Both officers bought (his or her / their) hats at the store.
2. Neither of the inmates had (his or her / their) fork or spoon.
3. Anybody can forget (his or her / their) handcuffs in the locker while dressing.
4. Did any of the inmates have (his or her / their) identification cards with them?

exercise 1   exercise 2   exercise 3

USING COMMAS CORRECTLY

INSTRUCTIONS: For each sentence pair, identify the sentence that uses commas *correctly* by placing an X in the space provided.

1. _____ After the shooting, Officer Jones turned over his gun to his supervisor.

   _____ After the shooting Officer Jones turned over his gun to his supervisor.

2. _____ The tall young blond-haired woman ran over to the officer when he arrived.

   _____ The tall, young, blond-haired woman ran over to the officer when he arrived.

3. _____ Before driving away from the station, I always check the fuel gauge.

   _____ Before driving away from the station I always check the fuel gauge.

USING SEMICOLONS CORRECTLY

INSTRUCTIONS: For each sentence pair, identify the sentence that uses semicolons *correctly* by placing an X in the space provided.

1. _____ The patrol was fairly routine; suddenly a car went speeding past the cruiser.

   _____ The patrol was fairly routine suddenly a car went speeding past the cruiser.

2. _____After stopping for the light; the car was struck from behind.

   _____ After stopping for the light the car was struck from behind.

3. _____ The property list showed the following items: a wallet containing $250, a MasterCard, and a Visa card; a small toolkit including a hammer, two Phillips-head screwdrivers, a pliers, and a box cutter; and a cigar box filled with twenty number two pencils.

   _____ The property list showed the following items: a wallet containing $250, a MasterCard: and a Visa card; a small toolkit including a hammer, two Phillips-head screwdrivers, a pliers; and a box cutter; and a cigarbox filled with twenty number two pencils.

USING COLONS CORRECTLY

INSTRUCTIONS: For each sentence, cross out the incorrect comma and replace it with a colon.

1. Inmates must comply with the following institutional rules, how to request books, how to mail a letter, or how to request pens or stationary.
2. Captain Bobbles insisted his officers follow uniform protocols, clean, pressed uniforms, shined shoes, clean weapons, and well-trimmed hair.
3. Officer Stanton hates doing paperwork, he often leaves all his reports until the end of the shift.

USING APOSTOPHES CORRECTLY

INSTRUCTION: For each sentence, add an apostrophe (if needed) in the appropriate place(s).

1. The officers report was very detailed and well written.
2. Mills vehicle was seen leaving the parking lot just before the fire started.
3. The evolution of policing progressed significantly during the 1990s.
4. The medical examiners autopsy report was critical to the success of the states case.
5. During the civil defense drill the officers formed into groups of fours and fives.
6. During the robbery the suspect stated "give me the money or you re going to die."

exercise 6   exercise 7   glossary terms

4

Taking Effective Field Notes

INTRODUCTION

As indicated in the chapter title, *effective* field notes are the focus of this chapter. While all police officers, and many correctional officers, prepare notes documenting activities they undertake and information they learned in the field, not all such writing is necessarily effective. Field notes can be handwritten notes, notes written in some form of personal shorthand, or tape-recorded verbal notes.

Many officers have tried to remember details from an incident without taking good field notes, only to later have difficulty remembering the details from the incident or the

The use of sound interviewing techniques and proper note-taking strategies will result in a more thorough investigation and accurate written report.
Source: Stockbyte/Getty Images

descriptions given by a witness or victim. The purpose of field notes is to refresh the memory of the officer when it comes to putting an investigation "together" or writing a report. Field notes must be organized in a fashion that facilitates ease of retrieval and report writing. Notes should be clearly written, with sufficient specificity to ensure that important points—such as the corpus delicti (body of the crime)—have been described and relevant descriptive information included. Police and correctional officers' notes do not, however, need to include extensive descriptions of what the investigating officer is wearing, or specific descriptions of an emergency medical technician (EMT) who might be providing a victim with treatment during a field interview. This chapter focuses on describing what are effective field notes and the relevant and important elements that go into creating them including organizing them, taking effective written notes while in the field, using field notes in writing reports, and using tape recorders and digital dictation systems.

THE IMPORTANCE OF GOOD FIELD NOTES

A good police or correctional officer's report should be detailed and accurate. Many agencies are so busy that officers do not have the luxury of stopping their duties to write individual reports as the information is received. Often officers go from call to call on their shift taking several reports and assisting on many others. Police officers working in even moderate-sized agencies routinely find themselves handling fifteen to twenty calls for service per shift. Similarly, correctional officers must handle numerous incidents during the course of a day and write reports on each of these to detail events or to be used as evidence in possible charges brought against an inmate. Many of the incidents investigated by police and correctional officers will require some form of documentation. At the end of a shift, an officer may have hours of report writing ahead or him or her.

When not handling calls for service, good police officers are *hunting*, proactively looking for activity in their patrol area that needs the attention of law enforcement. Similarly, correctional officers move around the facility, vigilant of any misbehaviors or dangers that may exist. This also limits the time an officer can spend writing reports. Once an officer becomes involved in an incident needing his or her attention, whether it is an intoxicated driver, contact with a crime victim, or a fight between inmates, another report must be generated.

At the end of a day, the officer must overcome the fatigue of a long, busy shift to accurately recall many facts, witness statements, as well as the various crime elements from several incidents and sit down to write his or her *reports*. It should be fairly obvious that a good report is required for an arrest or a significant investigation; it is also important to note, however, that incident reports are read by a number of different people. These individuals include peers, superiors (supervisors), prosecuting attorneys, and defendants' counsel. All of these people will judge the reports in terms of their accuracy, clarity, and utility in either legal or administrative proceedings. The only way an officer can effectively organize all of the shift's information is by taking good notes. Thus, effective field notes must be clear, concise, legible, and organized.

As was discussed in some detail in Chapter 1, technology is changing the way notes are taken by officers in the field (Foster, 2004). Many officers are using digital tape recorders and in-car video to capture field activity. Whereas many officers at first were skeptical of these technological innovations, digital devices in particular have quickly become integrated into the regular note-taking procedures of an increasing number of police agencies. *Narrating* notes on a recorder results in more complete information, and allows the officer to develop field notes rapidly and efficiently. Similarly many agencies are using in-car video to record events, especially in the face of an increasing number of civilian bystanders who regularly use their cell phones to record interactions between police officers and stopped suspects or traffic violators. The video can be reviewed prior to and while writing reports to allow more accurate recall of events and sequencing of events.

Like most people, police officers do not like to be recorded while in public. Whatever someone does or says in public is not private. If it can be seen or overheard, it can be lawfully recorded. Currently, an officer in a major city faces discipline for assaulting a bystander at a crime scene. The bystander was standing in a driveway (later discovered to be his driveway) as officers were investigating a burglary. The officer objected and forcefully took the camera away from the citizen. The citizen complained and the officer was suspended. The lesson to be learned from this and other high-profile incidents of police misconduct captured on videotape or audiotapes is this: If you would not want your *mother* to see or hear you acting or speaking in a certain manner, then follow the rules of your agency and act professionally!

TAKING EFFECTIVE FIELD NOTES

Effective field notes are complete and accurate accounts that are also legible and written using proper grammar and terminology. Notes should be taken immediately as the information is received or observed, not twenty minutes later or after completion of an interview. Officers sometimes miss the importance of producing legible notes, but must remember that these notes may end up in court, either as exhibits intended for the eyes of the jury or to be used to refresh the officer's memory on the witness stand. Notes may be read aloud in court or at administrative hearings; they may also be demanded during discovery in criminal trials and in civil actions. Officers do not want to be embarrassed in court by having to admit they cannot read their own handwriting. Worse still is when field notes are written so poorly that the officer cannot determine, after reading them, who the victim is and who the accused is, or when they contain extraneous information that complicates or confuses the actual case record. In a court case several years ago involving a fatal traffic collision, an officer was embarrassed to discover that his sketch of the scene done on a napkin had been introduced into evidence as the "factual diagram" by another officer! For this reason notes must be professionally maintained and officers should avoid keeping personal items in their notebook. Imagine having to explain a grocery list or a girlfriend's phone number that appears in a notebook to a jury.

Officers' notes are meant to refresh their memory. Officers frequently develop their own style of shorthand that includes acronyms and police jargon. Again, you should use caution in developing such shorthand note taking, because field notes may be read by a wide assortment of people and are *not* confidential records in most jurisdictions. Notations such as *R/P* (reporting party) are commonly used. Table 4-1 gives examples of other commonly used abbreviations.

Frequently, different agencies use slightly different forms for incident writeups. Often, these forms reflect a given agency's policies, procedures, and writing style and customs. As a new officer becomes acclimated to a department's note-taking customs and forms, using a copy of the face page from the incident report is an excellent way to capture all the information necessary to begin writing the report. Most agencies' *face page* is the first page of the report document (see Chapter 6 for more details on the face page). This page has all the information necessary to

table 4-1 Common Police Abbreviations

Common Abbreviation	Definition	Type of Report Used in Most Often
R/P	Reporting party—usually the person who calls the police	Crime, incident, traffic
CP	Command post	Crime, incident
POI	Point of impact	Traffic
DR number	Division of records number	All crime and incident reports are assigned DR numbers. Reports not open for public view (intelligence reports) do not have a DR number.
E/B	Eastbound	All
W/B	Westbound	All
ECL	East curb line	Traffic
WCL	West curb line	Traffic
DOT	Direction of travel	All

properly document an individual's personal information. This includes full name, date of birth, important addresses, and telephone numbers including cell phones; at least one West Coast agency asks for an e-mail address. E-mail addresses help alleviate the problem of incomplete information in the report by providing another method of recontacting the person for follow-up by the reporting officer or detective. A steno pad is an effective tool; however, there is a definite advantage to a note pad small enough to be carried in the back pocket or the pocket-sized spiral notebook that can be kept in an officer's shirt pocket. The advantage is that the small pad is always available. An officer will not have to carry a large pad or return to his or her car or office to locate something to write on—or worse, find it necessary to write on the back of a business card, scrap of paper, or napkin!

ORGANIZING FIELD NOTES

It is important that officers maintain organized notes. Every officer is likely to develop his or her own method of organization with experience. Generally, notes can be divided into *seven* logical areas or sections, which are outlined in the following text.

Administrative Details

The first field notes section contains administrative details that are important for record-keeping purposes. Details should include the incident date, DR number, time of call, time of arrival, and type of report taken. The acronym *DR* stands for **division of records** and stems from the early days of policing. Originally, division of records referred to a separate division in the police department. A records division still exists in most police departments. The division is responsible for maintaining the originals of police reports in a filing system. Additionally "records" keeps track of other enforcement documents, such as traffic citations. Finally, the records division keeps and maintains statistical data that must be reported to the state and federal governments. Nearly all agencies still use the term *DR* in referring to the criminal report number. A DR number is assigned to every report. The report is then managed or filed by the department records bureau based on that number.

Supplemental Crime Broadcasts

A second section in good field notes contains information useful for a **supplemental crime broadcast,** a radio broadcast that tells officers involved in an incident whether or not a crime has occurred, suspect and vehicle descriptions, and other valuable information that may have been unavailable when dispatch or call takers talked to the reporting person.

When an incident occurs, the initial responding officer quickly gathers information from the victim or witnesses that verifies a crime has occurred along with a description of the suspect(s). This becomes the basis of the supplemental crime broadcast, and the purpose of the broadcast is to assist units responding to crimes in progress or crimes that have just occurred. More details on supplemental crime broadcasts are provided in the section "What to Include in Field Notes."

Officer's Initial Impressions

The third section or area included in field notes is for the initial impressions of the officer's five senses. This could include unusual odors, smoke, debris or items littered about the crime scene, or anything else noteworthy that the officer sees, feels (touch), smells, tastes, or hears. Care must always be taken to not disturb the forensic evidence at a scene, but frequently officers can make important discoveries by just being observant.

For example, recently during a death investigation officers found a person who had been deceased for several days. While the outside temperatures had exceeded 100 degrees for a couple of those days, the body was in remarkably good condition which made the determination of time of death much more difficult. The initial responding officer had noted that the room was very cold. Further investigation revealed that the decedent had left the air conditioning on high, thus cooling the body and explaining the lack of decomposition.

In another case, an officer noted a man's cologne on entering the bedroom of a rape-homicide victim. This information was recorded and was an important part of the case against the person when he was convicted.

Victim's Identifying Information and Statements

A fourth section in an officer's field notes deals with the victim's identifying information and the victim's statements. The officer should record the victim's name, contact information, age, ethnicity, and the victim's description of what happened.

Witness Information

Witness information is recorded in this next section. As with victim information, this area should include all of the contact and demographic details, as well as a description of what happened from each witness's perspective. Witness comments should be recorded separately so the information does not get confused.

Officer's Observations of the Crime Scene

There should be a sixth section describing the officer's observations of the crime scene. These may include whether the crime scene seems viable or staged and if the victim and/or witnesses seem truthful, fearful, reluctant to speak, and so on. Some of this information will not make it into the final report because it may tend to show bias on the part of the officer and cause the report to lose its objectivity.

Additional Emergency Resources at the Scene

Finally, field notes should include information about any emergency services that responded to the scene or that were called by the officer. These may involve fire services, emergency medical services, special tactical units, and any other resources hazardous materials teams, ambulance crews, receiving hospitals, detectives, etc.

WHAT TO INCLUDE IN FIELD NOTES

Crime scenes come in basically two varieties, *hot* and *cold*. A **hot crime scene** typically involves arriving at a crime in progress or where an incident has just occurred. These situations can be quite dynamic. There may be injured victims, gunfire, people running in search of cover, and in general a lot of confusion. The first thing the officer must do is assess if additional officers are required and whether other services—such as emergency medical services (EMS) or special weapons and tactics (SWAT)—are warranted. Once sufficient officers and services are on scene to control the situation and make it safe, officers conduct preliminary investigation activities. Usually, a senior or supervising officer delegates various activities, including talking to witnesses and victims and developing a sense of what has occurred. It is very important that officers quickly establish whether or not a crime has occurred, and if a crime has occurred, whether it is a felony or misdemeanor. This must be relayed to responding officers as soon as possible. The classification of crime is extremely important, especially for special units such as K9 as it will impact the type of response they provide.

The officer should record the administrative information as previously described; information obtained at this time should be noted with the heading *Supplemental Crime Broadcast*. This includes the type of crime, if the suspect(s) fled in a vehicle, the vehicle's description, if the suspect(s) fled on foot, and outstanding suspect descriptions leading off with gender of offenders, clothing, and physical descriptions.

The next most important information to be recorded concerns weapons. This information will assist searching officers in making a legal detention and in being safe during any stops that may occur. Finally, names of suspects, potential vehicle descriptions, and direction of travel details must be recorded. This information must be given in a logical fashion for assisting responding units that will begin an immediate search of the vicinity for the fleeing suspect(s).

Once order is restored to the hot scene it begins to have more in common with a *cold crime scene*. A **cold crime scene** involves officers arriving on the scene after the crime has occurred (where the criminal activity has already ended). Once this has been established, the officer begins to sort out witnesses and victims. The officer should obtain and note information from as many people as possible who are at the scene. It is a common occurrence for witnesses to emerge many weeks after an investigation with completely different stories than the evidence indicates. Such a witness may severely impair his or her credibility if the responding officer has already interviewed the individual and has "locked" him or her into a story.

Next, the handling officer should take a moment to observe and note dissipating evidence. These notes should be under the heading "Initial Impressions." Responding officers may notice smells that may include an odor of perfume, cigarette smoke, body odor, or chemical smells. In the Vietnam War of the 1960s, North Vietnamese soldiers reported being able to smell the presence of American soldiers by the odor of cigarette smoke. This was also the method used to link a series of vehicle burglaries. Officers taking crime reports on the burglaries began to note the smell of tobacco smoke in the vehicles that had been broken into in a particular area. They captured that information first in their field notes and then in the reports. This allowed the series of crimes to be linked and, once a suspect was identified, the entire series was solved. The crime analysis unit used this information to assist investigators in closing several cases as well as providing a comprehensive list of property stolen in the thefts. The information provided a list of property to be seized when a search warrant was later served on the suspect's residence.

Officers may observe things such as tire tracks, or footprints, in surrounding mud puddles or may see broken objects or items that may have been used as weapons during a crime (pipes, bats, knives, guns, etc.). For example, at a burglary, the method of entry may have involved cutting a pane of glass with a glass-cutter so the burglar could reach in to unlock the deadbolt lock; or it may have been smashed using a brick. The pattern or method of cutting or breaking the glass so the burglar could gain entry may be distinctive and relevant to the investigation. In the case of safety glass, usually found in sliding glass doors or doors of a business, the condition of the glass should be captured in your notes as soon as safely possible because the small fragments of glass will fall from the opening, distorting the size and shape of the hole made by the object used to smash the window. Tiny drops of blood or human hair at a homicide scene may be immediately visible to the naked eye, and should be protected and recorded in the field notes. Failure to do this may result in evaporation, or in the case of hair, having it blow away. Although it is still somewhat controversial, areas where a suspect has walked or been present may provide evidence to K9 teams. The K9 may then be able to track a suspect with scent.

Unlike many television shows where the solving of the case always seems to revolve around locating some exotic piece of evidence, such as a rare blood type on a droplet of blood found at the crime scene, or a specially produced bullet cartridge for a modified military weapon, real crimes tend more often to be solved through good information obtained from witnesses and victims during the course of interviews in the field and first responders who pay close attention to the crime scene and the information it holds.

The following list is adapted from one offered by Palmiotto (2004) as some of the *essential* pieces of information an officer should include in field notes of an investigation:

- The time the officer received the call or complaint, and how this call or complaint was made.
- The name and identification of the responding officer and any other investigating officers on the scene.
- An exact description of the offense—this includes specification of the elements of the crime (the corpus delicti).
- The location and time of the crime and methods used during the course of the crime.
- A precise description of evidence items observed or obtained by the officer.
- A listing of all the official and/or agencies or services that were notified.
- The marking and disposition of each item of evidence obtained.
- A listing of photos, drawings, and sketches that may have been made, and measurements taken, as well as identification of who created or recorded each.
- Complete identification and contact information taken from each victim and witness.
- Descriptions and identification of the offender(s) offered by the victim(s) and witness(es).

- The details of any follow-up of leads or search to locate leads.
- The details of any arrest of a suspect or suspects made at or in the immediate vicinity of the crime.
- Descriptions of the mode of transportation and route use by the offender(s) to arrive and leave the scene (if available).
- The present location of the offender(s) if known.
- Any further actions that may be deemed necessary by the investigating officer. (pp. 96–97)

Witnesses at a crime scene often provide vital information that can assist in solving crimes and locating offenders. Accurately capturing witness testimony and information is essential to any investigation. This process should begin in the officer's field notes as soon as witnesses are contacted and interviewed.

WITNESS INFORMATION

Witnesses are sometimes hastily questioned on the spot at the scene of the crime, immediately after having seen or heard an emotionally charged criminal event. This can affect people in different ways, including causing them to be fearful, shocked, or even hostile and uncooperative (Berg, 2008). Nonetheless, witnesses possess potentially crucial information that may lead to the apprehension of the criminal offender; they must, therefore, be interviewed quickly so that a supplemental criminal broadcast can be issued.

Because witnesses have a variety of reasons to be willing or resistant to talk with the police, officers should be careful to record in their notes the demeanor of witnesses. A **recalcitrant** witness (defined here as a witness who shows stubborn

As witnesses are being interviewed pertinent information should be recorded in field notes for use later when drafting
Source: Aaron Roeth Photography

or defiant resistance to authority), for example, may be unwilling to speak with the officer because he or she is scared, or because he or she has something to hide. In some cases, it may be necessary to obtain a court order to require the witness to speak with the officer. Obtaining this order will take time, and the interview is likely to be handled by a different officer, so whatever information can be obtained initially should be recorded in the field notes and then transferred to the official report. Berg (2008, pp. 111–112) outlined the following witness categories.

Willing Witnesses

Willing witnesses generally cooperate with the police and furnish all information they have concerning a given event. They either seek out the police to furnish their information or cooperate fully when located and interviewed. Be mindful, though, that willing witnesses may not always be reliable and may have ulterior motives.

Eyewitnesses

Eyewitnesses are the most important types of witness. Allow them to state in their own words what they saw happen. Avoid asking them a lot of questions until they have completed recounting their story. After hearing an eyewitness's account, ask specific questions to clarify inconsistencies or gaps in their story.

Reluctant Witnesses

Hostility toward police, stubbornness, fear, indifference, or a relationship with the suspect may make a person reluctant to furnish information. A reluctant witness is one of the most difficult problems an officer can contend with in an investigation. Patience, tact, and persuasiveness should govern the investigator's conduct during this type of interview. Information from a reluctant witness may be the link needed to convict or clear the suspect in the crime.

Silent or Disinterested Witnesses

These individuals want to offer no information or assistance to the investigator. Some simply do not want to become involved in a police matter whereas others may fear any contact with the police or the courts. Still others may lack sufficient intellect to understand the need for their assistance or may be so oblivious to their surroundings that they can truly offer no information. There are also people who, for whatever reason, delight in seeing the police fail in their efforts, and they will remain silent. The interviewer must remain patient and persistent when working with such witnesses. Sometimes appealing to their sense of decency or fairness or attempting to have them empathize with victims in the case may help in obtaining information.

Unreliable Witnesses

People in this category may be deficient individuals, publicity seekers, children with vivid imaginations, or pathological liars. If you allow witnesses to talk freely, you can call to their attention obvious discrepancies in their statements. To establish the reliability of statements, the interviewer should try to learn how the witnesses came by the information, how good their memories are, and what interest they might have in the case or the people involved. It is also wise to determine their credibility, personal feelings, and honesty. If a witness appears to be a pathological liar, this witness should be reminded that lying to the police has serious repercussions.

Frightened Witnesses

Such people fear that suspects or their associates will seek revenge should they cooperate with the authorities. They honestly believe that someone is lying in wait to harm them, and they will suffer loss of sleep and appetite worrying about this threat of harm. Investigators should try to gain their confidence and assure them that retaliation is extremely rare. These witnesses should be told to notify police immediately if they receive any actual threats.

Biased Witnesses

Biased witnesses willingly furnish information, but their statements may be prejudiced toward the suspect or victim in some way. A close relationship between a witness and the suspect tends to bias the statement furnished by the witness. Often a desire to wreak personal vengeance on a suspect is very strong. When dealing with such a witness, investigators should consider the manner of conversation, the inherent likelihood of the story, the number and character of contradictions in the story furnished, and the nature and extent of the witness's interest in the case. When a biased witness makes statements that are obviously slanted to one side or the other, careful interviews can prove the statements inaccurate. For example, a friend of a suspect was present at a fight between two people. When contacted by the police, the suspect's friend said the victim had attacked the suspect with a hammer. In self-defense the suspect pulled a gun and pointed it at the victim. Fortunately several other people in the area saw the entire incident. They provided consistent statements regarding the occurrence, which involved an argument over a woman, and the person pointing the gun was arrested and successfully prosecuted for brandishing a firearm.

Hostile Witnesses

Hostile witnesses, who are not disposed to furnish any information to the police, are antagonistic and resist any form of questioning. Investigators should not let a hostile witness know that they resent this attitude. Instead, investigators should try to determine the reason for the hostility and then try to correct it. It is important to make such individuals feel that their information is greatly appreciated. Appeals to civic duty, personal pride, religion, decency, family, or justice may be helpful. Winning the cooperation of hostile witnesses may ultimately provide the margin of proof necessary to successfully prosecute a suspect.

Timid Witnesses

When witnesses are self-conscious or shy, lack confidence, or have poorly developed language skills, the investigator should make every effort to put them at ease. All conversations should be conducted in a relaxed manner and questions asked in a simple, straightforward manner.

Deceitful Witnesses

When an investigator encounters deceitful witnesses, the investigator must listen attentively to the story offered, but not immediately let on that he or she does not believe the story being offered. The witness should be allowed to recite many falsehoods before being confronted with them. Then the witness should have each false statement pointed out to him or her, and reminded that there are serious consequences for offering perjured testimony before a court of law. Tape-recording and playing back false statements can sometimes induce a deceitful witness to recognize the futility of deception. In some cases, asking the witness if he or she is willing to take a polygraph test (discussed later in this chapter) may result in a change of attitude and a willingness to speak more honestly.

When conducting field interviews with witnesses, it is important for the officer to be prepared to handle each of these various types of witnesses. In addition to noting the demeanor and possibly the relationship of the witness to the victim(s) and offender(s), when interviewing witnesses it is also very important to ascertain their *line of sight* during the events they witnessed. If a witness was not in a position to actually see what happened, this should be documented in the notes, regardless of how willing and forthcoming this witness may be. Conversely, when speaking with a witness who has an excellent and clear line of sight of events, this should be noted as well and the witness's physical location during the crime indicated in the notes. Given the types and variety of information that must go into field notes, more and more agencies have begun to use electronic recording devices to take more exacting notes. Officers should be familiar with how to effectively use this technology to accurately capture information in field notes.

USES FOR FIELD NOTES

While the primary function of field notes is to refresh the officer's memory of past events, field notes capture much more information than you might think. This information includes briefing information; information obtained from **crime analysis units**, or units tasked with the analysis and reporting of information relating to crime trends and patterns; task lists from supervisors; and information necessary for completing reports and notes taken from interviews with witnesses at incident and crime or accident scenes (Palmiotto, 2004). As indicated, notes taken in the field become the basis of the official report. Effective note taking, then, leads to better report writing. Furthermore, notes taken during one investigation may become useful to another officer in a subsequent investigation. Consequently, even information that may on the surface seem unimportant should be recorded in detail.

For example, during the course of a burglary-rape, a responding officer may notice that the lamp in the living room is unplugged from the wall socket. Because the officer recorded this information in the field notes, another officer was able to recognize this as part of a suspect's **modus operandi** (MO: the method of operation) from several other burglary-rapes he was investigating. In the other investigations, the suspect intentionally unplugged the lamps to prevent the victim from turning on the lights and potentially getting a better look and description of him. Because the information appeared in the notes, and subsequently in the report, the officers were able to determine that a serial rapist was victimizing their community. Also, as suggested earlier, officers must be mindful that notes can be "discovered" in both criminal and civil actions; thus, great caution should be used when recording confidential information from informants and other sources.

Although many officers rely exclusively on their memory, well-written notes provide consistently accurate information. The written notes can provide the actual address of a wanted person, not the commonly heard refrain "I don't remember the address but I can show where it is."

USE OF A TAPE RECORDER

The first rule in using a tape recorder to record field notes is that *if you don't have it with you, it's worthless.* The second rule is *if the batteries are dead—you might as well not have it with you!* Officers must check batteries for a charge and have additional batteries on hand just in case the batteries die during the course of an investigation. Before each patrol shift, a tape recorder function check should be performed. This includes checking the battery charge and recording volume, as well as the mechanical condition of the device. If you are using tape (rather than a digital recorder) you should additionally be certain to have several spare tapes with you.

In spite of working in a dynamic environment, law enforcement professionals have traditionally resisted rapid changes, particularly organizational changes and those centering on technology (Boyd, Melis, & Myers, 2004). Ironically, we are living during times of significant technological changes. For those who can recall watching *The Jetsons* cartoon program during their childhoods, many will likely recognize we are currently living in the *Jetsons era* with computers, video telecommunications, hovercrafts, Wi-Fi communications, DirecTV or Dish television, electrically powered vehicles, iPods, PDAs, digitized photography and audio recording, and more. Given these advances, law enforcement agencies as well as correctional institutions must learn to embrace technology and change. Stated simply, since the bad guys are keeping up with the changes, so too must the police.

DIGITAL DICTATION SYSTEMS

Many law enforcement agencies across the nation are beginning to mandate a move to digital dictation systems to create formal reports. These systems can increase the efficiency and accuracy of the reporting writing process. Reports are available faster and can be accessed online, which means officers in different departments and various locales can simultaneously share case information and coordinate their efforts to solve crimes.

The development of digital technology allows the agency several options regarding its dictation system. Current systems either use data from a digital recorder, or officers use a telephone line to dictate their reports. Reports are dictated in the field or in the police station by officers either onto a dedicated phone line or into an analog or digital recorder. Once dictated, either a contract company or in-house personnel transcribe the reports into the department's format. Using this kind of technology results in clear, easy-to-read reports that can be rapidly accessed or distributed. The days of eraser marks on a page or lines of correction fluid so thick the paper seems brittle will soon be numbered.

Tips for Dictating Full Reports

Dictation systems can be a great aid in capturing information for a report. The most important thing to remember before narrating into a recorder for dictation is to eliminate distractions and background noise. Frequently, when officers return to the station after an interesting case, a good arrest, risky contact, or some unusual or interesting call for service, they sit down to begin writing reports. Other officers may want to hear the latest installment of the patrol events much like storytelling at a family gathering. Laughter may break out, comments may be interjected, and mild shouts may even occur. If the officer is about to write his or her formal report, then this may or may not be a serious problem depending on the officer's powers of concentration. However, if the officer is using a dictation system, he or she can be reasonably certain that the noise from the *listeners* can be heard around the immediate area—and through the microphone or telephone receiver connected to the dictation system. The noise will make it difficult for a transcriber to clearly understand what the officer is dictating since the system also picks up extraneous noises. Noise and loud confusion will likely make many passages of the orally presented report impossible to hear and will not, therefore, allow for the production of an accurate transcription. The report will likely be returned to the officers with gaps and breaks that need to be edited before the report can be submitted for approval. So, the first tip for using a dictating system is to work from a quiet place; find a private location for dictating such as an unoccupied office or in a police car with the radio turned off. Some jurisdictions may have a designated dictation room designed to provide officers with a quiet venue for dictating their reports, similar to how many departments once provided a room filled with computers on which officers could write their reports.

A second tip involves planning. Do not simply sit down and start dictating off the top of your head; that's what field notes are for. Read through the notes and decide what needs to be put on paper. You may even want to draft a quick outline to allow yourself to focus and flow more smoothly. An outline is an essential element of a good report for the new officer. This can be a crucial step in report organization.

When officers begin to dictate, many officers have problems with organization. Without a clear idea of the organization of the report the end results may be confusing, or the report may ramble on from point to point with no apparent end. The best way to establish the order of the report is stick with the following steps: state how you got there, establish the elements of the crime, indicate what you saw at the crime scene, state what the witnesses told you, detail what you did to solve the crime, and state what additional resources were required. These steps are discussed in greater detail in Chapter 5.

Let's consider the process of dictation. Take a moment to think about dictation from the perspective of the transcriber. Generally, the person transcribing the report will not have the ability to talk to you about the case. All he or she can do is attempt to listen carefully and discern what you are trying to say. In fact, if you were to ask a transcriber how the report "sounds" to him or her after typing it, you might be surprised to discover that the transcriber does not listen to the report. Most don't remember any of the story they have just typed. They simply react to the spoken words and then type what they hear. With this in mind, speak slowly, loudly enough to be clearly audible, and with conscious concern about possible extraneous sounds. If an airplane, for example, is flying overhead during the dictation, stop dictating. One way to effectively check your dictation is to periodically play back the material to hear how you sound. If you have difficulty discerning what you are saying, imagine how it must sound to the transcriber. Transcribers often complain about these noisy backgrounds including dictation in a moving police car.

LEGAL STATUS OF NOTES

The legal status of notes may vary from jurisdiction to jurisdiction across the country. To be sure of the legal precedent in your area, you should check with your local district attorney or legal advisor for clarification.

The U.S. Supreme Court, in *California v. Trombetta* (1984), held that agencies are not required to keep certain items (in this case a breath sample obtained from a drunk driver) that may be part of a particular prosecution. Most states have come to similar conclusions when determining whether an officer's field notes are subject to discovery by the defense. The key element is that the officer accurately prepares the final police report. California, for example, has a long line of cases indicating that there is little risk as long as the notes are destroyed in good faith. This means that the notes are not destroyed to conceal information from the defense, the information from the notes is incorporated into the report, the report accurately reflects the notes, and the defense gets a copy of the report before trial. Make sure there are no restrictions in your jurisdiction regarding the retention of notes. Some local jurisdictions and states may require notes be booked into evidence or otherwise retained.

chapter summary

1. The focus of this chapter is on how to take *effective* field notes. The importance of taking good notes cannot be overstated. Notes taken that are inaccurate, illegible, or do not make sense are ineffective and will lead to a poorly written report.

2. Officers must develop good note-taking skills to be able to capture all of the information they receive during an incident or investigation. The use of abbreviations and shorthand in field notes is permissible so long as they can be accurately transcribed and are legible.

3. The use of an outline to structure your field notes will add clarity and completeness and ensure that you do not leave out important details in the final report.

4. The chapter provides a template for field notes that includes administrative details, supplemental crime broadcasts, the officer's initial impressions, the officer's observations of the crime scene, the victim's information, witnesses' information, and any additional resources used at the scene.

5. One of the primary purposes of field notes is for the investigating officer to record facts and observations that may be lost during the initial moments of an investigation. Important observations of evidence at the scene that may dissipate or the spontaneous statements of witnesses or suspects should be recorded in detail for later inclusion in the investigative report.

6. Information obtained from interviewing witnesses is vital to a thorough investigation. While interviewing witnesses or suspects, important information should be recorded in field notes.

7. During the course of any investigation many different types of witnesses could be encountered. Each type of witness can present the investigating officer with

different challenges. Officers should always evaluate a witness's motivation and role in the investigation. This will ensure that all the pertinent questions are asked and accurate testimony is obtained.

8. Tape recorders and dictation devices can assist in capturing information for notes and later completing reports. These devices require officers to organize their information and limit distractions and background noises before dictating or narrating information. This way an accurate and legible record of the information is captured.

Exercises: Taking Effective Field Notes

exercise 1

WRITING A SUPPLEMENTAL CRIME BROADCAST

INSTRUCTIONS: Using the following statements, write a supplemental crime broadcast for this possible street robbery and assault.

Statement 1:
While patrolling the parking lot of a grocery store, you are "flagged down" by a shopper who points to a woman sitting on the ground bleeding from the head. She tells you, "I was walking to my car when a blue van pulled up next to me and a white male reached out of the window and grabbed my purse. He pushed me and I fell. I think I hit my head on the ground."

Statement 2:
As you are taking this information, a citizen approaches who is very excited. He tells you he heard screaming and looked toward a woman (the victim) and a white male wearing a baseball cap in the parking lot. The woman was on the ground and the male was getting into a large blue commercial type van with a license plate beginning with the number "5."

_____

_____

_____

_____

_____

_____

_____

_____

_____

_____

_____

_____

_____

WRITING QUESTIONS FOR BROADCAST

INSTRUCTIONS: Write four additional questions that you would ask before "putting out" the broadcast.

_____

_____

_____

_____

_____

_____

CREATING FIELD NOTES

INSTRUCTIONS: Using the following picture, write field notes about what you see in the picture.

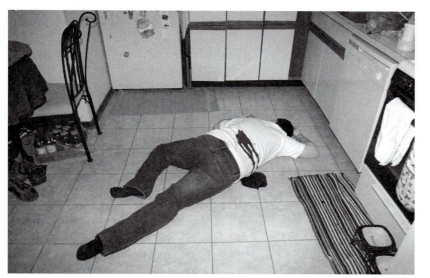

Source: © Chris Kerrigan

_____

_____

_____

_____

_____

_____

_____

_____

glossary terms

5

Writing a Good Narrative

INTRODUCTION

A good narrative is an accurate reporting of a good investigation. No matter how good an officer is at the technical writing process, he or she cannot write an acceptable report without a thorough and complete investigation. The contrary is also true. A good investigation will look like it was poorly done, shortcuts were taken, and that the officer just didn't care if it is not documented in a well-written report. To fully discuss what makes for a good narrative, more discussion on completing investigations is necessary. In this chapter the technical aspects of police report narratives are discussed as well as some investigation issues. We will look at the preinterview and interview processes, as well as the technical aspects of a report including chronology, active voice, objective narrative, word usage, and first- and third-person narrative.

THE REPORT WRITING PROCESS

Officers must first evaluate what type of situation they are attempting to document. Is this a report for department information, for documenting a crime, or for prosecution of criminal conduct, or is it something a citizen needs to have documented for insurance purposes, most commonly a traffic collision? These circumstances have a few things in common. Some level of investigation must be done and interviews with victims, witnesses, and/or suspects must be conducted. The information obtained from the investigation must be documented in a manner that fully tells the story of the incident or crime and is supported by the information discovered.

Interviewing Techniques

Let's look at the interview first. The investigating officer must decide who will be interviewed and in what order. At large scenes additional officers might be asked to talk with witnesses and determine who will be a good witness. Officers must determine who saw and remembered the most. It is vital that identifying information be obtained from every potential witness. Often follow-up investigation might become necessary. A person who does not at first appear to have relevant information may later be discovered to have very important information.

The Preinterview Process

Before beginning interviews of witnesses there are a few things that the officer should consider. The preinterview process should include a brief evaluation of whom you are interviewing, where you will interview the witnesses, and an estimate of how long the interview will take.

As you evaluate the witness, assess the person's motivation for speaking with the police, his or her age, the individual's ability to comprehend, and any biases he or she may have in a particular situation. The interviewer should be aware that many people will lie to the police. Nearly all new police officers are surprised at how often people try to manipulate the police. Typically it takes officers a few times of being deceived before they learn to carefully evaluate what they are being told. There is a saying among experienced police officers that people will lie even if the truth would get them out of trouble. Many people come forward because they are simply good citizens who want to help. Unfortunately, many others come to the police with questionable motives. While this is expected of suspects, others involved in an investigation may be motivated by a dislike of the involved parties, the perceived need to manipulate the police and the investigation for their own needs, and so on. Divorce and child custody situations are good examples of this, as well as situations where ownership of property needs to be established, or where a person with mental illness tries to report a crime or act as a witness to an event that did not occur. Officers should be extremely wary of any attempts by witnesses, victims, and suspects to influence or direct an investigation.

Obtain Incident Background Information   The interviewer should have a good understanding of the incident that is being investigated. Walking into an interview with only a basic understanding of an incident can result in an interview of minimal investigative value at best and disastrous results at worst. In such situations the subject may lead the interviewer away from essential information. A poorly planned interview will certainly result in the necessity of recontacting the subject to obtain additional information.

Select the Interview Location   The interviewer should attempt to control where the interview takes place. In many field investigations the interview will take place at the roadway curbside or at someone's kitchen table. Interviews should take place in an area free from distractions. Distracting conditions include the threat of suspects returning or acting out if they are detained nearby, other witnesses, chaos created by EMS in the case of a death investigation, and the proximity of the decedent and possibly the media. Locate somewhere out of view of the scene if possible. If not possible, then locate the witness back to the scene and away from overwhelming noise or scene chaos. If necessary, bring someone else for your security, as you will be concentrating on the statements of the witness and not on a larger scope of officer safety.

In a large-scale incident where there are numerous subjects, *where* becomes a problem. Police were faced with this problem when a person who was mentally ill and armed with a large sword walked into a grocery store where he was employed and began attacking people. Two store employees were killed and a dozen others were wounded before the subject was shot by responding police officers. More than sixty people were in the store at the time of the attack and each had to be interviewed as witnesses to the officer-involved shooting.

Think about where you would interview these people. A strong need exists to keep all separated or at least monitored to prevent these obviously upset people from sharing their experience with others and distorting everyone's recollection. You can see how impractical that is with so many witnesses. The inside of the store could not be used because it was a crime scene with lots of physical evidence, not to mention the potential impact on witnesses having to go back into the building they just escaped. Eventually the local transit authority brought some buses to the scene and the witnesses were taken back to the police station where interviews could be conducted.

Finally, you should consider how much time the interview will take. Try to give yourself time to conduct a proper and thorough interview.

Evaluate the Witnesses   A witness's age and ability to perceive are other factors in an interview that officers should be aware of and take a moment to evaluate. Young children are often witnesses to domestic violence. The effective officer will take time to work on his or her interview technique with children. Important factors include establishing that the child to be interviewed understands right from wrong and that he or she is giving you truthful answers. Thoroughly discussing the techniques for interviewing children would take another book.

Biases are another important factor to be recognized and weighed before the interview. Biases can arise from differences in lifestyle, socioeconomic status, gender, and race/ethnicity. Each of these biases affects not only how a witness relates the story to an officer but how he or she perceives the incident. Officer's biases also come into play. For example, a female officer taking a sexual assault report from a female date rape victim might be *more* sympathetic to the victim's plight. A male officer, who is the father of successful adult children, investigating an overdose where the victim's mother has let her twenty-seven-year-old opiate-addicted son live at home might be *less* sympathetic in this situation. In each of these investigations, the officers' personal biases should not influence how they conduct themselves or document these incidents.

Assess Environmental Factors   An assessment of environmental factors related to the witness's testimony is also important. The interviewer should look at where the witness was located in relation to an incident and determine if his or her vision or other perception could have been impaired. An assessment of lighting, visual impediments, direction of attention, and the stress of the incident is important because each can affect perception.

Develop an Interview Plan   The interviewer should take a moment to decide what kind of information is expected from the person to be interviewed. The interviewer should have a plan on how this information will be elicited from the witness. A skill that every successful street cop has is the ability to read people. This skill is essential in sizing up how information will be acquired from the witness. A tip for

Each witness to be interviewed should be evaluated and a list of questions developed to ensure that all pertinent questions are asked.
Source: © Mikael Karlsson

officers doing interviews is that the person you are interviewing as a witness may actually be a suspect! Although this seems obvious, our own biases and perceptions cause us to make the mistake of discounting this fact. Many officers are surprised to find that the witness later turns out to be the suspect. The results can be at the least embarrassing and at the worst, deadly.

Develop a Positive Interviewer Attitude and Demeanor   The last part of the preinterview is the officer's demeanor, which sets the tone of the interview. Officers should develop the ability to be friendly and open in word and demeanor while being vigilant and ready to employ necessary safety techniques should the need arise. Some of the best street interviewers are able to quickly and easily develop a rapport with those being interviewed. This skill can be learned. Field training officers are urged to take officers fresh from the academy to shopping centers in their beat. The trainees are told to go into a store and find out something personal and not job related about the first person they see. This is a test of their ability to talk to people. A good police officer must be at ease with all types of people to be effective at undertaking his or her daily duties. As a multicultural society, officers must be adept at communicating with people from many different cultures. While the proper demeanor for each situation will vary, it is necessary for obtaining information from interviewees. Officers need to be able to check their personal problems, biases, and worries at the locker room door.

The Interview

The interview should be distinguished from the **secondary crime broadcast**. In the secondary crime broadcast, the officer obtains information from a witness that establishes what crime has occurred to assist officers in deployment around the crime scene in likely avenues of escape and to assist those perimeter officers in locating possible suspects. The interview takes place once the scene is safe and officers have the time

The use of good interview skills cannot be over-emphasized. Successful investigations are developed through a series of interviews with witnesses and suspects.
Source: Aaron Roeth Photography

to carefully ask the questions necessary to establish elements, describe property, and attempt to identify suspects.

We suggest a three-step process for interviewing witnesses. The first step is to listen to the entire story. The second step asks the witness to retell the story while you take notes. In the final step you read back what the witness said from your notes and ask any clarifying questions.

Listen to the Entire Story   The first step begins with "what happened?" The witness should be interrupted only to keep him or her on task. Many times witnesses will get off the topic and begin to tell you about the 1967 Ford Mustang they once owned and not how the victim was assaulted in the fight between parents at the T-ball game. Listening to the story all the way through is much more difficult than it sounds, but it essential. This allows the witness to process observations and describe them in detail. Officers have the tendency to interrupt this process when they hear a piece of information that may be key to the elements of the crime. This is the proper time to make a note so you can return to the information later.

This is also a good time to note any nonverbal communication of the witness. Is his or her level of nervousness appropriate to the situation? Does the witness avoid eye contact and stare at the ground or off somewhere behind you? Avoiding eye contact is different from looking about at the crime scene and other distracters. If you see these characteristics you might start to consider the veracity of the witness's statement.

Repeating key points back to the witness is a good active listening technique that will help you remember what the witness said and ensure that you get the information correct. You should know if you have a good witness or someone who happened along after the incident occurred. This can be best illustrated by the witness at a car crash who tells the officer that he saw the incident. Using the first step, the officer may find out that the witness only *heard* the collision and went to the scene afterward. Hearing a car collision is generally not key information to the investigation. Remember to *listen* to the entire story!

Have the Witness Repeat the Story   In the second step, have the witness repeat the story but this time ask clarifying questions of the witness. At this point you should firmly establish the elements of any crime you are investigating. Clarifying questions might include obvious ones such as "When he yelled 'give me your watch' did you feel frightened?" Remember that fear is an important element of robbery. This brings up the point of becoming a student of police work. Make sure you are sound in all necessary parts of the job, such as criminal law in this case.

Clarify the Witness's Story   The last step is to make sure you correctly understand the witness's statement. Read back the statement to the witness as you have captured it in your notes and clear up any discrepancies. Multiple witnesses will have different perceptions of the same incident. If you get multiple statements that are exactly alike you should start to get suspicious of how this occurred.

Remember to obtain complete witness information or the grumpy old sergeant will "kick back" the report and you will have to recontact the witness to obtain missing information. Those in police work love those boxes on forms, so be sure to check off all relevant information. Many agencies still require officers to strike through all irrelevant boxes to indicate the boxes are not applicable.

Police officers frequently must complete reports in the field or at the scene of incidents.
Source: David R. Frazier Photolibrary, Inc.

Writing the Report

Departments differ dramatically in the technical aspects of report writing. Some agencies have comfortable rooms with multiple computer stations for report writing whereas others have decades-old report writing areas with only a couple of computers for officers to use. Although most agencies have some type of report writing software and allow officers to type reports or at least face pages, some require handwritten reports from officers. No matter what technology you have at your disposal, from a pencil to a computer or even, if you are blessed, to a digital dictation system, the report is the same. The following text explains how to format a crime report. Although some modifications may be necessary for different jurisdictions, the format fits the basic crime report and the complex report.

The days of a crime report containing only a few lines of basic information are long gone. Officers are expected to produce thorough and accurate reports with sufficient depth to clearly outline the crime, list witnesses and their statements, and document the actions taken by the officers to solve the crime. Although significant differences will exist in the report styles between agencies, generally crime reports have a basic format.

The first, or introductory, paragraph explains how the officer learned of the report call for service and where he or she contacted the reporting party or the victim. The next paragraph establishes the elements of the crime, and the third section documents statements from eyewitnesses to the crime provided they are discovered during the initial investigation. Next, the officer's observations are documented, including a discussion of the steps the officer took to solve the case as well as additional resources utilized, such as crime scene investigation (CSI), crime lab, K9 search teams, detectives, or SWAT. The importance of all the officers writing their own supplemental reports cannot be understated. We will talk about arrest reports and special reports in later chapters.

Write the Introductory Paragraph   All reports should have some type of **intro-ductory paragraph** to orient the reader to the activities of the officer and how the officer arrived at the scene to begin his or her investigation. A typical example of a report of an armed robbery might start with this:

> My partner Officer Smith and I were dispatched to the report of an armed robbery at Larry's Supermarket, 123 Main Street, at approximately 1300 hours. Upon arrival I found victim Larry Smith standing in front of the business.

Since police departments are twenty-four-hour-a-day operations, the use of military time or a twenty-four-hour clock is the standard.

Compare the opening paragraph of an arrest report to the opening paragraph of an "on-view" arrest report (an on-view arrest is a self-initiated field contact that develops into an arrest; these reports are discussed in more detail in Chapter 7). The opening paragraph might be necessary to set up the reasonable belief of occurring criminal conduct for an investigatory stop. The introductory paragraph might look like this:

> At approximately 2230 hours I was on routine patrol in full police uniform, in a marked police vehicle. I was W/B on Walnut when I saw a blue Ford Mustang weaving back and forth in the No. 1 W/B lane of Walnut.

This is obviously the opening paragraph of a driving under the influence (DUI) investigation. The preceding paragraph establishes the essential initial elements of the incident. Another example might be:

> At approximately 0730 hours I was conducting a vehicle burglary investigation at 4541 Campus when I looked into the window of a red Chevrolet minivan to see if it too had been broken into. I noticed a semiautomatic handgun similar to the distinctive design of a Glock protruding from under the driver's seat.

The previous example may be the beginning of robbery investigation. Each of these introductory paragraphs orients the reader to how the officer began the investigation. They include the essential questions of who, what, where, when, and how. The concept of chronology, the time orientation of all the participants in the incident, is discussed in a later section.

Establish Crime Elements   The second section of a report documents the **elements of the crime**. Elements are the necessary components of a criminal statute that estab-lish a violation and subject the perpetrator to criminal liability. Preparing to write this paragraph requires a solid knowledge of criminal law. Usually, the victim or reporting party will help the writer establish the elements. Their statements can contain the necessary information to establish the elements.

Generally, the elements for burglary include entry into a specified structure with the intent to commit a theft or felony therein. After interviewing the resident of a home where you called for a report, the second section of the report might look like this:

> Jones told me that she left her house locked and secured at noon on 07-12-07. She left on vacation and returned at 2300 hours on 07-19-07 to find that the window to kitchen had been broken. She saw footprints on the kitchen counter near the window and

> floor. Further inspection of the house revealed that several pieces of
> jewelry had been taken from the master bathroom

The previous paragraph is an example of the elements of burglary. This is of course an easy example of establishing the elements. There will be reports that take several paragraphs and statements of multiple witnesses to establish the basic elements of a crime. An assault may look similar to the following:

> Smith told me that he was drinking with suspect Johnson. They
> began to argue about the score of the Independence High School
> football game. Suddenly, Johnson stood up from the bar and struck
> Smith on the side of the head with a closed fist.

Although these are examples of basic crime reports, a complex homicide may necessitate using the statements of several witnesses, the results from an autopsy, and the interpretation of physical evidence to establish the necessary elements. When sheriff's deputies were called to the discovery of a deceased woman who had been thrown into a ravine next to a roadway, they prepared a death report. Because the cause of death was not readily visible, the coroner had to document the cause of death and make a determination that the death resulted "at the hands of another" through a post-mortem (after death) examination. Additionally, the victim had to be identified and that documentation prepared. Being unable to identify the victim, detectives had to publish the information to other agencies via a police teletype system. Once those steps were accomplished, the sheriff's department detectives discovered the body matched the description of a woman who had been reported missing from her home in another county by her husband three days before. Establishing the elements of this murder took several reports, several statements, an examination of the body, and a report from another agency. This investigation resulted in the successful prosecution of the husband for the murder of his wife.

Summarize Witness Statements   The third section of a report should include **statements from witnesses** who are located at a crime scene—the written or verbal accounts of what witnesses saw or heard. It is important to remember the idea of chronology as you document witnesses' statements. Briefly, chronology is the order of events experienced by the actor in the report. Accurately capturing witnesses' statements is critical. Many an officer has been embarrassed on the witness stand when a nonbiased witness now says something completely different from what the officer had written in the report. This underlines the importance of taking notes and tape recording investigations for later review.

Witness statements have two purposes: to gather information and to lock in or document the witness's version of the events. Imagine a witness who is friendly to the suspect. At the scene she tells you the suspect "had been drinking beer all day and went crazy when the Raiders lost." Later, realizing that her friend has some criminal liability, she relates that the suspect had been drinking water all day and that he was suddenly attacked by an out-of-control Packers fan. Accurate notes, and in this case a tape-recorded interview, will be of great assistance to the prosecutor as the case is evaluated for trial l.

In a thorough investigation all bystanders should be sorted out for those who saw something relevant to the investigation. In a significant investigation information should be obtained from each person in the vicinity. Tape-recorded contacts are important here. Locking a person into a statement can be vital to the prosecution later, especially when a person changes his or her story dramatically or suddenly becomes a witness who saw it all.

Document Officer's or Investigator's Observations   The fourth section of a report is used to document an officer's or investigator's observations. Officers will make several observations at the scene that should be documented. Experience will tell you what needs to be noted. In a burglary investigation you will talk about the point of entry, how the suspects moved the property from the location, how security systems were defeated, and how the suspect left the location.

The officer who is skilled in criminal law will recognize that there are several ways to establish entry with intent to steal. In a residential burglary the method of entry alone may establish this key element. With this in mind, all officers at the scene should be aware of the surroundings as they pass through the areas of the crime scene. One of the authors has many experiences of other officers finding important evidence that was missed in the initial sweep and a few where he is the one who missed the evidence!

This may also include unsuccessful attempts to locate witnesses. Noting the locations searched, as narrowly as possible, such as by address assists detectives who later come back to a scene and do another "canvas." Officers often think, "If they said something important I would have written it down!" This can make it more difficult for detectives doing follow-up investigation

In large-scale investigations officers might want to record the statements of individuals who deny witnessing an incident. While these statements may not be fully documented in the police report, the information on those people who were contacted and interviewed should be noted. These details can be used later to impeach those who were initially interviewed and later attempted to make a statement regarding the incident. This technique played a role in an officer-involved shooting case where a person interviewed at the scene denied any knowledge of the incident, but later attempted to testify to facts regarding the person's role as a witness. The witness was prepared to give testimony that would have been career ending for the officers and possibly expose them to criminal liability. Once the tape was transcribed, serious conflict arose regarding exactly what the person could have seen from the vantage point he or she initially claimed to be in at the time of the shooting.

Use Additional Resources in the Investigation   This section should deal with any additional resources you needed to complete your investigation. It may include something as routine as a CSI technician to the not-so-routine SWAT call out. The CSI tech should be identified by name and a reference regarding whether a supplemental report will be prepared by the technician. Some crime scene investigators prefer the reporting officer to report on the work done at a scene. Although it saves the investigator from having to write a report, it can cause serious problems in court. We have all played "telephone" where someone whispers in the ear of another a few words and then they are passed on to the next person. Writing reports for others has the same effect. Imagine how difficult it would be for both the reporting officer and the CSI officer if mistakes were made on a report that ends up in court. As a brief aside, in complex investigations involving many officers who prepare supplemental reports, one officer should be assigned to gather the supplemental reports, read them, and make sure each one is accurate. Then a supervisor should read and approve the entire case to prevent conflicting versions of the incident being written. This can be tricky, especially where the report-writing process may take several hours to complete. To restrict overtime, the supervisor who was on scene may not be available to read the report. Agencies should take steps to ensure that the supervisor on scene is the person who reviews the final report since they are the most familiar with the case.

This section of the report also contains EMS (emergency medical systems) information as well as where a victim might have been transported to and the name of the attending physician. Regarding EMS and doctors, this section should mention whether the victim signed a medical release form. This can be a very important piece of information in certain prosecutions, especially domestic violence. Although most doctors don't like being listed in reports because of their dislike for testifying, this section provides the necessary information for the district attorney or investigators. With this information the proper hospital can be served with a request for information when a release has been properly obtained from the involved parties.

CHRONOLOGY

The report writer must recognize that reports will include several different **chronologies** or time sequences. Numerous people may have been involved with the events documented and each person may experience or record the events in his or her own sequence. Each chronology must be accurately represented in the report. Even the simplest of reports may have more than one person's experience. Many officers have trouble with this and prefer to write in the present tense, which can result in a report that is difficult to read, especially if it moves back and forth between past and present tense.

When writing reports, some officers do not sequence the events from the perspective of witnesses and sometimes from their own perspective. This leads to a report that doesn't flow well and can be confusing to the reader. You can avoid this by carefully maintaining the sequence of events from the perspective of the witnesses. Document their statements individually and avoid the temptation of jumping back and forth between witnesses. This will cause significant confusion for the reader.

Take an on-view vandalism report as an example. An officer on patrol sees a broken window of a business. The officer's chronology starts at that moment. She sees the damage, makes an assessment regarding the type of crime, and decides how to handle the incident. Among other things the officer will request that the property owner be located through resources available to dispatch. She will also try to locate witnesses and obtain their statements. All of these witnesses will have to be documented and will have their own chronology that must be accurately recounted. So far in this situation the officer has done three separate things, in order: making the initial observation, contacting an owner, and locating witnesses.

When the responsible party makes a statement, his or her chronology will probably start when he or she last saw the window intact, which will be before the officer found it broken. The witness will have a chronology that also precedes the officer's chronology.

The report might look something this:

> On 06-11-08 at approximately 1930 hours I was patrolling the Hidden Valley Shopping Center. I noticed the front window of Barney's Jewelry store had been broken. I looked at the broken window and I saw that the hole was approximately the size of a brick. I saw a brick on the floor on the inside of the business adjacent to the window. The hole was not big enough for a person to have entered the store.

I requested that dispatch locate a responsible party and within 30 minutes the store's owner Barney Smith arrived. Smith told me he had left the store locked and secured on 06-11-08 at approximately 1705 hours. At that time the window was intact. Smith told me that there was no apparent loss from the inside of the business. Smith said that on 06-11-08 at approximately 1100 hours he had a customer in the business who was very upset about the store's return policy. Smith is not sure that this subject was involved in the vandalism. The subject was described as a male in his early 30s. Identifying information on this subject was not available as the store's computer system is not available at the hour of the report. Smith will check his records for further information on this subject and the disputed purchase.

As I was examining the broken window, witness Johnson approached me. He said that at approximately 1900 hours he was walking his dog in the area. As he was walking through the Hidden Valley Shopping Center he saw a female sitting in a black Mercedes-Benz in the parking lot. Approximately 10 minutes later he saw the woman walking toward the front of the stores carrying what appeared to be a brick in her hand.

As you can see, this example contains the chronology of the officer, the store owner, and the witness. While the report writer could try to write in strict chronological order from the time the owner had the confrontation with the upset customer all the way through the last thing the officer does in the investigation, this becomes very confusing to the reader, seriously inhibits the flow of the report, and makes writing in a narrative style difficult. Arrest reports will be covered in more detail in a later chapter. These reports can become quite complex because of the several different chronologies that must be documented.

ACTIVE VOICE WRITING STYLE

The terms *active* and *passive voice* indicate the relationship between a verb and its subject in a sentence (Glenn & Gray, 2007). *Voice* suggests whether the subject of the sentence is performing (doing) the action or the subject of the sentence is being acted on. It is proper to use an **active voice** when a subject is the person or thing performing the action. In contrast, a passive voice is used when the subject is the receiver of the action. A **passive voice** is best used when the writer wants to emphasize the recipient of the action rather than the actor.

Officer Smith wrote the traffic collision report. [active voice]

The traffic collision report was written by Officer Smith. [passive voice]

Of these two examples, the active voice sentence construction sounds much clearer.

Police and correctional officers routinely write about incidents that involve someone or something engaged in some form of action. The purpose of these reports is to describe actions by a suspect or inmate that might constitute a criminal or administrative violation. Writers must be very clear and precise about what they are describing and who the subject of that action is. When describing the actions of another person the use of active voice is much clearer.

> Mr. Jones wrote in his sworn statement that he was not home at the time of the fire. [active voice]
>
> In his sworn statement, Mr. Jones wrote that the fire was started by someone else. [passive voice]

It is essential that the structure of these sentences leaves no doubt as to what the officers observed or what was revealed from their investigation. If a sentence is unclear, or leaves room for interpretation, a defense attorney or judge might find reason to file a motion, not find probable cause for an arrest, or dismiss a case for lack of evidence. Writing police or correctional reports using an active voice often provides greater clarity and communicates information more effectively. By directly linking a subject to the action the reader has no doubt about the relationship or action being described. The following sentences demonstrate how confusion in relating the testimony of witnesses can be created by using the incorrect voice.

> Officer Green saw Mr. Graves quickly leaving the building at 123 Market Street while the burglar alarm was ringing. [active voice]
>
> As the burglar alarm was ringing, Mr. Graves was seen quickly leaving the building at 123 Market Street by Officer Green. [passive voice]

The first sentence written in an active voice clearly relates testimony from the security guard, Officer Green, about witnessing a suspect, Mr. Graves, leaving the scene of a burglary. The second sentence (passive voice) might be interpreted as Officer Green and Mr. Graves leaving the building together.

Police writers should strive for absolute clarity to prevent confusion. They have the best understanding of what they are writing about. It should never be assumed that the reader is going to have the same level of understanding. A report should be written as clearly and concisely as possible so that the reader is brought logically to the same conclusion as the writer. This is just as important when writing about your own actions or observations.

> While traveling southbound on Route 401 at mile marker 201, I observed the suspect's vehicle swerving erratically from lane to lane. [active voice]
>
> While swerving erratically from lane to lane on Route 401, the suspect's vehicle was observed southbound at mile marker 201. [passive voice]

The first sentence (active voice) clearly states what the writer observed and where the observation took place. The second sentence (passive voice) is not as clear, and does not communicate clearly who observed the action and where he was when that occurred. It is not clear if the officer was southbound or the suspect's vehicle was southbound or both. If the officer was called to testify to this incident several months later a poorly worded narrative might cause confusion or doubt as to his testimony. Sentences constructed using passive and active voice can influence the meaning being conveyed by the writer. The proper use of these styles can alleviate confusion and improve the clarity of writing.

OBJECTIVE NARRATIVE WRITING

Objective narrative writing is best described as "let the facts speak for themselves." The professional model of policing saw the advent of the objective report. In the objective narrative the officer is not trying to persuade the reader to come to a conclusion about an incident. Rather, the officer is letting the statements of the witnesses and the officers' observations provide a window to the crime scene. Through this window the reader can see the alleged acts of the suspect and come to his or her own conclusions (Frazee & Davis, 2004).

Some officers write persuasive reports. These expose the officer to some really tough moments of cross-examination. The line of questions will probe whether the officer "had it out for" the defendant, if the officer believed the defendant was guilty before the investigation was complete, and similar lines of questioning. These types of reports can damage the credibility of the officer in the eyes of the jury.

A persuasive report interprets what the officer sees at the scene, what the witnesses say, and how they say it. While this may seem like a good way to approach a report, it tends to show bias. The reader should come to the conclusions based on the information you gather. For a crime report, persuasive language makes the reader consider whether the elements actually exist or if the writer is trying to influence him or her into coming to the same conclusion as the writer. In an arrest report this takes on an additional aspect because it appears that the writer is trying to influence the reader's interpretation of the evidence against the accused.

WORD USAGE AND EFFECTIVE WORDS

Report writing should be clear, concise, accurate, and complete. Historically, police and correctional report writing has been characterized by two extremes: Officers were either too wordy (verbose), or too brief and direct in their writing. The first extreme, being too wordy, can result in a confusing or rambling narrative that takes up space on a report form but fails to provide the needed elements or accurately explain the actions or observations of the writer. The second extreme, being too brief, leaves out important details and uses shortcuts to save space and time.

Examples such as *Saw drunk, arrested same* can be found in many nineteenth-century police arrest records. Conversely, statements such as *The suspect appeared inebriated and was acting in rude, profane, and disorderly manner while in public* frequently find their way into today's police reports. Neither of these statements provides adequate detail to draw a logical conclusion or apply a set of criminal elements to a suspect's actions. Effective writers should detail observations and facts to provide the reader with a clear image of what is being described.

> I observed the suspect standing on the front sidewalk of the business. He was staggering and appeared unbalanced on his feet. When I approached him, I smelled the odor of alcohol on his breath and he was shouting profanities at other citizens in a loud voice.

In this descriptive narrative readers are left with a better understanding of the events and should have no question about the veracity of the facts or the motives of the officer.

Reports Must Be Clear

A well-written investigative report should be easy to read and understand and each sentence should convey the intended meaning. Every reader should interpret the same meaning from what was written. Shorter sentences tend to be easier to understand. When sentences are too long, or run on, they tend to confuse the reader. Too many sentences in a paragraph can also confuse the meaning. Five to ten sentences should be adequate to convey what is being communicated in that paragraph. Any more might be too wordy and affect the intended meaning.

In an attempt to include everything necessary to secure probable cause, some officers will try to mimic the language of legal statutes or jury instructions in their arrest reports or affidavits. This use of legal terms or phrasing is sometimes referred to as using *legalese*. Usually this is done to give the appearance that all of the required elements of the crime are mentioned. This can result in a lengthy narrative that is hard to follow and contains legal terms or phrases that might be confusing to the reader. For example:

> The suspect manifestly endeavored to conceal himself or his person within the structure and avoided visual detection by officers searching the building for him.

This could be simply stated as:

> *The suspect hid inside the building while officers searched the area for him.*

The second example conveys the same information in a much clearer way. While the first example might sound more *official*, the meaning is not as clear as the second version. Clarity in writing ensures that the reader will understand what is being conveyed.

Police and correctional writers should try to avoid legalese. These terms are written primarily for use by attorneys and judges and often are misinterpreted by lay readers. For instance, a sentence such as *I searched the curtilage of the suspect's home* is easier understood if written as *I searched the area directly around the suspect's home*. When discussing *prima facie* evidence it is better to simply write *direct* evidence. The use of terms derived from Supreme Court decisions, such as *Terry Stop* or *Carroll Doctrine,* should also be avoided. It can only be assumed that trained officers and attorneys will understand that these terms refer to legal decisions that allow officers to stop suspects based on *reasonable suspicion,* or motor vehicles based on *probable cause* (Bennett & Hess, 2007). A police report should be easily read and understood by juries which are usually made up of ordinary citizens. The use of some legal terminology in reports is sometimes unavoidable, but it should be strictly limited.

Reports Must Be Concise

Effective writers should strive to be economical with their words while providing sufficient details in a format that is easy to read and understand. The length of the report is not as important as the quality of the writing. Being concise in writing is the best way to make every word count without omitting important facts and observations. One of the best ways to reduce wordiness is to leave out unnecessary words. For example: *The suspect's coat was gray in color.* This statement can be shortened to *The suspect's coat was gray*. Using too many words in a sentence can be confusing and hard to read. Consider this example:

> The suspect made a furtive movement with his right hand into his right front pocket of his pants.

This statement is too wordy. This sentence could be shortened as follows:

> The suspect reached into his right front pants pocket.

These examples are basic ways to simplify sentences to add clarity and eliminate unnecessary words.

The correct choice of words is very important. Choosing words that are easily understood by the reader makes for a better and more effective report. Police and correctional writers sometimes use words that may have multiple meanings or are not clear. For example, the word *contact* has multiple definitions. It can mean the act of communicating, the act of making a physical connection, or the interaction between people. Officers often use the word *contact* to describe physically approaching a suspect, calling someone on the telephone, or simply speaking to someone. Each use of the word in these examples has a different meaning and could be misinterpreted. Words that could have multiple meanings are referred to as **abstract words**. Words that convey a clear meaning are referred to as **concrete words**. Writers should always use concrete words in their reports. These words are easily understood and are less confusing.

Another way to be concise in writing is to leave out unnecessary details. Information that might be interesting but is not related to the investigation should be left out. Statements such as *The suspect was belligerent and used profanity* might be appropriate for an arrest report for disorderly conduct or obstructing an officer but are unnecessary for a narrative detailing an arrest for shoplifting. If the information does not add factual support for the offense being charged or provides useful information, it should be left out.

Specific witness information such as date of birth or home address should be left out of the narrative portion of the report. These details should be written in the witness information portion of the report form. One of the best ways to be more concise in writing is to properly identify the subjects in your report without overusing the abbreviations *Mr., Ms.,* or titles such as *Director* or *Principal*. Simply using the last name of the person being described instead of surname or titles is appropriate for most reports. If a person's title is important for the reader to know, it can be written at the point in the narrative when the person is first mentioned. The title can then be left off after that point. If two individuals with the same last name, such as a husband and wife or siblings, are listed in the report it is acceptable to use first names and last names to distinguish between subjects.

Victims, witnesses, and suspects must be clearly identified in the narrative portion of the report. This is so that the reader understands the actions being described and what role each person plays in the investigation. It is appropriate to label the roles for persons being described in the narrative the first time they appear in the narrative (e.g., *victim, witness, reporter,* and *suspect*). Multiple victims, witnesses, and suspects can be listed numerically to distinguish them (e.g., *victim #1, suspect #2,* etc.). Once each person has been identified he or she should then be referred to only by the last name throughout the remainder of the narrative. This allows the reader to clearly distinguish who is doing what and the role each person plays.

A complete detailed description of a vehicle along with tag number and vehicle identification number should not be included in the narrative portion of the report unless this is critical direct testimony.

> Moss told me that the tag number on the suspect's vehicle was HVT 231. He was able to write down this number as the vehicle fled the scene.

If, however, the vehicle is listed in the report only because it was involved in the investigation, such as a traffic crash or wrecker tow record, it can be described in detail in the section of the report that lists vehicle information.

Police and correctional writers also frequently use abbreviations to shorten the narrative of their reports. This practice is sometimes problematic and can cause confusion. Some abbreviations such as *St.* for *Street* or *TN* for *Tennessee* are universally recognized and understood. Others such as *DOT* could mean *direction of travel* or *department of transportation* and can be confusing. If there is any question as to the common understanding of an abbreviation, the word or phrase should be spelled out.

By eliminating unnecessary visual distractions, details, or descriptions, the report's narrative section remains uncluttered and easier to read. It is important to remember that the investigative narrative should address who, what, where, why, and how (if known) and lead the reader logically but quickly to a conclusion.

Reports Must Be Accurate

All of the details in the world are worthless if they are not accurate. The true measure of an investigative report is its accuracy. A neat and well-organized report that contains inaccuracies and factual mistakes is of no value in a criminal prosecution. If the information related to times, dates, locations, or people detailed in the report are inaccurate it leaves the reader wondering if *anything* contained in the report is credible. Police writers must be extra vigilant about checking the accuracy of addresses, times, and facts related to their investigations. When obtaining information from persons involved in the investigation, always confirm the validity of the information. Confirm spelling of names, dates of birth, and addresses from driver's licenses or other forms of identification. Check addresses against property records to ensure accuracy. When interviewing witnesses or victims, repeat back to them information communicated verbally for confirmation.

An officer's assumptions or educated guesses have no place in an investigative report. A fact describes an actual occurrence, or something known, and is not an assumption, belief, or opinion (Biggs, 2008). Investigative reports should be written objectively. It is not acceptable to try to slant or bias the facts to achieve the desired result. Opinions or beliefs also have no place in an officer's report. Reports should describe witness testimony, physical evidence, and tangible investigative findings. Leaving out important facts can also show bias or a lack of objectivity. Let *all* the facts of the case being investigated speak for themselves. This shows objectivity and is the hallmark of a professional investigative report.

Certain words or terms can indicate bias or a *lack* of objectivity. For example: *The suspect claimed he was not near the scene of the robbery.* The word *claimed* can leave the reader with the impression that the statement might not be true. Unless this is established by fact, or other testimony, it could indicate bias. It would be more objective to write *The suspect stated he was not near the scene of the robbery.*

Descriptions of suspect behavior should also be objective and based on actual observations. For example: *The suspect showed signs of deception when questioned about the burglary*. This wording cannot be supported by facts, so it should be reworded. You may have seen detectives in movies and television who have the *ability to tell* when someone was lying. In the real world *no one* can definitively detect deception from outward appearance. These statements simply provide defense attorneys with opportunities to attack the credibility of investigators and create doubt in the mind of juries. It is better stated objectively: *The suspect gave varying accounts of his whereabouts at the time of the burglary*.

The use of derogatory language when describing suspects or witnesses is unprofessional and can show bias. The use of the terms *boy* or *girl* when describing adults can sound demeaning and unprofessional. Using the terms *men* and *women* or *young man* or *young woman* is more appropriate. Terms that demonstrate prejudice or insensitivity to race, gender, ethnicity, or sexual orientation should be avoided. Statements in written reports that exhibit bias or prejudice, or lead the reader to a conclusion not supported by facts or testimony, should be reworded or omitted.

Reports Must Be Complete

An incident or arrest report must contain a detailed narrative of the events to provide detail and clarification. If critical details are glossed over, left out, or poorly worded, the reader does not get an accurate account of the events. Describing details and observations paints a picture for the reader's mind. The richer and more complete the detail, the clearer the picture will be. For example, a description of an intoxicated suspect might be written as *The suspect looked drunk*. It would be better to write *I smelled the odor of alcohol on the suspect and he appeared unsteady on his feet*. The second sentence details two observations of characteristics that would indicate a suspect was intoxicated. The first sentence provides no factual support. When testifying in a driving under the influence trial, an officer using first statement might leave the jury questioning exactly what the officer saw. The second statement leaves no doubt about the observations of the officer and provides a clearer *picture* of the event.

Often in their haste to just get the report done and turned in, officers might omit important details or shorten events. This lack of patience and attention to detail can be a critical mistake. Officers may have to rely on these reports months or even years later when testifying at deposition or in a trial. It is much better to take the time to write a detailed narrative now than to struggle to remember important details later.

NARRATIVE WRITING IN FIRST AND THIRD PERSON

First, we need to define the **third-person narrative** as when the writer describes the events from a position *outside* the events that are being reported. This was a very popular method of reporting prior to the 1980s. The typical report would read something like *The reporting officer saw* . . . or *This officer*. . . . Third-person narratives appear to have come from the common method of writing in the search warrant. Most jurisdictions have abandoned the third person in the search warrant, but some persist. The final approval on the use of first- or third-person narrative for search warrant affidavits always rests with the district attorney for that jurisdiction.

Thankfully, this practice has been all but eliminated in modern police report writing. The old practice was confusing and tedious. Report writers are now encouraged to write in the first-person narrative. The first-person style of writing best describes what *you*, the investigating officer, saw, did, and heard. The person writing the report becomes the narrator of the incident. Each of the examples in this chapter was written in the first person. The following example is written in the first person and also the active voice:

> Upon arrival I contacted witness Johnson who told me that he was standing on the corner of Associated Rd. and Brea Blvd. He was preparing to walk westbound on Associated Rd. He was facing a red light for westbound traffic on Associated when he saw the red car (V1) driving W/B on Associated. The red car drove through the red light and struck the blue car (V2) on the driver's door. From his vantage point Johnson said he clearly saw the signal for W/B Associated and it was red.

The officer in this paragraph clearly states that he contacted the witness. The witness's point of perception is established and the individual observations of the traffic signal are also quite clear. The officer uses the first person to describe his actions.

chapter summary

1. A good narrative is an accurate reporting of a good investigation. No matter how good an officer is at the technical writing process he cannot write an acceptable report without a thorough and complete investigation.

2. The investigating officer must decide who will be interviewed and in what order. At large scenes, additional officers might be asked to talk with witnesses and determine who will be a good witness. Officers must determine who saw and remembered the most. It is vital that identifying information be obtained from every potential witness.

3. The report writing process is a multistep process that involves identifying, locating, and interviewing witnesses.

4. The preinterview process should include a brief evaluation of whom you are interviewing, where you will interview the witnesses, and an estimate of how long the interview will take.

5. Interviews involve a three-step interview process. The first step is to listen to the entire story. The second step asks the witness to retell the story while you take notes. In the final step you read back what the witness said from your notes and ask any clarifying questions.

6. Writing the report is also a multipart process that begins with developing an introductory paragraph which introduces the reader to the incident. Elements of the crime must then be detailed and supported with testimony from witnesses and physical evidence. The investigator's observations at the scene must be described and documented. Any additional resources such as forensics investigators or other supporting personnel should be recorded.

7. One of the most effective methods to document an incident is to use a chronology or time line of the event. The writer simply begins the report with his or her involvement or the first known event in the incident. The report then develops the timeline through a systematic detailing of the different events or actions in the case being documented. This allows the reader to understand what happened and when events in the incident occurred.

8. The terms *active* and *passive voice* indicate the relationship between a verb and its subject in a sentence. *Voice* suggests whether the subject of the sentence is performing (doing) the action or the subject of the sentence is being acted on. It is proper to use an active voice when a subject is the person or thing performing the action. A passive voice is used when the subject is the receiver of the action. A passive voice is best used when the writer wants to emphasize the recipient of the action rather than the actor.

9. In the objective narrative the writer is not trying to persuade the reader to come to a conclusion about an incident. Objective writing lets the statements of the witnesses and the officers' observations provide a window to the crime scene. Through this window the reader can see the alleged acts of the suspect and come to his or her own conclusions.

10. Report writing should be clear, concise, accurate, and complete. Choosing words that communicate clear meaning to the reader is essential. Using words that are offensive or indicate bias on the part of the writer should be avoided.

11. The use of first- or third-person writing styles indicates what perspective the writer is using to describe his or her own actions. First-person writing describes what *you* saw, did, and said. It is the preferred method of police and correctional report writing. Third-person writing is a style of writing that describes all actions from the perspective of a third person. It is frequently used in search warrant affidavits and court documents. This style of writing typically uses *this officer* or *this writer* to describe the actions of the writer in the narrative.

Exercises—Recognizing and Writing a Good Narrative

RECOGNIZING ACTIVE AND PASSIVE VOICE

INSTRUCTIONS: In the space provided, write an **A** if the sentence uses the active voice, and write a **P** if it uses the passive voice.

1. _____ Suspect Smith was apprehended at 10:30 A.M. in front of his house.

2. _____ Lieutenant Malory apprehended suspect Myers in front of the suspect's house at 10:30 A.M.

3. _____ The first fire truck arrived at exactly 10:00 P.M.

4. _____ The fire hydrant on the corner of Wilshire Dr. and North Shore Rd. was turned on at 10:10 P.M.

5. _____ The Cadillac Escalade crashed into the Toyota Corolla's left rear bumper.

6. _____ The Toyota Corolla's left rear bumper was hit by the Cadillac Escalade.

7. _____ The house was broken into at 11:35 P.M.

8. _____ An unknown suspect broke into the house at 11:35 P.M.

9. _____ The vehicle was searched by Officer Jones.

10. _____ Officer Mills apprehended the suspect in a field adjacent to 431 Old Market Rd.

WRITING IN THE ACTIVE AND PASSIVE VOICE

INSTRUCTIONS: Rewrite the sentences from Exercise 1. If they are in the active voice change them to the passive voice, and if they are in the passive voice change them to the active voice.

1. _____

   _____

2. _____

   _____

3. _____

   _____

4. _____

   _____

5. _____

   _____

6. _____

   _____

exercise 1

exercise 2

7. _____

   _____

8. _____

   _____

9. _____

   _____

10. _____

    _____

exercise 3

WRITING A CHRONOLOGY OF EVENTS

INSTRUCTIONS: In the space provided, write a detailed narrative using the following events. These events all occurred on October 23, 2011, beginning at 7:00 A.M. and ending at 11:00 A.M.

Place them in the proper chronological order for the following times: 7:00 A.M., 7:20 A.M., 7:29 A.M., 7:32 A.M., 7:40 A.M., 7:45 A.M., 7:50 A.M., 7:55 A.M., 8:30 A.M., 8:35 A.M., 8:50 A.M., 10:30 A.M., 11:00 A.M.

- At your request, crime scene investigator Mills arrives to process the scene. She photographs the back door and begins to process the interior of the store for latent prints and other physical evidence. [7:50 A.M.]

- You conduct a search of the interior of the store and find that the shelves have been ransacked and the counters moved. You observe several areas on the glass countertops that appear to have fingerprint smudges. [7:45 A.M.]

- Detective Holmes informs you that he has responded to the Anytown jail and has interviewed suspects James and Floyd. They have both confessed to committing the burglary at Martin's grocery store. He will complete a supplemental report to your case and charge them both with burglary. [10:30 A.M.]

- You receive a radio call to respond to Martin's Grocery Store, 321 Main Street, Anytown, MN. [7:20 A.M.]

- Officer Webb from the midnight shift radios you with information about a traffic stop of a red Ford pickup truck he and his partner made at 3:30 A.M. at the rear of a grocery store in the western part of Anytown. The two suspects had a crow bar, a cash register, lottery tickets, and cartons of cigarettes inside the vehicle. He arrested the driver, Jesse James, for driving with a suspended driver's license, and his passenger, Billy Floyd, for outstanding felony warrants. They are currently being held at the Anytown jail. [8:30 A.M.]

- Based on CSI Mills's findings and the information relayed from Officer Webb you call Detective Holmes and relay the information to him. [8:50 A.M.]

- You examine the back door of the business and find that the door lock has been pried open and the door forced open. [7:40 A.M.]

- You are Officer Johnson working the dayshift for the Anytown, MN, police department patrolling the east side of Anytown. [7:00 A.M.]

- You arrive at 321 Main Street. [7:29 A.M.]
- CSI Mills radios you that Mr. Martin has reviewed the videotape from his surveillance camera at the rear of the store and may have captured evidence of the burglary on tape. [8:35 A.M.]
- You leave the scene and respond to the station to complete paperwork and meet with Detective Holmes. [11:00 A.M.]
- You speak with Fred Martin, the owner. He says he arrived at his business at 7:00 A.M. and discovered that his store had been burglarized. He checked the inside of the store and found the cash register missing and the store ransacked. Several cartons of cigarettes and a roll of lottery tickets were also missing. [7:32 A.M.]
- You conduct a canvas of the area and interview Eddie Smith, the clerk from the Good Times liquor store, located at 325 Main Street. He states that he heard a loud crash at about 3:00 A.M. He then saw a red pickup truck leaving the back of the grocery store a few minutes later. [7:55 A.M.]

WRITING IN THE FIRST AND THIRD PERSON

INSTRUCTIONS: Rewrite the following sentences in the first-person style (you are Officer Johnson).

1. This officer responded to the corner of Elm Street and Sycamore Drive.

   _____

   _____

2. Lieutenant Sanders handed the firearm to this writer.

   _____

   _____

3. This officer was directed to the scene by witness Summers.
4. Officers Johnson and Ramirez searched the building for the suspect.
5. This writer smelled the odor of burning marijuana coming from the interior of the suspect's vehicle.
6. Upon this officer's arrival, the suspect fled southbound on foot through the field.
7. Officers Santiago, Morgan, and Johnson were present when the suspect was apprehended.
8. Witness Green advised this officer that she was the owner of the vehicle.
9. Detective Brown met with this officer at the scene and took over the investigation.
10. Officer Stevens and this officer were assigned to a traffic detail on Route 401 and Highway 85.

exercise 4

117

WRITING WITH CLEAR, CONCISE, AND CONCRETE WORDS

INSTRUCTIONS: In each sentence, circle the abstract word. Then in the space provided, replace the abstract word with a concrete word.

1. I contacted the suspect at his place of employment.

   _____

2. The witness indicated that the suspect's vehicle was a gray-colored sedan.

   _____

3. Sergeant Smith advised that roll call would begin at 1400 hours.

   _____

4. Officer Randle stated that he was not present when the vehicle was searched.

   _____

5. Witness Paulson placed the suspect at the scene of the robbery.

   _____

6. The suspect revealed that he was a convicted felon on parole for murder.

   _____

7. Officer Burns detected the suspect hiding in the bushes.

   _____

8. Detective Morris detailed his involvement in the case.

   _____

9. The suspect proceeded to his vehicle and drove out of the area.

   _____

10. The victim related that he was in fear for his life when he saw the handgun.

   _____

glossary terms

6

Writing Crime and Incident Reports

INTRODUCTION

The previous chapter discussed the format for crime reports at some length. In this chapter we will go into depth about describing *people, property,* and *evidence* as well as describing events. We will provide some suggestions for areas of inquiry of witnesses and victims in preparing the supplemental crime broadcast described in Chapter 4. We will also cover the development of descriptions of people and property both in the initial response and in the report and will discuss tips on describing items in the final report.

Police officers gather information upon their arrival at a crime scene that must be disseminated to other assisting officers. This chapter is organized by dealing with the supplemental crime broadcast and its necessary elements first, the detailed descriptions of suspects and property next, and finally, the report itself. Many officers overlook the importance of descriptions, often because eliciting the information and documenting it can be tedious work.

Officers should pay particular attention to the descriptions they provide. This is one area where most officers spend the least amount of time and effort. The lack of *workable* descriptions on crime reports is due in part to the poor descriptions provided by victims, but it also relates to a lack of effort on the part of initial investigating officers. The result of poor descriptions of suspects and their method of escape is frustrating for units arriving at a scene to assist, who then waste precious radio airtime as first responders ask multiple questions to clarify what they are looking for. Additionally, detectives who are taking the descriptions from the initial reports and doing follow-up investigation experience great difficulty in trying to use the information provided in the crime report. Poor descriptions of property make it all but impossible to recover property for victims. Many patrol officers forget their *responsibility to the victim to recover their property* whenever possible. All of law enforcement should keep recovery of property as a primary goal. As we look at descriptions, we must realize that they are taken in at least two distinct circumstances, each with a different goal.

DESCRIPTIONS AT CRIME SCENES

Following are some ideas for the development and capture of good, usable descriptions that will hold up in court and under cross-examination. The witness at the scene may have the information, but it is the responsibility of the officer to obtain it. The witness seldom knows what is important in descriptions; only the proper series of questions will bring out that information. Whether an officer is getting information for a report or obtaining important information for the supplemental crime broadcast, the officer must know what he or she is looking for in a description.

Supplemental Crime Broadcast

The accuracy of the first description taken when a crime is unfolding or upon the arrival of the initial officers at the crime scene is extremely important to apprehending the suspect(s). This information could provide the reasonable suspicion for a detention or probable cause for an arrest. Dispatchers usually take the information from the reporting parties. This information is often inaccurate. The initial caller may not have witnessed the incident and is only calling at someone's request, or the caller is overcome by the event and cannot give accurate information beyond what has happened to him or her. Once the call is dispatched to officers, they respond to the area and, in the case of serious crimes, respond quickly, taking positions on a perimeter or in the path of a fleeing suspect. The first unit in the area should go to the scene, make contact with victims and/or witnesses, and as soon as possible obtain information for a radio broadcast. In this situation the best description contains information that describes something distinctive about the suspect or about his or her method of leaving. Typically you will see descriptions of people and vehicles. Clothing descriptions can be valuable, but suspects often peel off a layer of clothing as they flee.

The officer then takes this information and provides a supplemental crime broadcast to other responding units (the supplemental crime broadcast was discussed in greater detail in Chapter 4). The officer providing this information can make a case at this point or ensure that the suspect will not be identified in the field by responding officers. It is important to remember that the longer it takes to get this information out, the more likely the suspect will pass by the perimeter units and escape. The supplemental crime broadcast must be sent out quickly and accurately.

Descriptions of fleeing vehicles should include make, model, color, license plate, and any distinctive markings. Does the vehicle have window stickers? Does it have a distinct sound such as loud mufflers? Does it have extremely dark window tinting? Each of these questions may serve to quickly identify a fleeing vehicle. And you can see the need for the officer to be creative in the questioning of witnesses. Don't rely solely on the basic description of make, model, and color. Table 6-1 gives some examples of distinctive markings that could be used to describe vehicles.

It is important to logically approach the crime scene. The first officer on scene needs to prioritize the manner in which he or she obtains information. With the suspect gone, the officer must decide what information is needed to immediately locate and lawfully detain him or her. If witnesses report the suspect is fleeing in a vehicle, then vehicle information is the most important. If the suspect is on foot or on a bicycle, then direction of travel, clothing, and a brief physical description are most important, as these are things that perimeter officers should be looking for.

Many suspects will wear multiple layers of clothing, only to drop jackets, sweaters, and even pants as they flee. This affects how the area is searched. Additional witnesses could be located along the suspect's path of flight. These witnesses can verify a change in clothing or a lack of change in the clothing description. At a recent bank robbery in the Los Angeles area, a suspect entered a bank and demanded money. He was wearing a black hooded sweatshirt and baseball hat with a particular logo on the hat. Several officers were in the area of the bank at the time of the alarm. A perimeter was set for officers looking for a subject in a black hooded sweatshirt

table 6-1 Areas of Inquiry on Vehicles

Window tinting	Broken or cracked windows	Roof or ski racks
Special rims or tires	Missing or unique bumpers	Raised 4 X 4 trucks
License plate brackets	Vehicle damage	Stickers or decals
Exhaust systems	Unique paint	Trailers or campers
Running boards on trucks	Box trucks or vans	Utility racks

and black hat. Investigating officers quickly went to a nearby store and obtained video of the suspect taking off the hat and sweatshirt as he walked away. This significantly changed his appearance and allowed him to slip away undetected.

As an aside, this is extremely important information for a crime report. It tends to show that the suspect planned the crime, although this may vary by region to some extent. Compare clothing worn in Los Angeles in August to clothing worn in January. It is not uncommon to see someone in a T-shirt and shorts on the coldest days in Los Angeles, whereas a person walking at a fast pace from a crime scene dressed in a T-shirt and shorts should raise some suspicion in January in Boston.

In describing people at crime scenes, officers often get bogged down in details that don't help in the immediate apprehension of fleeing suspects. While general height and weight information can be helpful in the extremes, it generally is not something an officer searching for a suspect in a crowd is going to use to base a suspect identification on. Style and color of clothing as well as color and length of hair are important and should be obtained first. Then general descriptors should be obtained. The information contained in the initial and supplemental crime broadcasts are essential when officers justify the reasonableness of any detention arising from those descriptions (*Terry v. Ohio,* 1968). Officers cannot rely on their *gut feeling* that a person is involved in a crime. A detention must be based on individualized suspicion. Inaccurate or poor descriptions will cause a court to invalidate the detention.

We should take a moment to talk about descriptions of property in the supplemental crime broadcast and how they differ from information obtained for the actual crime report. The most important information for responding officers is the information that will give them the legal right to detain a potential suspect. This is the information described previously. Included in the information given to other officers is the "loss"—for example, "cash," "in-dash car stereo," and so on. This can usually be done quickly, and detailed descriptions are not necessary. Once a suspect is detained a more complete description of the property can be made.

DESCRIPTIONS IN POLICE REPORTS

Officers should never forget that the purpose of thorough descriptions in police reports is to catch criminals, incarcerate predators, and recover property. Once a scene has been stabilized, the reporting officer must begin to collect detailed descriptions of possible suspects, their vehicles, and the involved property. Many officers think of property descriptions as that involving stolen property. Property descriptions include stolen property as well as weapons or even implements that were used in the crime. Good modus operandi (MO) information can be obtained from a detailed description of many weapons, especially homemade weapons.

Providing Accurate Descriptions

There are several important administrative issues in obtaining and documenting complete descriptions in reports. All law enforcement agencies in the United States contribute crime data to the **Uniform Crime Report (UCR).** The UCR is maintained by the FBI and is a compilation of nationwide crime statistics that contains information on reported losses from a range of crimes against persons and property crimes. This is effectively the report card of success or failure for police agencies. Their rate of clearing or solving crimes as well as the frequency of crime occurring in their jurisdiction is frequently obtained from UCR data. The value of this information can be severely affected by poor and inaccurate reporting by initial report takers, and the data can affect the reputation of an agency. Inaccurate data may label a city with an inaccurate crime rate or an inflated rate of loss.

The second issue is the expanded use of multiagency databases. In the past few years many agencies have begun to share information with other agencies. This is often done between a few cooperating agencies, or on a countywide basis. In the past, agencies held their data from contacts, arrests, and reports very closely. It was not uncommon for agencies to discipline employees who released crime information to other agencies. Thankfully, today many agencies are providing data for retrieval of information. Imagine looking for a person named "Carl" who committed a crime and was observed fleeing in a brown Ford Escort. Using a countywide database, all traffic tickets issued in the county or field contacts or persons listed in crime reports can be searched, often from a patrol car with an MDT (mobile data terminal) or computer. Complete and accurate descriptions lead to more arrests and more recovered property.

The third issue in providing accurate descriptions is **intelligence-led policing (ILP).** ILP is a crime-fighting strategy that uses real-time crime information and analysis to detect crime trends and patterns. This analysis is then used to make tactical decisions about officer deployment and investigative resources. Data obtained at crime scenes will help crime analysis units prepare tactical and strategic information for use by patrol on investigations.

The ability of officers to locate and recover stolen property and contraband depends on accurate descriptions in reports. With this in mind the old U.S. Navy Seal adage "Attention to detail" best describes how officers should approach property lists. A properly documented property list is an important part of the report writing process.

Unfortunately, full, accurate descriptions frequently get overlooked by officers who take shortcuts due to high call volume, lack of interest in the case, or plain laziness. Many agencies let officers *get by* with reports that lack detail. While low standards on reporting quality may seem like a necessary balance in a busy city or area, low standards result in unsuccessful prosecutions and increase the potential for successful civil suits against agencies as entities and officers as individuals. This is especially true in incidents that may take years to get to a court of law. Agencies that allow the standards of property lists slip soon allow the overall report writing standards to fall to the bare minimum.

An example of the necessity to obtain complete descriptions of stolen property is in the area of sexual assault investigation. The East Area Rapist has been linked by DNA to dozens of sexual assaults and murders in the state of California that occurred in the 1970s and 1980s. The suspect would find objects in the residence to use as the murder weapon and then leave with the weapon. These items have not been found. Although he is still unidentified and thus still at large, imagine an investigator who did not work on any of the original cases who later finds himself or herself faced with preparing a search warrant of a potential suspect's property working with poor descriptions of the believed murder weapons stolen by the suspect. These items could be essential in corroborating the DNA found at the crime scenes and proving the suspect is the murderer. Some might argue that investigating officers would take great care on the murder investigation because of the importance of the crime. The East Area Rapist is believed to have begun his crimes as a residential burglar.

Describing Property

A significant number of crimes investigated by law enforcement involve stolen property. It is very important for officers to describe property accurately in their crime or incident reports. Good descriptions in a crime report will help achieve the primary goals of law enforcement agencies which are arrest of suspects, recovery of property, and successful prosecution of cases. Professional investigations including thoroughly described property should be a priority for all officers. Agencies with active crime analysis units have higher expectations for full descriptions of property and suspects on reports. With the advent of multiagency databases the thorough and accurate capturing of this information is even more important. Crime analysis units rely on the information gathered by officers for linking crimes for more in depth analysis, such as geographic (geo) profiling, information sharing with other agencies, and informational bulletins for their agency. This is a critical component for ILP.

Frequently, property descriptions in police reports lack important detail. Many officers find obtaining good descriptions a tedious process. Imagine sitting at the dinner table of burglary victim who has lost heirloom jewelry, electronic equipment, and various identity-related paperwork. In this situation it is a long process to obtain descriptions of the property. Some officers ask the victim for a general estimate of loss and then leave a property form. After giving brief instructions on the completion of the form, the officer will leave, asking the victim to describe the property on the form and return the form to the police department.

One practice that leads to poor or, at least, imprecise descriptions is the method used by each department to record information on its report forms. Most police report forms have boxes that prompt officers to enter specific information. This results in the officer thinking that items such as sex, race, height, and weight are sufficient for a good description. Report forms also have fixed boxes for property descriptions. Most of these boxes prompt such items as the article number, quantity, serial number, *description*, and value. Table 6-2 shows a typical property list. Many officers believe if they put something in each box they have sufficiently described the involved property.

This form works well for property that is serialized, meaning it has a serial number, such as an Apple iPhone or a Dell computer. But take a moment to think about your iPhone or similar device. Is there something on your phone that makes it unusual or unique? Perhaps you have a sticker, or a document contained in the phone's memory that identifies the phone as yours. This information would be valuable to the investigator who recovers the phone.

The widespread availability of computer systems has significantly enhanced the ability of law enforcement to identify stolen property. By simply running a serial number through the system, the status of a piece of property can be established rapidly. Of course this means obtaining an identifier that is recognizable by the stolen property system in use and having it properly entered in that system. This is usually a serial number provided by the product manufacturer or an **owner-applied number** (**OAN**) applied by the victim—typically a social security number or driver's license number.

Often officers do not want to wait for a victim to find a serial number for items, as they want to get back in the field for the next call. Imagine the frequently repeated situation of the car stop where the officer sees a laptop computer in plain view on the rear seat of the detained vehicle. After asking for consent to look at the laptop she runs the serial number that returns "clear." An investigation begins and

table 6-2 Typical Property List

Item #	Quantity	Brand	Serial #	Description	Value
1	1	Sony	Unknown	PSP	$150
2	Miscellaneous	N/A	N/A	Miscellaneous women's jewelry	$10,000

the driver cannot tell the officer the make or model of the computer, where it was purchased, or how long it has been in his car. He tells the officer that the computer belongs to his father and that he was taking it to be fixed. The officer then asks the subject to start up the computer to see if she can find identifying information on the owner. The driver says, "No, it won't start and data might be lost if a startup is attempted." The investigation into the true owner of the computer is over. Had the officer who took the original burglary report taken the time to wait for the victim to search and find paperwork on the computer that contained the serial number, the officer who made a good observation on a car stop would have a felony arrest and the property would have been returned to the victim.

Statewide stolen property identification systems will return a *hit*, or query response, on a serial number when it is entered into the database. Then the person who is running the number—the officer, a dispatcher, a records clerk, or a detective—will have to sort through the responses to find matching property from a further description of the stolen items listed in the response. Officers should remember that some products do not use a unique number, so an additional in-depth description beyond a serial number is also necessary. Bicycles are an excellent example. Frequently the same manufacturer will use the same number over and over. It is not unusual to run a bicycle serial number and get more than a couple of hits. After contacting the victims it is later discovered that the questioned bicycle is not one of the listed stolen bicycles. This is more frustrating because the officer has not proven that the item in question is not stolen, but only that the item is not in the stolen property system.

The next best description is the OAN. This can be any unique number. Some people use their social security number, their driver's license number, or any other number they can use consistently. It is recommended that the social security number not be used for the simple fact that it is not traceable by local police and can also expose the victim to the secondary crime of identity theft. The driver's license number is the preferred number. It is traceable by police in almost the entire country. This is important when property has been stolen and the victim does not know of the theft. When officers find the property, run it through a stolen property system, and it comes back clear, they have one more investigative step. The driver's license number usually stands out as such and the owner can be identified. Once the owner is contacted, the status of the property can be determined.

Describing Property without Serial Numbers

Trying to describe jewelry stolen in a burglary using the boxes in a preprinted form is simply not helpful. It presents an obvious problem, because significant time should be taken to describe the jewelry for the detectives who might try to trace the jewelry in pawnshops or attempt to locate the property online. The lack of space on the form should not prohibit you from using a separate form and describing items in detail. When you sit down with the victim, ask for photos of property; often you will find that pictures have been taken with the victim wearing or holding the property. Although photos are the most helpful, you might also consider a picture drawn by the victim. Other items that may provide good descriptions are written appraisals and even original receipts of purchase.

Some items can defy identification. Golf clubs are frequently stolen because they are easily sold to retail golf shops. Unless there is an OAN or a label with owner information, there is little chance that the clubs can be recovered even if they are located. Seldom are OANs on golf clubs, as the etching may affect performance of the club.

Describing Property Seized in an Investigation

Officers are frequently called on to record and describe property seized in the course of an investigation. Items come into the custody of the police in several situations. The first is the result of a search done pursuant to a search warrant. Property seized from the execution of a search warrant must be carefully documented. A document called a *Return of Search Warrant* must be prepared soon after the search and will be filed with the court. This document tells the issuing judge about the results of the search. We will discuss the search warrant process and required reports in greater detail in Chapter 8.

The second property list documents property seized from some other search that

Accurately describing property seized during investigations is an essential part of report writing.
Source: © Mikael Karlsson/ Arresting Images

will be used in court. When listing property as *evidence*, accurate descriptions are very important. In some jurisdictions property can be released to the victim prior to the case going to court. Photos are taken of stolen or recovered property. A good description may save a case in court if the photos are later lost, which unfortunately does happen.

Finally, there is property that is found or abandoned. Often the legal status of the property is not always clear. These items are frequently referred to as *property under investigation*. A reasonable attempt can be made to determine the status of these items before releasing the property to the last person in possession of the property.

Property lists begin to get more difficult when trying to describe mass-produced items without serial numbers. Here the officer might be able to find something that makes the item unique. This is limited only by the imagination of the officer and the witness. This information cannot be captured in any searchable database, however, and whatever makes it unique is only as good as the memory of the officer. While a noted unique item might be easily located in a pawnshop, the information is probably not going to help officers at a car stop.

Describing Persons

Police officers and detectives must frequently describe the people involved in their investigations. Do not limit your thinking about descriptions to suspects. Victims might need to be described, especially in kidnapping cases or missing persons investigations. When third parties are reporting criminal activity they might have observed, they might also need to provide descriptions. You might think that the description is limited to the memory of the witness, but this is not exactly true. It is the responsibility of the investigating officers to ask questions of the witness that might stimulate and refresh the memory.

Keep in mind these considerations when obtaining descriptions of people. If the information is being taken for a supplemental crime broadcast, time is of the essence. Simple questions that give arriving officers the best chance of finding a fleeing suspect are the best. Clothing is the most frequently used descriptor, although many criminals will change their outer clothing when they can. The suspect's race, sex, height, and weight are sufficient information for perimeter units. Officers should never *assume* the race or gender of the suspect based on subjective criteria. This information should always be obtained from eyewitnesses and confirmed if possible through multiple sources. If the race or gender of the suspect cannot be determined through witness testimony, that information should be indicated in the narrative of the report.

Perhaps this is a good place to briefly discuss the issue of **racial profiling**. The following example may help illustrate how racial profiling can interfere with conducting a professional investigation and apprehending the correct suspect:

An officer arrives at the scene of a crime. The suspect has fled the area. The officer quickly establishes a crime and obtains a description of the suspect from the victim. She then puts out the following information in the supplemental broadcast. "The suspect is described as a male black wearing a black T-shirt." Is the use of race in this supplemental crime broadcast an example of unlawful racial profiling? The U.S. Department of Justice provided this definition of racial profiling in its pamphlet *A Resource Guide on Racial Profiling Data Collection Systems* (Ramirez, McDevitt, & Farrell, 2000):

> [A]ny police-initiated action that relies on the race, ethnicity,
> or national origin rather than the behavior of an individual or
> information that leads the police to a particular individual who has
> been identified as being, or having been, engaged in criminal activity.

With this definition in mind, is the officer in the previous scenario practicing racial profiling? The answer of course is no. The officer is reporting information that may lead the police to the suspect, not a suspicion based on race, ethnicity, or national origin of the suspect.

If, however, the officer—based *only* on his or her knowledge of the area and his or her history of dealing with a certain race of suspects—*assumed* that the suspect was a black male and disseminated that information to other officers, the action would constitute racial profiling and would be considered unlawful.

Describing Suspects

Suspect descriptions for reports must be more detailed and accurate. Two approaches are frequently used by investigating officers. The officer asks a witness or victim to describe the suspect and asks him or her to provide a flowing narrative. The officer can then make notes on how the suspect is described. The advantage to this approach is that the witness will talk about the details that made the greatest impression in his or her encounter with the suspect. This method has a tendency to turn up fine details the victim might have forgotten and the officer would not have known to ask about, such as a limp in gait or visible body piercings. The downside of this method is that many times the witness will provide details in a disorganized manner. This requires

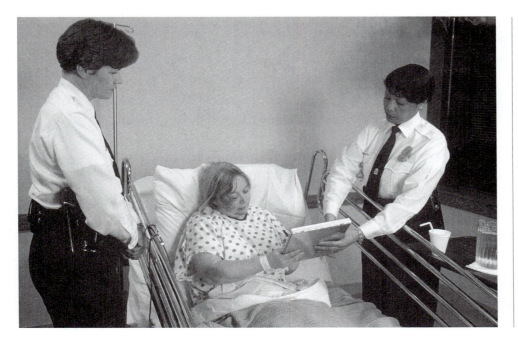

Accurately describing people involved in investigations is a critical part of report writing.
Source: David R. Frazier Photolibrary, Inc.

that the officer go back and carefully review the details to be sure an accurate description has been provided.

Another effective method for interviewing witnesses is for the investigating officer to systematically ask the witness questions starting from the top of the suspect's head and moving downward. The following list may help in organizing an approach:

- Was the suspect wearing a hat? If so, what style? Were there any logos? What color? What was the condition of the hat?
- What was the hair color and hairstyle of the suspect?
- What color were the suspect's eyes and how were they set in the face?
- Describe the suspect's nose, its size, and whether it was straight or crooked.
- For men, did the suspect have a mustache? For women, did the suspect have fine facial hair?
- Were the suspect's teeth discolored? Straight or crooked? Were any teeth missing? Any gold fillings?
- Did the suspect's mouth have an unusual shape?
- Did the suspect have any facial scars?
- Was the suspect's chin prominent or weak?
- Was the neck unusually long or thick? Any scars?
- Describe the suspect's shirt: What style? Button-up or T-shirt? Patterned or logo? What was the color of the shirt and its condition?
- Did the suspect have any scars on arms or exposed body parts?
- What was the condition of fingernails? Painted? If so, what color?
- Did the suspect have any visible body piercings?
- Was the suspect wearing any jewelry? If wearing rings, which finger? Any necklaces, religious medallions, or body jewelry?

- Did the suspect have tattoos? Were they artistic or crude? Describe the tattoo: Was it discernible or faded? Where was it located?

- Was the suspect wearing a belt? Did it have a distinctive buckle?

- Describe the suspect's pants, shorts, skirt, or dress. What color and style?

- Was the suspect wearing shoes? If so, were they dress or athletic? What brand or color? Was there a logo or unusual tread design?

This list is certainly not exhaustive but is sufficient to provide a solid description. One thing that is commonly missed in describing suspects is what they *say*. The witness should be pressed on this issue. The exact words serve a couple of purposes. First, the words used can provide important MO information and can be used to link crimes by crime analysis. This is especially important for geo profiling. Second, the exact words may be used in later identification procedures. The words spoken to a victim may become a significant part of the victim's memory. When hearing the suspect say the words, memory can be heightened.

Estimating Property Value

Obtaining accurate property values is important to the reporting process. First, they establish necessary elements of crimes such as grand or petite theft. These numbers are used by the FBI's Uniform Crime Reports to establish losses for all reporting agencies. There are several different ways to determine the value of a piece of stolen property. Items that are stolen from retail stores should be valued at the price the piece is offered for sale. This is referred to as **retail value**. So, in our shoplifting case in Chapter 4, if the suspect took a shirt that was offered for sale at $40, the proper value in the police report would be $40. You would not use the cost to the store when it was purchased from the wholesaler. You would also not include the sales tax the suspect would have paid if he or she had purchased it.

When placing a value on the items stolen from people or residences the proper method of valuation is **fair market value**. This is usually an estimate that is made by the victim as to the actual value. While many victims look at replacement costs, fair market value is the best approach. Police officers seldom find it worth the time to haggle over value with the victim. This can result in the victim filing a personnel complaint against the officer and, while the victim can seldom support the alleged value, the officer can't prove what he or she thinks the property is worth either. Eventually, the insurance company will adjust the value before settling any claim. It is recommended that officers ask for proof of value, especially when the claimed value seems overstated; however, officers shouldn't argue with victims. Detectives and insurance companies will look at the report and establish the proper value.

The next area concerning property values is property taken from other commercial businesses. This could be anything from panels used to power the electricity in a building to computers. Often receipts for the items are available as well as other documentation to establish actual value.

Again, officers are often confronted with victims overstating the value of items. Years ago the police received reports of residential burglaries with the only loss being "imported Persian rugs." Values were stated in the tens of thousands of dollars. The officers felt these values were inflated for insurance purposes, but they generally did not possess the expertise to challenge these claims. The officers believed the values stated were being used to defraud the victim's insurance carrier. The real discussion of value occurred when the insurance company received a claim for $30,000 to $40,000.

Another possible type of property resulting in disputed values is jewelry. Here the officer clearly would have no idea what the value may be for a piece of jewelry. Thus, receipts or appraisals are the best way to determine value. Don't forget to ask for pictures with the victim wearing the item. A photo provides a good description of the item and helps determine the actual value.

DESCRIPTIONS OF EVIDENCE: COMPLETING EVIDENCE REPORTS

Keep in mind a couple of things when documenting the seizure of evidence. The first is that you must provide a solid legal basis for the search. If a search occurs, remember that *plain view* is not a search. Another way officers frequently conduct a search is of a vehicle that is being impounded. While the policy reason for allowing the search is to protect vehicle owners from theft of property and to protect tow agencies and the police from false claims of theft, any contraband that is located can be seized and used against the owner in a criminal prosecution. These searches are constitutionally permissible when the department has a policy requiring vehicles to be searched and the searches are always conducted when a vehicle is stored and documented. Properly documenting the evidence requires that all officers clearly understand current search and seizure law. Officers must then apply that knowledge in the field. Second, you must accurately document how and where the items were found, including who found the item, who took it into custody, and finally, how and by whom the item was put into the property division of the police department. This is known as the *chain of evidence*. A poorly documented chain of evidence gives defense counsel the opportunity to "impeach" the evidence and demonstrate that the investigation was conducted in a sloppy fashion. **Chain of custody** and its importance in the report writing process is discussed in depth in the following text. We define it as establishing and documenting the possession of evidence from the point of seizure until the evidence is introduced at trial or final disposition.

When serving search warrants, search teams are usually divided and given responsibility for the search of particular areas of the target location. In this type of search several officers may find key pieces of evidence in different locations. The "case investigator" is notified of the find, and then looks at the location where the property is located. The investigator will make some notes and then the evidence is collected by another officer. Some agencies will document the finding of the evidence as being done by the case investigator. The idea is to limit the amount of court time by various officers in establishing the chain of evidence as well as to not overburden the case officers in doing the entire search themselves. This practice is discouraged as it creates the potential for some embarrassing testimony if the officer is asked the wrong questions by the prosecutor or the right questions by defense counsel.

The recommended practice is for the person who finds the items to report the find to the case investigator. The case investigator then records who found the item and where it was found. Another officer collects the item and books it into evidence. The evidence report will reflect the observations of the "finder" and who collected the item and placed it into the evidence system at the police department.

Each agency has its own policy on the booking property and every piece of evidence should be booked according to this policy. The policy will include how the property is handled prior to packaging, the method of packaging the item, and where the item is to be secured. Closely adhering to your agency's policy eliminates the need to explain unusual booking practices.

Documenting the Chain of Custody

Before a piece of seized property may be entered into evidence in court, the item must be proven to be authentic and trustworthy. This is known as the *foundation*. Only after the foundation for the item can be established will a judge allow the item entered into evidence. The item must be what it is purported to be. While this is courtroom process that the district attorney is responsible for, you can make his or her job a lot easier by strictly following proper procedures in handling and storage of evidence.

There are three ways to establish that an item is what it is *purported to be*. First is by the testimony of an eyewitness. Here the witness is able to testify to factors that make the item unique. An example would be the rightful owner of stolen jewelry identifying the piece from the item's unique design. The second method of establishing the proper foundation is by the markings that a witness may have made on the item. An example would be a Rolex watch. While there are lots of Rolex watches, this one may have a special engraving on it or a manufacturer's serial number. You can see the importance of waiting as a victim of a burglary finds the serial number for items that have been stolen.

Most agencies "tag" certain items, such as firearms, with identifying information. Some agencies still have officers carve or etch initials or serial numbers in the item itself with an engraving tool. The idea is that the officer can identify the tag or etching as his or her own and "authenticate" the item for court. You can see that this is not the best practice when dealing with an item that may be returned to the rightful owner at some later time.

Finally, and least desirable, is the chain of evidence method of establishing that an item is what it is purported to be. Multiple witnesses may be required to testify to complete the chain. With each witness the possibility of the defense finding a discrepancy in testimony increases. Good defense counsel will use any discrepancy to attack the case of the prosecution. This calls for a very long day on the witness stand.

DESCRIPTIONS OF INCIDENTS

The next few sections will discuss the preparation of the crime report starting with the face page. In preparing crime reports it is easy for officers to get distracted and not do a complete job. Often these reports get returned to the officer by supervisors for correction, but sometimes they don't.

Take, for example, an incident in California where the officer investigating a fatal traffic collision involving a young mother turned in a sketch of the scene done on a napkin as the factual diagram by officers who thought they were providing some reference points. This diagram turned up as a piece of evidence in a civil suit years later. You can imagine the embarrassment of the two officers who prepared this sketch when they appeared for a deposition. Preparing the report involves the property lists, the face page(s), and the narrative. We have talked about property lists and now move on to the face page and narrative.

Completing the Face Page

When the reporting officer sits down to actually write the repor, the first document completed will be the **face page**. The face page identifies the incident type and the date, time, and location of occurrence. Also included on the face page is *demographic*

figure 6-1 Felony Crime Report

Robbery	1. CASE NO.
Felony Crime Report **Jackson Police Department**	07-1024

2.CODE SECTION	3. CRIME	4.CLASSIFICATION	5. REPORT AREA
211a PC	Armed Robbery	Market w/revolver	5

6.DATE AND TIME OCCURRED - DAY	7.DATE AND TIME REPORTED	8. LOCATION OF OCCURRENCE
06/29/07 0700 Friday	06/29/07	100 North "C" St., Jackson 92410

9. VICTIM'S NAME LAST, FIRST, MIDDLE (FIRM IF BUSINESS)	10. RESIDENCE ADDRESS	11. RES. PHONE
McDaniel's Market		

12. OCCUPATION	13.RACE-SEX	14. AGE	15.DOB	16. BUSINESS ADDRESS (SCHOOL IF JUVENILE)	17. BUS. PHONE
Grocery Store				Same as 8	555-1505

CODES FOR BOXES 20 AND 30   V = VICTIM   W = WITNESS   P = PARENT   RP = REPORTING PARTY   DC = DISCOVERED CRIME

18.CHECK IF MORE NAMES IN CONTINUATION [X]

19. NAME - LAST, FIRST, MIDDLE	20. CODE	21. RESIDENCE ADDRESS	22. RESIDENCE PHONE
McDaniel, John Joseph	RP	1234 Elm Avenue	555-3210

23. OCCUPATION	24. RACE -SEX	25. AGE	26. DOB	27. BUSINESS ADDRESS (SCHOOL IF JUVENILE)	28. BUSINESS PHONE
Owner	MWA	54	9/9/52	Same as 8	555-1505

29. NAME - LAST, FIRST, MIDDLE	30. CODE	31. RESIDENCE ADDRESS	32. RESIDENCE PHONE
Johnson, Mary Lois	W	955 North "C" Jackson	555-1433

33. OCCUPATION	34.RACE-SEX	35. AGE	36.DOB	37. BUSINESS ADDRESS (SCHOOL IF JUVENILE)	38. BUSINESS PHONE
Housewife	WFA	48	12/12/58	None	

MODUS OPERANDI   (SEE INSTRUCTIONS)

39. DESCRIBE CHARACTERISTICS OF PREMISE AND AREA WHERE OFFENSE OCCURRED
Large groc. mkt. in downtown area next to hotels. Alley in rear, Pkg. lot on E. side

40. DESCRIBE BRIEFLY HOW OFFENSE WAS COMMITTED
Climbs fire escape on adjoining hotel, jumps to roof of mkt., drills out 20" hole in roof, lowers self
via rope to floor of store, waits till opening, forces mgr. to open safe, locks victims in walk-in
cooler, leaves through rear alley exit.

41. DESCRIBE WEAPON, INSTRUMENT, EQUIPMENT, TRICK , DEVICE OR FORCE USED
2" B/S Rev. 1-1/4" drill, chisel, hammer, rope

42. MOTIVE - TYPE OF PROPERTY TAKEN OR OTHER REASON FOR OFFENSE
Money & Checks

43. ESTIMATED LOSS VALUE AND/OR EXTENT OF INJURIES - MINOR, MAJOR
$8,110.

44. WHAT DID SUSPECT/S SAY - NOTE PECULIARITIES
"This is a robbery, behave and you won't get hurt. Get over here 'fass'."

45. VICTIM'S ACTIVITY JUST PRIOR TO AND/OR DURING OFFENSE
Opening Store

46. TRADEMARK - OTHER DISTINCTIVE ACTIVITY OF SUSPECT/S
Ate on premises, drank Vodka

47. VEHICLE USED - LICENSE NO. - YEAR - MAKE - MODEL - COLORS (OTHER IDENTIFYING CHARACTERISTICS)
None seen

48. SUSPECT NO. 1 (LAST, FIRST, MIDDLE)	49. RACE- SEX	50. AGE	51. HT.	52. WT.	53.HAIR	54.EYES	55. ID. NO. OR DOB	56. ARRESTED
S-1 Name Unknown	WMA	30-35	6'	200	Dk	brn		YES ☐ NO [X]

57. ADDRESS, CLOTHING AND OTHER IDENTIFYING MARKS OR CHARACTERISTICS
Work clothes, wore flashy ring with large brilliant stone

58. SUSPECT NO. 2 (LAST, FIRST, MIDDLE)	59. RACE- SEX	60. AGE	61. HT.	62. WT.	63.HAIR	64.EYES	65. ID. NO. OR DOB	66. ARRESTED
S-2 Name Unknown	WMA	30-35	5'8	180	blk	brn		YES ☐ NO [X]

67. ADDRESS, CLOTHING AND OTHER IDENTIFYING MARKS OR CHARACTERISTICS
Work clothes, Army type boots, small blue dot left cheek under eye

68. CHECK IF MORE NAMES IN CONTINUATION ☐

REPORTING OFFICERS	RECORDING OFFICER	TYPED BY	DATE AND TIME	ROUTED BY
Samons #18 / Jacobs #35	Jacobs	mmk	06/29/07 1300	Owens

FURTHER ACTION				
[X] YES	[X] DETECTIVE	[X] C11		
☐ NO	☐ JUVENILE	☐ PATROL		
	[X] DIST. ATTNY	☐ OTHER_____	REVIEWED BY	DATE
	[X] SQ./ P.D.	☐ OTHER_____	Moore, R.L. Lt	6/29/07

information on the victim and witnesses. If there are multiple victims or witnesses an additional page for this information should be completed. In the past this information included name, address, and telephone number in addition to business address, telephone number, and occupation. Many agencies have recognized the widespread use of e-mail and cell phones and include this information on report face pages as well. Officers should recognize the importance of these identifiers as they provide information that may be needed to contact involved parties in the future.

Figure 6-1 shows a sample felony crime report. In addition to the information mentioned earlier, some other obvious information is included in the report. This includes reporting and approving officers' names and rank, suspect description, and suspect vehicle description. Additionally, there are several boxes marked modus operandi, or MO. These boxes primarily assist the records division in fulfilling mandatory reporting requirements for UCR.

The information shown in Figure 6-1 can be vital to both investigators and crime analysts. Linking a series of crimes can often be tedious; this linkage is important in distinguishing unrelated crimes from serial crimes. Often suspects will use similar language when engaging victims. For instance, consider the statement of the robbery suspect in Figure 6-1: *This is a robbery, behave and you won't get hurt. Get over here "fass."* Most of the statement is unremarkable, but the term *fass,* a slang derogatory term for a person, and the use of the word *behave* might help in the linkage of other robberies. Sex offenders are known to use similar language each time they confront victims. Good reporting accurately captures these words.

Some departments no longer use MO boxes on reports; records personnel glean the required UCR information from the full report. Although this seems to take more time of the clerical personnel, the information obtained has a tendency to be more accurate because records personnel are more familiar than the patrol officer with information needed. Refer to your department's report writing guidelines as you prepare the face pages. Usually instructions are available telling you how to proceed.

The goal in both incident and crime report writing is to accurately capture the events that have occurred. Generally, crime reports and arrest reports, to be discussed later, will by nature be more complete and thorough than incident reports. Officers should remember that crime reports will provide the basis for the eventual arrest of the involved party. Taking away a person's liberty is a serious business. The crime report is the first step in this process.

Writing the Narrative

An old-time sergeant once told a new officer to *paint the picture,* using long, sweeping hand motions as though he were painting the side of a house. Officers should remember to write in a fashion that would let a reader *see* the scene. This means that an officer should be thorough and provide all elements of a crime, including details that indicate the state of mind of the offender. The victim and at times the officer will ensure a **filing** (the formal filing of criminal charges) and successful prosecution. Officers must be able to identify factors that tend to establish guilt as well as those that establish defenses and indicators of innocence, known as **exculpatory** evidence (*Brady v. Maryland,* 2000). If the district attorney is not armed with this knowledge before a case is filed, then the case is doomed to fail in court. Unfortunately the officer who completed the investigation and wrote the report stands to be the most embarrassed.

Officers should remember to always write in an objective manner. For example, in the description of a bloody crime scene, the phrase *there was blood everywhere* is emotionally charged. A more objective statement might be *I saw a large amount of blood on the walls and floor.* As stated in Chapter 4, the first section of a police report establishes how an officer arrived at an incident. Generally, this occurs in one of two ways for the patrol officer. First, the officer may respond to a radio call. Second, he or she she may observe something during patrol that requires further investigation. Finally, the officer may have been alerted to a circumstance by a citizen.

Establishing the Elements of the Crime

The next section of the report narrative should establish the elements of the crime being investigated. Again, knowledge of criminal law is essential. Usually this paragraph begins with the reporting party's statement. This is often the victim or, in the case of a noncriminal report (an incident report), an involved party. This statement frequently establishes the elements of the crime being documented. This, of course, varies depending on the type of crime or incident. As an example, you are not going to be able to obtain statements from victims in all homicide cases, but you will be able to obtain statements from the victim in most robbery cases. You will generally have an idea of what type of case you are investigating during the initial interview. Using the three-step interview process described in Chapter 4 and taking good field notes helps determine exactly what occurred. Once you have established that a crime has occurred, you can then proceed with an interview that will provide you the details that make the report complete. These details will vary for the type of crime being investigated.

The elements of the crime must be clearly documented. Many new officers will write reports and fail to properly outline crime elements. They rely on the original dispatch information to determine the crime type. An example would be shoplifting. Generally, anyone who takes the property of another with the intent to permanently deprive is guilty of theft. However, a call dispatched as a shoplifting could actually be a burglary when it can be proven that the suspect entered with the intent to steal. Each state establishes its own laws and the elements for each crime. Officers should refer to their jurisdictions for a comprehensive list of crimes and the elements necessary to establish them.

Documenting Witness Statements

The next part of your report includes what witnesses and others involved in the investigation tell you during the course of your investigation. A report may have several statements. As an example, a business owner may have hired a security guard to assist with loss prevention. The security guard sees a juvenile conceal an item in his backpack. The juvenile then makes a purchase from a cashier of other items not concealed in the backpack. He leaves the store and is confronted by the security guard who has to chase the juvenile for several blocks where the juvenile stops and pulls out a knife. Then another police officer arrives and takes the juvenile into custody. He is returned to the store for your report. While this may seem like an easy shoplifting report that requires only the statement of the security guard and potentially the suspect, several other components are involved and a couple you may have not noticed.

First, who called the police? Was it a citizen watching an adult chase a minor? Was it the security guard as the crime was unfolding? Do you need to document how the security got there, meaning how important is the owner's statement? Take a moment and make a list of the people you think should be interviewed and their statement contained in the report. Here are a few examples of people who might become important.

The most obvious witness is the security guard. He has witnessed more than one crime in this incident. He is the person who will establish the elements of the crime(s) for you. Without this witness you might be filing an incident report because no one can tell whether or not a crime occurred. His statement is important and can establish whether the crime is a simple petty theft, a misdemeanor, an armed robbery, or a felony. The statement of the security guard will give you the necessary information to establish the elements.

Here is another statement from a police report: *Spelman, the loss prevention officer, told me she detained Russell when Russell stole the CD.* While this seems to encompass the elements of the crime of shoplifting, it does not objectively develop the events that prove the crime. This is a good example of an officer being **conclusory** in her report. This means that the officer has stated the conclusion that Russell stole or shoplifted, without supporting it. The officer should document what the loss prevention officer saw so that the reader—a police supervisor, a city or district attorney, or a defense counsel—will come to a logical conclusion. Hopefully, this conclusion will be one that is shared by the officer.

From time to time officers get "stuck" at this phase. They know that something has happened and they have the person who is responsible detained, but without the crime elements they will likely be unable to arrest a suspect or provide the information to prosecute the crime. A look at the state's penal (or criminal) code is helpful here. The elements should be apparent as you read the statute that you think applies. If you don't have the elements, don't give up; you may be dealing with a different crime. Another important resource is the state's jury instructions. They will tell you what the prosecuting attorney (the city attorney or the deputy district attorney) has to prove in court to obtain a conviction. This is a resource that most police departments should have readily available. Jury instructions are also available at any law library. Once you establish the crime, you can then determine if the evidence, both physical and oral, proves the elements of the crime.

The previous shoplifting scenario was fairly straightforward. Remember, your report may not start with the security guard. One of the witnesses may lead to the security guard. Keeping the order and chronology correct for each witness in a crime is essential to the readability of a report. We discussed chronology in Chapter 5, and it is a critical part of the report writing process.

Now look at the cashier. Is his statement important? In this instance it is very important because the suspect paid for other items. The cashier is necessary to determine what the suspect paid for and how payment was made. In other words, including the cashier's observations will depend on whether or not the security guard observed the suspect walk past the registers without paying. If the guard didn't, then this is an important statement.

Take a moment and think about the bystanders. If someone saw something that helps develop your case or provides a defense to the charge then it must be included (*Brady v. Maryland*, 1963). This is true even if you have multiple people saying the same thing. Always remember that the *Brady* decision requires the prosecutor (and you) to pass on any exculpatory information to the defense team during the discovery phase. That is, information that might show a person's innocence. Discovery is the time in the criminal proceeding that the prosecution must turn over all information it has for the case. This includes your police report and any reports written by other members of your department or the DA's investigators. Failure to do so results in an acquittal and sanctions against the DA.

Now what about the bystander who says he didn't see anything other than the handcuffed juvenile once the police arrived? Should you include this statement in your report? This is where good field notes come into play. Imagine the witness who tells you he only saw the suspect sitting on the curb handcuffed after the arrival of the police. Clearly, this does not help with the elements of theft and assault with the knife nor does it provide a defense to the crimes. Thus, it does not need to be in the report. Now, several weeks later that witness appears at trial and says he saw the police place a knife in the suspect's pocket. Your field notes would be very helpful at this point. You may or may not remember the witness; however, if you have the person's name and statement in your field notes it can be used to help refresh your memory while on the witness stand. This may be enough to refute the witness's newfound recollection of the incident. Of course, it would be even better if you had a tape-recorded statement from the witness at the scene.

A very important statement is the one the actual victim makes. In this case it is the store owner. The store owner must agree to support prosecution of the suspect. Some jurisdictions will prosecute only with a cooperative witness, meaning someone who wants to press charges. So you must ask and document whether or not the owner is interested in prosecution.

In this chapter we talked about obtaining important information for responding units to a crime scene. We also discussed the importance of good property descriptions for the recovery of property and the successful prosecution of offenders. Writing the report was also discussed, as well as some information on the forms used by agencies.

chapter summary

1. Police reports contain several distinct sections. We have spoken of the parts of the narrative, but just as important are descriptions of property and people. Descriptions should be carefully obtained and reproduced.

2. The initial description taken at the scene of the crime should be sufficient to broadcast to other responding officers in the form of a supplemental crime broadcast.

3. The true purpose of descriptions of property in police reports is the recovery of property. This is an essential task for all police agencies as it not only lessens the impact of crime on the public but also assists victims as they recover from the effects of crime.

4. Property values should be established with receipts or other documents when possible. If those are not available, then fair market value is the best way to establish value. Often values are in dispute. Officers should allow investigators and insurance companies work out the final value. Officers should avoid arguments with victims.

5. One of three ways to establish an item is what it is purported to be. Of the three discussed in this chapter, chain of evidence is the least desirable.

6. Police report narratives should fully describe the incident being reported. Crime reports should pay particular attention to the elements of the crime. A report without clear crime elements is not a crime report, it is an incident report and cannot be used for prosecution.

Exercises—Writing Crime and Incident Reports

exercise 1

DEVELOPING A LIST OF WITNESS QUESTIONS FOR A SUPPLEMENTAL CRIME BROADCAST

INSTRUCTIONS: The following victim statement was taken at the scene of a domestic violence call. Using this statement, develop a list of questions you might ask the victim to develop a supplemental crime broadcast.

Victim statement:
The suspect has fled the scene prior to the arrival of the police. The victim is found with a large laceration to her forehead. The victim tells you that her husband has fled the scene prior to the arrival of the police. His car keys are gone, but due to crowded parking on their street it is not known where his car was (or is) parked.

_____

_____

_____

_____

_____

_____

_____

_____

_____

_____

_____

_____

exercise 2

COMPLETING A PROPERTY LIST

INSTRUCTIONS: Using the information listed in the narrative, fill out the blank department property list.

An officer makes a lawful stop of a vehicle for a vehicle code violation. Upon contact with the driver the officer smells the odor of an alcoholic beverage and begins a DUI investigation. The officer ends up arresting the driver for DUI and then searches the vehicle incident to the lawful arrest of the driver. During the course of the search the officer finds an open bottle of bourbon, a loaded handgun, and a plastic baggy containing methamphetamine. She seizes all of these items and locks the items in the trunk of her police car.

The officer books the arrestee and obtains a blood sample for testing by the crime lab. She intends to ask for the following charges: (1) possession of a controlled substance, (2) driving while impaired, (3) possession of a loaded and concealable handgun, and (4) possession of an open container of alcohol. She then books the property into evidence following the procedures laid out in her department's policy manual. The case is filed by the local prosecutor and is now at trial. The prosecutor is attempting to enter the items into evidence. Assuming the jurisdiction does not require the production of the actual open container and will rely on the testimony of the officer as to the condition of the bottle and the fact that the liquid in the bottle smelled like alcohol, name the methods for entering the items into evidence.

During a search of the vehicle, the officer found 1 gram of methamphetamine, a Glock, Model 19, semiautomatic handgun loaded with 15 rounds of 9 mm ammunition, and one half-empty bottle of Jim Beam bourbon. Remember, value is not necessary on most seized property unless it is U.S. currency.

Anytown, MN, Police Department   Property Form 2011-01

Item #	Quantity	Brand	Serial #	Description	Value

exercise 3

IDENTIFYING CRITICAL ELEMENTS FOR A CRIME REPORT

INSTRUCTIONS: The following paragraph describes an incident that an officer might encounter while on patrol. Using the information in the paragraph, list the facts that might be important in a crime report. Not all of the information contained in the paragraph is necessary for a crime report. List only the facts that are necessary for a report.

While on patrol an officer, working day watch at seven o'clock in the morning, is dispatched to a theft report at the reporting parties' residence. He arrives and Dave O'Neal tells them that he left his car parked on the street. It was parked overnight after he returned from a party. He always locks the car, a red BMW with Tennessee license plates. He had been drinking at the party and left his laptop computer on the front seat. When he awoke he watched several football games before he tried to find his laptop. He remembered he left it in his car. Later in the day he went to his car and discovered that someone had taken his computer. The driver's window was shattered and a small chip of porcelain laid on the ground next to the window. A crime scene investigator was called in to investigate.

_____

_____

_____

_____

_____

_____

_____

_____

_____

_____

_____

_____

_____

_____

WRITING A CRIME REPORT NARRATIVE

INSTRUCTIONS: Using the elements from Exercise 3, create a detailed narrative for a crime report. Make sure you develop the report using some of the ideas and guidelines discussed in this and previous chapters.

_____
_____
_____
_____
_____
_____
_____
_____
_____
_____
_____
_____
_____
_____
_____
_____
_____
_____
_____
_____
_____
_____
_____
_____
_____
_____
_____
_____
_____
_____
_____
_____
_____
_____
_____

exercise 4

glossary terms

7

Writing Arrest Reports

INTRODUCTION

Writing arrest reports presents a challenge for police officers because of their technical nature and the detail that they entail. Many, if not most, officers walk blindly through the steps of an arrest with little regard for the nuances of criminal law, search and seizure, or suspects' admissions and confessions. They rely on past experience, a limited knowledge of the intricacies of the law, a belief in right and wrong, and luck to guide them.

As an example, after an officer made a great observation of a stolen sport-utility vehicle being driven down a Southern California freeway, he attempted to stop the SUV. A pursuit ensued involving several officers. The pursuit continued for several miles before the suspect abandoned the vehicle and was then chased on foot by the officers. The officers caught the suspect and took him into custody in a large field that was a muddy quagmire due to a recent rainstorm.

Now the officers faced the task of getting the suspect back to the police cars, as no access was available to the field by vehicle due to the muddy conditions. After lugging the uncooperative suspect through the field, the officers had to negotiate a six-foot chain-link fence with a handcuffed suspect. Once they had overcome this obstacle, the officers, who were covered in thick mud, handed the suspect over to another officer who was not involved in the vehicle pursuit or foot chase. While both the suspect and the officer were standing behind a police car on a freeway that had slowed to a crawl as motorists gawked, the officer asked the suspect why he ran, where he stole the car, and what was he going to do with the car. Although this was meant as "small talk" the officer was not thinking about his legal obligations. Even a basic knowledge of the law of admissions and confessions tells you that the officer should have given the suspect his Miranda warnings before uttering a word. His attempt at small talk was clearly custodial interrogation which violates the rules on questioning of in-custody suspects (*Miranda v. Arizona*, 1966).

Another example of an officer lacking technical knowledge of the law regarding arrests is a simple car stop that results in the arrest of one of the passengers. A typical reason for stopping a vehicle might be the observation of a mechanical defect that constitutes a violation of the state's vehicle code. In this case, the officer notices the car has a burned-out taillight so she initiates a car stop with her red lights. Because the car stop is occurring in an area known for high crime including acts of violence on police, the officer takes her gun out of her holster and places it out of view hidden behind her back. Upon making contact she smells the faint but distinctive odor of burning marijuana. The officer orders all of the occupants out of the vehicle and conducts a limited search for weapons that reveals one passenger is in possession of a small amount of marijuana. She asks for consent to search the vehicle, which the driver gives, and the officer begins a search. She finds a loaded, concealable handgun wedged between the back of the front center console and the driver's seat, an area accessible to all passengers in the vehicle. She then interviews each occupant inquiring about the ownership of the gun.

This is typical of thousands of car stops that occur in the United States every day. Officers preparing arrest reports must be aware of all the potential defenses to criminal charges as well as the criminal procedural issues raised in the reports. While this is not a book on criminal procedure, there are at least seven different issues that an officer must be aware of when writing arrest reports. The issues range from knowledge of the state's vehicle code, to the impact of taking a gun from the holster even though it is hidden from the driver's view during a contact where a later search is based on consent or the impact of the officer's firearm being in her hand on statements made by the suspects to the various theories of searches of motor vehicles and the application of each. As officers write arrest reports they must realize that these legal issues need to be addressed in the report. This must be done in a plain, straightforward manner. Deputy district attorneys are generally burdened by large caseloads and often see the reports for the first time the morning before the cases come before a judge or a jury. Clearly written reports that detail the issues presented in a case will assist the DA in preparation and presentation of a case.

Every arrest involves issues of proof, conformance to constitutional procedure, and a thorough investigation that is properly documented for an arrest to result in a successful prosecution. A good educational foundation in criminal procedures and investigative techniques provides an important step in avoiding the pitfalls described previously.

Not only must the report objectively paint the picture of the encounter, it must also reflect the officer's understanding of the facts and circumstances at that time. State of mind can be important in several ways. The courts have consistently stated that an officer's state of mind is not important to the establishment or existence of probable cause to make an arrest or obtain a search warrant. Probable cause is an objective standard based on reasonableness. The courts will make their determination of probable cause based on what a reasonable person would believe, not the officer or the suspect.

The officer's state of mind is very important in cases involving the reaction to a suspect's resistance, also known as use of force. While the propriety of the use of force to overcome resistance is based on the officer's state of mind, the force itself must be objectively reasonable (*Graham v. Connor,* 1989). The officer's report must support **objective reasonableness**. The question a court will try and answer is "would a reasonable police officer in that position use that amount of force?" In writing an arrest report where force has been necessary this standard must be kept in mind, and fully developed in the report, as the officer prepares the case for prosecution. Failure to do so or making conclusory statements can lead to lawsuits. Going through any civil lawsuit as a defendant is a very unpleasant experience that can be even more unpleasant when trying to defend a poorly written report.

Correctly documenting the facts or circumstances which led to making an arrest will help secure a successful prosecution.
Source: Brand X Pictures

DOCUMENTING THE ARREST

Arrests generally result from several types of situations. Let us consider the types of arrest situations and the reports and reporting styles necessary in documenting them. Arrests occur in field observations, also known as on-view arrests, calls for service, investigative follow-ups, and arrests based on **judicial authority**—the warrant arrest. Each type presents its own requirements for proper documentation. The arresting officer should keep in mind whether the report establishes each of the following:

- Why and how the police became involved.
- The elements of the crime(s) to be charged.
- Sufficient facts and circumstances that meet the requirement of **probable cause**.

To establish probable cause, an officer must prove that it is more likely than not that the person arrested has committed the crime to be charged.

When possible, officers should identify the variables of the report and create a plan for how they are going to address them. In a complex arrest, a brief outline with headings for each of the legal issues and investigative points that prove the crime elements and establish probable cause makes it easier to ensure that each area is covered. In complex arrests, especially those involving several officers, it is a good practice to have another officer look over the outline to make sure all of the issues at hand have been recognized.

ARRESTS MADE ON CALLS FOR SERVICE

Officers face unique challenges in arrests generated from calls for service including development of the case from a third party, usually the victim or a representative of the victim business. This was discussed at length in the shoplifting scenario in

Chapter 6. There you can see that great potential for confusion exists in the report writing process in arrests that result from calls for service. In these cases, clear, well-thought-out reports must be prepared to avoid this confusion. Usually, but not always, the report must include the elements of the crime, as you would in a crime report, but also the pieces of information that led to the establishment of probable cause. At times one officer may take an initial crime report and a second officer will document the arrest. Although the arrest report will refer to the crime report, it is not necessary to rewrite the crime report in a second report. The first report has the elements of the crime and the second documents the arrest.

The development of the case is just as important as writing the report, and case development will directly affect the written document. Officers need to take a moment and decide what issues they are facing as they develop the case. Too many officers don't stop to think about the legal issues, evidence requirements, statements of involved parties, and the potential for additional witnesses and how they all should be addressed in the final document. The officer who carefully plans his or her reports will follow the basic report writing steps.

An example is the anonymous informant. Informants must be dealt with carefully in the report-writing process to maintain their confidentiality. Some officers may take the easy way out and simply not include the informant in the report. This could leave a big hole in a case that gives defense counsel a series of questions that can make the officer appear as though he or she is being untruthful or is trying to conceal information from the defense, thus exposing the officer to *Brady* issues (*Brady v. Maryland*, 1963). Often witnesses will supply information that starts the investigation process but is not material to the defense. It is acceptable to omit these witnesses in the final report.

The officer may have to look to other sources of information to establish the portion of the arrest that originated from the informant. As an example, a patrol officer makes an arrest for possession of a controlled substance. The officer does an outstanding job and spends some extra time talking with the arrestee about his drug habit. The conversation includes topics such as the arrestee's drug of choice, how he began using illegal drugs, how the drugs are ingested, what other types of drugs the arrestee uses, and how he obtains the drugs. As you can see, the conversation accomplishes a couple of things. First, it establishes rapport with the arrestee. This may prove useful later during the investigation or if the arrestee provides information as to his sources or the location of other contraband. Second, the conversation increases the officer's knowledge in the area of drug abuse and should be included in a file the officer keeps on his expertise. Finally, the underlying reason for this discussion is to develop information on how and where the drugs were obtained. During this discussion the arrestee tells the officer that he may have information regarding a "drug dealer who sells to children." Many agencies may require the original officer to include a detective in the discussion at this point. The arrestee agrees to tell the officers the information with the promise of "consideration" in his current arrest. This means that the officers will tell the judge, who will hear the current arrest of the arrestee's cooperation in the new investigation. The informant says he will do this only on the condition that he remains anonymous in the future case. The arrestee then tells the investigator that he was talking to a person (and he names that person) on the corner of Sweet Rain and New Brook Streets when two kids about 12 years old approached. The subject went into his car (which he also describes) and produced two small plastic bags containing marijuana. The kids each gave him some money. The arrestee said he saw at least 20 more similarly packaged bags of marijuana in the subject's car.

This is an example of material information. Unless the detectives can build a case for a search warrant without the information provided by the arrestee, the information provided would be material to the affidavit for a search warrant. The defense has the right to know that a confidential informant is being used and certainly would want to cross-examine the witness (we will discuss confidential informants in greater detail in Chapter 8).

Compare the previous example to the following. Officers were called to the residence of a woman who lived alone. She complained of loud noises coming from a neighbor's garage late at night. She reported seeing people coming and going. These people would walk in the house, stay for only a minute or two, and then leave. She feared they were selling drugs and told the officers she saw people leave the house who appeared to be obviously under the influence of a substance. Her observations were consistent with drug-selling activity and might be used as part of an affidavit to support a search warrant. However, she requested that she remain anonymous, as she feared the resident's reprisals.

Officers have a few options in this instance including surveillance, lawfully stopping vehicles leaving the residence, or doing some background research on the residents of the house. The officers chose the latter and discovered that people who lived in the residence had significant criminal records. Two of the residents were on parole and state parole officers were contacted. A parole search was conducted and stolen property that had been taken in residential burglaries along with a small amount of drugs was found in the residence. In this instance the reporting person did not provide material information, which required her testimony and as such was not considered a confidential informant.

Arrests are frequently made during major incidents. These can sometimes be violent and chaotic which can add to the challenge of writing a detailed and accurate report.
Source: © Mikael Karlsson/ Arresting Images

In an arrest that occurs as a call for service from a third party, many things have already occurred that the reporting officer cannot change. In the case of an employee who has stolen or embezzled from his employer the officer will likely have the opportunity to interview witnesses who will provide the elements of the crime as well as look at paperwork supplied by the employer or a bank that has evidentiary value in proving both the crime and who is responsible.

There are a few calls that most officers are not fond of handling. Domestic disputes and traffic collisions top the list. But most officers are less than pleased when they are called to take the report of fraud. These cases are often very complex with lots of witnesses and sometimes the "victims" are involved in some conduct themselves that is at the minimum unethical. For these reasons the cases may be difficult to investigate and ultimately to prosecute. Fraud comes in many forms, but the rules and format of report writing still apply. The most important thing in properly documenting these calls for service is organization. The elements of the crime must be clearly laid out in the report. This takes a clear understanding of the statute that has been violated and any evidence needed by the DA to prove the case.

You might receive lots of documents from the reporting party. Often officers book the documents into property as evidence but forget to attach copies for the investigator to read. Each document should be copied and a copy attached to the report. A list labeled "attachments" should identify the documents and each should be referenced properly in the report. It is extremely important to keep this information clear and organized. Carefully noting what part of the document is being referenced can help the reader understand the implications of the document. You should also think about your mental approach to these cases. The lack of interest by officers in this type of investigation manifests itself in poor reports. Remember from earlier chapters, many people read these reports and judge the individual officer by this work product. With this in mind, an officer can set himself or herself apart from other officers by conducting good investigations and producing well-written reports.

ARRESTS MADE DURING MAJOR INCIDENTS

The majority of police calls for service involve routine matters such as theft or burglary reports, lost property, various disputes that need to be documented, or traffic collision investigations (reporting of traffic collisions is subject for an entire separate book). However, officers frequently find themselves involved in the investigation of serious crimes that stem from calls for service. Various law enforcement agencies may work differently in these investigations. Some may require that responding officers stabilize the scene and provide security until detectives can be called to handle the investigation. Other agencies require the assigned officer to prepare the initial case, and detectives are assigned the case after the approval process, only being called to the scene in the event of a major crime. Even in agencies that do not require the assigned officers to handle the investigation, supplemental reports that document officers' observations are going to be required. First responders should carefully observe the scene and take proper notes for completion of the report. Even the smallest initial observation can be extremely important to the overall case. Taking the time to make notes of those first impressions are very important. This, of course, assumes a cold crime scene, which is safe to work in. Suspects are either in custody or gone from the scene and bystanders are not hostile.

When responding to "in-progress crimes" officers can easily be overwhelmed with sensory information. They must process this information quickly and efficiently. In doing this they often miss information or simply pass it by as they try to comprehend the totality of the incident and grasp information that is perceived as more important. Many agencies have in-car video with audio capability. Activating this equipment as early in the incident as possible will help capture the event as it unfolds. Even though the video camera will probably not be facing the incident, it should capture all of the audio. In agencies that don't have mobile video, it is essential that officers invest in a good digital recorder. These can be obtained for a reasonable cost and the audio can help in keeping notes and later in the report-writing process.

Because incidents can unfold quickly, some information will be missed. Large incidents will have more than one officer involved. For these reasons alone it is important for all officers involved in this type of an incident to participate in a "debrief" of the incident. The purpose of a debrief is not to have officers get "their stories straight." It allows for the coordination of supplemental reports and puts into perspective each officer's actions and observations of the total incident.

Several years ago officers responded to a disturbance in a small amusement park. Several members of a family decided that they wanted to fight with the police upon their arrival. Officers made several arrests in the chaotic scene, which included actions that occurred in many areas of the park. Once order had been restored, officers had to write five arrest reports and justify the use of force in other incidents. Officers did not debrief the incident and each wrote separate reports. Unfortunately, the confusion caused by uncoordinated reports resulted in the DA not being able to file the cases. Because the cases were not filed, the persons who were arrested filed lawsuits against the involved officers, supervisors, and the department. The resulting civil action required officers to be away from the job for weeks both in preparation for the trial and to testify at the trial. This cost the department numerous staff hours and thousands of dollars to defend the suit. Officers were subjected to untold stress while the legal issues were sorted out. Eventually a jury found for the department and the officers. In this example, if the officers had debriefed their roles and coordinated their actions before writing reports the cases might have been successfully prosecuted and civil action avoided.

One officer should be designated as the lead officer. In the case where a detective is brought in to handle the case, he or she should be the lead officer. The leader officer should be responsible for the crime report (or arrest report if a crime report has already been taken) and coordinating all supplemental reports. This officer should direct thedebrief so that all officers have complete knowledge of the case. In major incidents officers are frequently surprised to find that they do not know exactly what happened in an incident until all of the facts are put together.

As mentioned before, this type of report must be written in a quiet location away from distractions. Officers writing reports with other employees in the same room can make it very difficult to keep focused on a complex case.

Another potential area of confusion in report writing is that of language barriers. It is always best that officers provide translation. They understand the nuances that may be needed for proof of a legal issue and understanding human nature. In many areas of the country an officer from an adjoining agency may be able to provided necessary translation. The next option would be a translation service that is contracted by individual agencies. The service is contacted by the agency when needed and services are provided over the phone. The least satisfactory option is to use friends or relatives at the scene. Several problems can occur using this approach. One is that the translator may have his or her own motivations for talking with the police. Another issue that the translator may also be a witness and insert his or her observations while translating.

Most agencies require that a supervisor review and approve all reports prior to being given to the records bureau for distribution, or to the DA. A good supervisor will ensure that the report is complete and that all elements are present and all legal issues considered. This is the last place that a report can be altered before it is distributed to other areas of the department and the DA. One supervisor should approve all related reports in an incident. One person doing the final approval will be able to see if there is anything missing from the entire case.

ARRESTS RESULTING FROM DOMESTIC VIOLENCE INCIDENTS

Another frequently challenging incident to investigate is domestic violence. Due to the nature of family violence it is not uncommon for many victims to recant the statements they initially make to the police. This is an area that requires good investigation and interviewing techniques and strong report writing skills. Each of these components can work together to complete an effective investigation and arrest. As an investigator you are trying to locate evidence that will support the allegations made by the victim. As an interviewer you must work to establish trust with the victim and witnesses who may be young children. As a report writer you must thoroughly document what your investigation has revealed. This call becomes more challenging when you consider the number of cases where an arrest is made but no prosecution occurs. The sheer volume of these calls with often frustrating results can cause some officers to "shortcut" the investigation and the service they provide. This can be a critical error. Domestic violence cases frequently develop into more serious incidents and can escalate over time into felony assaults, child abduction cases, or homicide investigations. Initial investigative reports related to any and all prior incidents will be reviewed and police actions scrutinized. A well-written report will withstand this scrutiny and protect the officer and agency from criticism.

ON-VIEW ARRESTS

An "on-view" arrest is a self-initiated field contact that develops into an arrest. Although some agencies continue to use the number of on-view arrests as a benchmark of an officer's performance, this practice has largely been done away with in the current era of community policing. Still, officers who are proactive and generate good arrests are always looked on in a better light than those who drive around aimlessly waiting for a call for service from dispatch.

Documenting the on-view arrest has some areas that need extra attention. First, the officer must justify the contact. It is important to understand search and seizure law here. While this is beyond the scope of this book, we again must mention that all officers need a good working knowledge of this area of the law, and we will only briefly touch on a couple of issues frequently encountered. Although a contact with consent requires just that, *consent*, the officer must set the stage for the contact and how the consent was obtained. Included in this passage should be details such as how many officers were present, how many people to be contacted were present, whether officers displayed firearms prior to asking for consent, and what was said by the officers to obtain consent—although a vast majority of police reports say something like, *I saw suspect Jones and did a consensual contact*. This is a good example of a conclusory statement in a report. The officer has not described the contact in a way that establishes a consensual encounter. A better approach would be, *I saw suspect Smith standing on the sidewalk of 11th Avenue. I was alone and I approached him and asked, "May I speak to you for a moment?" to which Smith replied, "Sure."* In this version, you can see where consent is clearly established. This can be more thoroughly established only with an audiotape recording so a judge, and later a jury, can hear the officer's tone and demeanor.

The police interact with the public in three ways. The first way is described in the preceding paragraph and is known as the *consensual encounter*. The next is the *detention*. When a person is detained, meaning a level of police intervention more than a consensual encounter and less than an arrest, it is necessary to justify the detention in the report. For the detention to be valid a certain level of proof is necessary. A detention is lawful only if reasonable suspicion exists that criminal conduct is occurring or was about to occur and the person is somehow involved exists (*Terry v. Ohio*, 1968). The reporting officer must ensure that this level of suspicion is clearly outlined in the report. Failure to do so will result in the district or city attorney not filing the case. If it does get filed and a complaint is obtained, the case will soon be lost in court with the proper actions by defense counsel. While knowledge of what type of criminal activity is occurring is helpful, it is not necessary. Only the suspicion that the person is about to or has recently been involved in criminal conduct is necessary.

As an example, an officer watches from outside a store as a suspect picks up an item in the store and leaves without paying for it. Are there possible explanations that make the actions lawful? Absolutely, but it is reasonable for the officer to detain the person based on what he or she saw. Compare this with the officer who stops and detains a person because he or she looks homeless. Agencies frequently get calls for service of this nature from people who are frightened by the appearance of the person who appears homeless. Clearly, it is not illegal to be homeless, thus a detention would not be justified without some other information since homelessness alone is not criminal conduct. Keeping this in mind is very important as the officer writes the report.

Finally, there is the arrest. Once a person is consensually contacted or detained, several things can happen that may rise to the level of making an arrest. The arrest is the highest level of intrusion on a person by the police. During a contact the officer may discover that there is judicial authority to arrest the subject, also known as an *arrest warrant*. Frequently, officers will do a search that reveals contraband on the subject. This leads to probable cause and an arrest. The reasons for the search, whether it is based on consent or one of the other legal justifications to search a person, must be correctly documented. Knowing the reasons you may stop a person or a vehicle or enter a building, not to mention the reasons for valid searches, is critical to a good report. The report of an on-view arrest will document all of this information.

The report writing process for an on-view arrest requires the officer to carefully plan a logical approach to the event. In the written report beginning with the actions of the officer, the chronology is very important. Confusing the chronologies of the officer and the person arrested will lead to a confusing report. Take a look at the first couple of paragraphs of this arrest report.

> Douglas was seen walking down the street with what appeared to be a handgun tucked under the front part of his shirt. He later said he found the gun after his car broke down on the interstate. It was in the bushes next to the road.
>
> On 04-01-10 at 1015 hours I saw a subject walking on Sand Canyon Avenue north of the I-40 interstate. He appeared to be concealing something under his shirt as he walked. I parked my marked police car behind the subject, later identified as Douglas, and approached him on foot. I said, "Hey can I talk with you?" Douglas turned and said nervously, "Yeah sure." This was recorded on my personal audio recorder. The digital recording was booked into police evidence.
>
> I immediately saw the handle of a gun protruding from the waistband of his pants. I secured the weapon, a Sig Sauer P220 .45-caliber

semiautomatic pistol. The magazine contained only four live rounds and there was an additional round in the chamber. The weapon was in excellent condition with scratches or weathering on the weapon. It did not appear to have been in the environment for any period of time.

As you read this you can see this arrest is a bit confusing. While the officer attempted to list the chronology of events as they actually occurred, it sounds like the observations in the first paragraph provided him with information that led to the stop. Had the officer used his chronology, the following order of the report would have been recorded. First the officer's observation of the suspect, followed by a lawful consensual encounter, next the observation of the gun are all in the initial section of the report. The approach of a citizen who tells the officer of seeing the man with a partially concealed gun and then an interview with the suspect finishes the reporting of the initial contact in this arrest

WARRANT ARRESTS

A **warrant arrest** is an order from a judge that certifies probable cause exists to make an arrest and commands any officer to do so. A warrant may be in the physical possession of officers or located in cyberspace, waiting to be accessed by a police department computer and a hard copy "pulled." When there is a warrant "in the system" an arrest can be made for the violation described in the warrant.

Agencies vary greatly on the amount and quality of documentation necessary for a warrant arrest. Some agencies require only a notation regarding the location of the arrestee's vehicle, if any, the disposition of the arrestee's vehicle, and the location of arrest. Other agencies require documentation of the circumstances of the initial contact and any other actions taken by officers during the course of the contact.

When preparing a report in a jurisdiction that requires a complete report outlining the facts and circumstances of a contact, the report should completely describe the incident. This should include the lawful reason for the stop or contact, whether the contact was the result of a traffic stop on a "jaywalker" or in response to the report of domestic violence. Investigating officers should also include information as to how the warrant was discovered. Finally, the report should detail the disposition of the subject (booked at jail, released on citation, etc.) and any vehicles or passengers as appropriate.

WARRANTLESS ARRESTS

Warrantless arrests are frequently called *probable cause arrests*. This is, in fact, a misnomer. No arrest can be made without probable cause, so all arrests are probable cause arrests.

Look to your state's requirements for warrantless arrests. Generally, an officer cannot arrest a person who commits a misdemeanor without a warrant unless that offense occurred in the presence of the officer. There are numerous exceptions to this rule, depending on the state. In California, for example, warrantless misdemeanor arrests can be made for driving under the influence, domestic violence, some weapons offenses, and offenses involving schools when certain criteria are met.

A person who commits a felony can be arrested without a warrant even if the offense did not occur in the officer's presence. This is commonly called a *probable cause arrest*. When making such an arrest, officers must establish probable cause just as they would for misdemeanor arrests. Let's look at an example of a warrant-less arrest for a felony.

> The victim arrives home late one evening, at about midnight. As he enters the house he sees a "figure" run out the back door of the residence. The victim runs to the back door and hears a noise that sounds like a person jumping over the back fence of the residence. The victim runs to the fence but the person is gone. Using his cell phone he immediately calls the police. While talking to the police the victim discovers his expensive watch is missing from the counter of the master bathroom. Officers arrive in the area and begin searching for the suspect. Some officers attempt to contact neighbors to determine if they have noticed anything unusual. The neighbor who lives to the rear of the victim's house tells officers that at about 11 p.m. she saw a white Chevrolet pickup truck parked in front of her house. She thought it was unusual, as she has never seen the truck on the street before. At about midnight she heard a loud noise from the rear yard. She saw nothing in her backyard.
>
> While the officer is talking with this witness, another neighbor comes up and says that at about midnight she was looking out her front window and saw a white Chevrolet pickup truck occupied by one person driving away from in front of the first witness's house. She noted that it had a personalized license plate, but the truck was driving away and she could not read it. This information is broadcast in a supplemental crime broadcast.
>
> Another officer who is driving through the area sees a white Chevrolet pickup leaving the residential development where the victim lives. The officer begins to follow the vehicle and sees that it has a personalized license plate. Based on the time of day, the relatively light traffic in the area, the close proximity in time to the crime, and the vehicle matching the general description of the suspect vehicle, the officer makes an investigatory traffic stop. Both witnesses are brought to the scene of the traffic stop and identify the truck as being very similar to the truck parked in front of the house and leaving the scene. With this information the officer arrests the driver and sole occupant on suspicion of burglary. A subsequent search of the truck reveals the victim's watch, which he is able to identify.

As you can see, the information provided by the victim to dispatch and then dispatch to the officer provides a basis for believing that criminal conduct was occurring and that the person in the truck was somehow involved. When added to the officer's observations about the surroundings, the detention can be justified.

This is a rather typical probable cause arrest. The officer made the arrest for a felony—burglary—even though it did not occur in his presence based on the statements of the victim and the witnesses. A valid search of the vehicle incident to the arrest revealed the victim's watch.

Each officer who will be writing reports must be aware of what the other officer's reports on the same incident are going to describe (discussed earlier). One officer will likely write a crime report, another will write *supplemental reports* involving the witness statements, and another will document the arrest. The officers have several legal issues that they must be aware of as they write the reports. Without careful consideration of these issues the arrest could be found to be illegal which will likely result in the **suppression**—excluding or throwing out—of evidence that was seized and is necessary to obtain a conviction (in this case the watch recovered from the suspect's vehicle) from court by the judge.

Private Person's Arrest

All states have rules regarding the right of a private person to make an arrest for a criminal offense, or a **private person's arrest.** Often this is misnamed a "citizen's arrest." A person does not have to be a citizen to make an arrest. To make a private person's arrest the crime must have occurred in the arresting party's presence. Although arrests are made by citizens during domestic and neighborhood disputes, the most common citizen arrest is by a merchant or the merchant's agent (security guard) for shoplifting or other theft from the business.

Department reporting requirements vary widely in the case of private person's arrests. One department may require a full report for all such arrests, while another department may require only a face page and a written statement from the arresting party. Still others may use a combination of both sets of requirements. The decisions on what reporting procedures are followed come from collaboration between the local district attorney and the law enforcement agency.

The law of private person's arrests is quite complex and the degree of civil liability for officers and their departments can vary depending on state law. It is recommended that officers obtain an in-depth knowledge of the law before becoming involved in these arrests. These issues include the status of property (evidence) seized by private persons to support arrests and whether or not an arrest is mandatory. Careful research is necessary to avoid exposing your agency and yourself to civil liability for false arrests.

When documenting the private person's arrest in a full report, officers should use the same report format discussed in Chapter 5. The full report must document the officer's arrival, establishing the elements of the crime and the physical evidence as well as the witness statements that have led to the arrest of the suspect(s). Care should be taken to establish probable cause for the arrest. Without probable cause the arrest will not stand up in court. This could lead to exposure to *civil liability* for the arresting person, your department, and potentially you. In this way the report is similar to any crime and arrest report.

Some agencies allow the officer to prepare a face page and then have the arresting party write an arrest report. Generally, you see this reporting process allowed when the arrestee is released at the scene with a citation or notice to appear. This means the person arrested is given a ticket with an appearance date in court, which limits **civil damages** (the amount a person or entity has to pay a person who is harmed and then sues) in the event of a false arrest and subsequent lawsuit. As you can see, the report written by a layperson may lack any or all of the parts necessary for a complete, prosecutable case. Officers must review these witness statements for the essential elements of a good report.

Motivation of the Arresting Party   As you develop your case for a private person's arrest you should consider the motivation of the arresting party. Are he or she truly a victim? Is there something motivating the person to make a false accusation? Unfortunately, poor business relationships, divorce and child custody, and many other factors can often lead to false arrests. Be aware of this as you investigate the crime.

In a recent stalking case the "victim" called the police accusing an ex-boyfriend of several crimes including illegal immigration, emotional and physical abuse, and sexual assault. The victim said that the suspect had called and said he was on the way over to her apartment and threatened to assault her again. The first responding officer initially believed the accusations and asked for additional officers to cover this incident. Only after extensive investigation did the officer realize that revenge was the motive for the victim to file a false report with the police.

WRITING CLEARLY AND CONCISELY IN ARREST REPORTS

Although this chapter has focused on how to write the various types of arrest reports, a bit of review on how to write good reports is needed. Following the reporting steps outlined earlier and in prior chapters might not necessarily result in a clear and concise report. When writing arrest reports, you must keep a few things in mind and avoid some other pitfalls.

First, whether you are taking a report in the field or completing an assignment in class, get organized and stay organized. At any crime scene you will have multiple tasks to complete. These vary from developing a rapport with a victim or suspect to restoring order from the chaos of an incident. Once your scene is secure and you can work safely, or once you are in a quiet environment where you can concentrate on your assignment, remember the organizational sections of an effective report. Your plan might be to describe how you got to the scene, establish the elements of the crime, obtain the witness statements, and document what outside resources you used and what they provided for you. This is a good framework from which to build your investigation and report. With this information you can be clear in your report and build the reader's concept to a logical conclusion.

Use clear and direct language. Often reports have vague details that end up confusing the reader. This occurs when officers think too far ahead as they write; they leave out important information that would help a sentence or paragraph make better sense. Following is an excerpt from an actual police report of a domestic violence incident. This is a classic example of where vagueness in a report can be confusing to the reader. When you read it, ask yourself, Who is waiting for the police?

> On 10-15-10, at 0852 hours, Officer Ray #294 and I along with Officer Franks #314, were dispatched to a domestic disturbance in progress. The reporting party, Alice Larisa, said her husband had threatened to break her nose and was waiting to contact officers outside the residence.

This passage lacks clarity. Is the reporting party waiting outside or is the husband waiting? While trying to be concise, the writer left out some key words that could lead the reader to question the intended meaning. In the previous example, adding the pronoun *she* would have clarified who was waiting. When you see pronouns such as *it, they,* and *them,* it is possible that confusion might arise in the mind of the reader; it is time to be more specific.

Here is another example of a report that lacks clarity.

> Alice and Charlie met in the year 2001 at a conference in Russia. They married later that same year in the United States and currently

have one child in common together. Their child is Marc who is 7 years old and was present during today's incident. Alcohol and drugs were not a factor in today's incident nor has it been a factor in their relationship. Charlie is currently 75 years old and according to Alice is depressed and is having mental issues.

Here you should have identified the unnecessary information as the 2001 conference in Russia, the fact that they married in the United States, and Charlie's age. The first two sentences could be shortened to *Alice and Charlie married in 2001.*

As you write, we suggest you read back what you have written. This works best if you read the passage aloud. As you read it ask yourself, Are there any questions that might come up when someone else reads it? This will help you avoid passages that are not clear and will help identify passages that are overly wordy.

Finally, remember to be logical in your presentation. The reader, whether it is a teacher, a supervisor, or someone from the court system, must come to the same conclusion that you did after reading the report. A reader who finds a report conclusory might also wonder why the officer wrote the report that way. Is there no evidence? Is the case too complex? A report that says *Gordon violated section 211 of the Penal Code and was arrested* without explaining how you came to that conclusion will result in the case not being filed by the DA.

chapter summary

1. To successfully write arrest reports a full and complete knowledge of several technical areas of the law is essential. This is an area of police work that officers cannot shortcut and rely only on the limited training given in academies and field training programs. Knowledge of case law and legal guidelines for arrests and seizure of evidence must be regularly refreshed and reviewed.

2. Generally, arrests come from the radio call for service, the on-view arrest, the investigative follow-up, and executing arrest warrants. Due to the nature of each type of investigation the reports can be quite different, but all have several things in common.

3. Reporting formats may vary from agency to agency and are dependent on the type of incident and guidelines set by the individual agency.

4. Major incidents present many issues including scene safety, hostile witnesses, and the necessity of supplemental reports from more than one person involved in the investigation. When reporting an incident with several supplemental reports it is a good idea to have one person designated as the case agent to coordinate the reports.

5. Warrantless arrests generally occur in three circumstances: felonies, misdemeanors occurring in the officer's presence, or misdemeanors not committed in the presence of the officer but allowed by state statute.

6. Reporting requirements for private person's arrests vary from state to state. In states where only a "citizen's statement" is required, officers must carefully read the statement to make sure it contains the necessary elements.

Exercises—Writing Arrest and Crime Reports

WRITING AN ARREST REPORT

INSTRUCTIONS: Watch an episode of a police reality show on television and select a specific arrest. Research the elements of the crime (i.e. possessing drugs, failing to yield to police, evading arrest) in your state using your state's criminal code. Use the information from the arrest and write an arrest report. Be careful to include the reason for the stop and fully develop the elements of the crimes involved and the necessary probable cause for the arrest.

_____

_____

_____

_____

_____

_____

_____

_____

_____

_____

_____

_____

_____

_____

_____

_____

_____

_____

_____

_____

_____

_____

_____

_____

_____

_____

_____

_____

_____

_____

_____

_____

_____

_____

_____

WRITING A CRIME REPORT

INSTRUCTIONS: Using the following information, write a crime report.

Kendra Jensen, who lives at 1329 S. Jefferson in an apartment above a small retail shop, hears a commotion at about 2 a.m. She looks out her window that overlooks Jefferson and sees a fight between four or five men all wearing the same type of shirt and a single male wearing a soccer jersey and scarf. She calls the police and asks for paramedics.

The victim (Jeffery Williams) is a rabid soccer fan. Whenever he watches a game he wears his team's scarf. He and several of his friends take a trip to another city to attend a game between Williams's favorite team, Williamette United, and Cascadia FC. The fans of Cascadia FC are known to be quite rowdy.

After attending the match, Williams and his friends stop at the O'Dey Tavern, a well-known hangout for fans of Cascadia FC. After closing time they leave and begin to walk back to their hotel. Then Williams gets separated from his friends and is walking down Jefferson Avenue, a well-known commercial area. The stores are closed for the evening. He is approached from the front and sides by four white men all wearing FC shirts. The tallest man says, "Let's take his scarf!" Williams, a two-tour Marine Corps combat veteran, says to himself, "These guys are not getting this scarf from this Marine!" A fight ensues and Williams is successful in maintaining possession of his scarf but sustains several cuts and bruises.

You and other officers arrive to begin first aid and start an area search for the suspects. After paramedics arrive, you notice a video camera that is on in the storefront window of an electronics shop at 1631 Jefferson. Closer inspection reveals the camera is pointed in the direction of the incident, the red "recording light" is on, and the images captured by the camera are being displayed on a nearby television monitor. The store is closed. No suspects are located.

The area has several apartments above the ground-floor retail stores. You contact Alex Johnson who lives above the electronics shop. He was awakened by shouting and heard a male voice say, "Take his scarf." By the time he looked outside he could not see anyone in the area. He did hear a motorcycle driving away at high speed. The view of Jefferson is partially blocked from Johnson's view.

_____

_____

_____

_____

_____

_____

_____

_____

_____

_____

_____

_____

_____

_____

exercise 3

WRITING A SUPPLEMENTAL ARREST REPORT

INSTRUCTIONS: Assume that you are waiting by an on-ramp for Interstate 40 on Magnolia Street, near the crime scene, watching for the pickup truck when you see one drive by. The vehicle was stopped for a broken taillight. The driver was wearing an expensive watch. He tells you that it belongs to his brother. You ask to see the watch and observe it has engraving on it. You verify that the stolen watch had a similar engraving. Assume the crime report is being written by another officer. Based on these new facts, write an arrest report narrative.

glossary terms

8

Writing Search Warrants

chapter outline

INTRODUCTION

A vast majority of searches undertaken by the police are done *without* warrants. Generally, the government (the police) may search only with a warrant, consent or exigency. The preferred method of any government search is a warrant. A person, however, may consent to abandon his or her right to privacy and allow the police to search. Finally, the police may search in the event of an emergency. Many cases have been heard by the courts regarding the various circumstances that may constitute an emergency. The fact that some don't consider is that once the emergency is over, so is the right to search and no search can be conducted beyond the scope of the emergency. **Scope** in this instance refers to the extent or range of the legal limits of a search. The scope of the emergency limits the areas the police can search and the items they can seize.

The courts have recognized the impact on effective law enforcement should a search warrant be required every time the government makes an arrest, tows a car, or contacts a person who may be armed. Because of this realization, the courts have developed a series of exceptions. Unfortunately, officers tend to look to the exceptions to the search warrant requirement in the Fourth Amendment of the U.S. Constitution rather than complying with the requirement and attempting to obtain a warrant.

The U.S. Supreme Court in *Katz v. United States* (1967) stated that a search without a warrant is **per se** (in itself) *unreasonable* (Samaha, 2011). This means that the prosecution must convince a judge that a warrantless search is allowed under existing law. The Court went on to say that warrantless searches must fall under carefully defined circumstances before any evidence obtained in the search will be admitted into court. While these exceptions require another entire course to begin to understand, it is highly recommended that any law enforcement officer take these classes to become familiar with the rules of constitutional criminal procedure.

Search warrants are surrounded with many myths and inaccurate information. A search warrant is *judicial authorization* to

A search warrant authorizes law enforcement officers to make entry into a person's home or business and conduct a search for evidence or suspects.
Source: © Mikael Karlsson

conduct a search where a person has an otherwise **reasonable expectation of privacy** (the legal standard to judge when a person can be free from government interference) and no court-recognized exceptions to the search warrant rule exist (Samaha, 2011). Since *Katz* the courts have limited warrantless searches to a limited set of circumstances. This chapter will discuss the search warrant and what goes into the preparation of the various documents involved in a search warrant, as well as some of the relevant laws guiding search warrant preparation.

The Fourth Amendment to the U.S. Constitution has two major provisions: reasonableness and the search warrant requirement. We will talk about how to satisfy the requirements of obtaining a constitutionally valid search warrant. The law on search warrants is quite expansive, therefore this chapter cannot cover the law of search warrants in all states and federal jurisdictions. When preparing an actual affidavit and request for a search warrant, it is suggested that you refer to your local DA for more information.

PURPOSE OF A SEARCH WARRANT

[N]o Warrants shall issue, but upon probable cause, supported by Oath or affirmation, and particularly describing the place to be searched, and the persons or things to be seized.

U.S. Constitution, Fourth Amendment

In colonial days, the king's officers were allowed to obtain warrants to search any property at any time. These were known as **general warrants**. *Writs of assistance* also authorized searches and were issued by the sheriff and allowed for searches. In England these searches were authorized for publications that spoke out against the government.

The British government used these warrants in the colonies in an attempt to control smuggling in the American colonies. The concept of general warrants and the impact on privacy were the motivation for the authors of the Constitution to include the warrant clause of the Fourth Amendment to the U.S. Constitution.

The Fourth Amendment is one of several limitations on government power that our founding fathers sought to put in place. The intent was to limit searches by the federal government. Later court cases expanded the Fourth Amendment to the states. A literal reading of the Fourth Amendment seems to indicate that unreasonable searches violate the Constitution. Although controversy existed over whether searches that were reasonable could take place without a warrant, it is clearly established today that the search warrant is the preferred method for police to conduct any search.

Components of the Fourth Amendment

The Fourth Amendment warrant requirement has three components. First, a search warrant must be based on probable cause; writs of assistance could be obtained merely on a government agent's suspicion. Next, a search warrant must be supported by the oath of the officer seeking the warrant. Finally, the warrant itself must describe the places to be searched and the items to be seized with "particularity." This requirement was meant to restrict government officers from the execution of "general" warrants issued to search for any criminal or seditious material. The good news is that most of the law in the areas of probable cause, oath, and the particularity requirement is fairly well established. It should be no trouble to prepare a request for a search warrant that meets these requirements.

Necessity of a Warrant

Today, warrants still must comply with these requirements. Because states are bound by the Fourth Amendment (*Mapp v. Ohio*, 1961), it is important to understand its intent. Law enforcement officers should seek to comply with the Constitution. Unfortunately, there are many legal and police training professionals who seek to teach officers how to "get around" the need to obtain a warrant. Knowing that the search warrant is the preferred method and seeking to obtain a warrant can "save" cases that would otherwise be lost to suppression hearings.

In *Mincey v. Arizona* (1978) an undercover narcotics officer was murdered during the course of an investigation. During an attempted narcotics "buy," a gunfight erupted resulting in the officer's death. Detectives arrived on the scene after the shooting and began a crime scene investigation that took four days to complete. The search was done without a warrant. Clearly, there was time to obtain a warrant, but officers relied on the belief that the search was lawful because they were investigating a crime. The court denied a so-called crime scene exception to the search warrant requirement. The defendant's conviction was overturned for lack of a warrant.

Certainly the officers who made the decision to search Mincey's residence did so believing they were acting reasonably. Had they taken one more step in their investigation, the conviction would have been preserved.

PREPARING THE WARRANT APPLICATION

Only a law enforcement officer or a federal law enforcement agent can apply for a search warrant. This means if a private person believes he or she has probable cause to believe that contraband is in a particular location, the individual cannot ask a judge for a warrant to search the property of someone else. Only a judge can authorize a government search based on a search warrant. An application for a search warrant consists of two documents. The first is the search warrant, which is a form that varies in format from state to state. In this section we will discuss the constitutional requirements for the warrant. The second document is the affidavit. The affidavit is a narrative stating the reasons the officer believes that probable cause exists to find certain items involving a crime, fruits of the crime, evidence of the crime, or items that prove a crime has occurred in a certain location. The affidavit is the section of the search warrant that most frequently results in court challenges.

The Warrant Process

Search warrants are obtained for many different types of searches. The items to be seized can include a wide variety of things such as illegal drugs, stolen property, and illegal or illegally possessed weapons. Other less obvious items might include **indicia** (items that show a relationship) of drug trafficking, ownership of a piece of property or residence, access to storage spaces, computer account information—such as **Internet service provider (ISP)** addresses, social network accounts, and activity on weblogs—and telephone account information as well as bank account information or business information. The applicant must decide what evidence might be found that will help prove a case against a defendant.

As an example, a citizen notices that people are coming and going from a neighborhood residence that is being rented by a man named Scott. These visitors stay for only a few minutes and each time Scott looks up and down the street before he lets the person into the house. Sometimes the citizen sees the visitors carrying items such as televisions, computers, or other valuable property into the house and then they leave without the property. The neighbor tells you that once he saw someone carrying a medium-sized safe into the residence. This person left the house within a few minutes without the safe and the citizen is concerned that it was stolen property based on the way the subject and the neighbor were looking around. The citizen becomes concerned that illegal activity is occurring. The citizen then contacts the local police or sheriff's department. This scenario is a common beginning to a narcotics investigation.

Investigators take the information supplied by the neighbor and conduct surveillance. The surveillance verifies the informant's observations. Investigators then do some further investigation and once they have developed enough information to prove probable cause, and if they desire to perform a search for additional evidence, they may decide to seek a search warrant.

The first step in this process is to prepare the documents that are required for the warrant. Remember that only a government law enforcement agent can request a search warrant. When a police officer believes he or she has enough information for a warrant, the officer prepares the warrant face page first. Although search warrant face pages vary from state to state, all warrants order a police officer to search a specific location and look for specific items. In many states the face page contains sections that meet the particularity requirement of the Fourth Amendment. These sections ask for a description of the location to be searched and the property to be seized.

The next document that must be prepared is the affidavit. The affidavit is the officer's statement of probable cause and must be carefully prepared. It must logically and clearly demonstrate why the items to be seized will be found in the places to be searched.

The affidavit begins with a statement of the officer's experience. Many officers call this the **hero sheet**. The purpose of the hero sheet is to establish the officer's identity, training, and experience. The officer's training and experience may become necessary to establish that the officer is an expert, so opinion evidence can be used. Expert testimony may be necessary to establish why the officer believes that the search will result in finding the items to be seized in the places to searched. The judge may need an expert to explain why certain clothing or actions or language are important to establishing probable cause.

The affidavit continues with how the investigation began, the statements of witnesses, the officer's observations, and other observations or resources. Any other collaboration should be included—remember that all information must be included in the affidavit.

Local custom varies between jurisdictions regarding the next step. Many agencies require that officers take the affidavit to a representative of the agency who will prosecute the case. This can be a deputy district or the city attorney. They will review the affidavit and must concur with the determination that probable cause exists. If further investigation is needed they will outline what is needed and send the officer back to do the additional work.

As previously stated, taking the affidavit and warrant to a deputy DA does vary from jurisdiction to jurisdiction. However, it is a good practice because it can eliminate warrants that lack probable cause and lessen the risk of rejection by a judge. A worse scenario are warrants signed by a judge when the warrant lacks probable cause and the warrant is later overturned by the judge presiding over the case (most often the signing judge will not hear the case except in small jurisdictions).

Once the DA agrees that the affidavit has the proper information to reach the standard of probable cause and the warrant is correctly filled out, the officer takes the warrant to a judge. This is not especially difficult while court is in session; however, many investigations move very quickly and warrants are often sought at night and on weekends and holidays. Judges usually rotate "on-call" duties to review warrants during those times. The judge then reads the affidavit and the warrant. If the affidavit states facts that reach probable cause and the warrant is correctly prepared, then the warrant is signed. This step is critical because, once a warrant is signed by an impartial magistrate, the good faith rule applies. This means that even if a later court finds the affidavit lacking probable cause, the service of the warrant is considered valid and the items that are listed on the warrant that are seized may be used in court against the defendant (*U.S. v. Leon,* 1984).

When serving a search warrant, the face page is the portion of the warrant that you give to the person in possession or charge of the location you are searching. Unless your state requires it, the affidavit does not have to be given to the person in possession. This portion notifies anyone who reads the warrant the location to be searched and the items to be seized, as well as the name of the judge who authorized the search.

Telephonic Warrants

Much has been said about the ease of obtaining search warrants in general. **Telephonic warrants** are those issued by a judge after hearing the affidavit over the telephone. It is not merely a matter of picking up the telephone and talking to a judge for a few minutes and getting the okay to search. The process is a bit more complex and relieves officers only of the necessity of going to a judge. In some jurisdictions, the officer must still contact the judge in person to have the warrant signed before it is filed with the court.

In many jurisdictions, the DA's office must be contacted prior to calling the judge. This call is to discuss probable cause and talk about the process with the officer. Once the DA is convinced that probable cause exists, the officer contacts a judge by telephone and is sworn in. The DA may be involved in a conference call with the judge, and the conversation must be recorded to be preserved for later transcription by a court reporter. The officer then makes an oral statement that would otherwise be the written affidavit.

With this in mind, the officer should write out the affidavit prior to talking with the judge. Writing out a warrant affidavit prior to reciting it to the judge over the telephone is just as time-consuming as writing the affidavit before it is given to the judge for review, but it helps eliminate mistakes. If an officer leaves out information that is later determined to be material to the establishment of probable cause, the legality of the warrant may be in jeopardy.

The judge then listens to the affidavit and asks questions if needed. If multiple officers or affiants are involved, each one is heard. Once the magistrate has heard the affidavit he or she will make a determination of probable cause and state on the tape recording that he or she has found probable cause. If the judge does not find probable cause, the judge, the officer, and the DA, if present on the call, will discuss what is lacking. The officer can continue the investigation to build the information that is required to reach the level of probable cause.

How the signing of the warrant and authorization for the search is accomplished varies across the country. Another formality that varies is the actual warrant that is left with the owner of the property to be searched. Once the warrant is served, the officer will file a document known as a *return of search warrant* with the court. This tells the judge what was found during the search. When the return is filed at the court, a transcript of the phone call to the judge is also filed with the court.

The importance of writing the affidavit first cannot be stressed enough. If the officer should leave out information or accidentally misrepresent facts because they are not organized, the warrant could be held invalid and the officer could be held liable for any damages sustained during the search or suffer liability for violation of a constitutional right.

Some states have requirements that must be met before a search warrant can be issued. In California, for example, a warrant can be issued only when the investigation can show that one of ten circumstances is present. These will cover most areas of conduct where a warrant to search might be desired, but they are more limited than other states that require only that the property being sought is evidence of or fruits of a crime.

Preparing the Warrant

In this section we will discuss the preparation of the warrant in greater depth, as well as the descriptions of the places to be searched and the items to be seized. We will also discuss the hero sheet and the importance of writing a thorough and logical affidavit. Any officer who is preparing a search warrant affidavit must keep in mind that each piece of evidence set forth in an affidavit is a necessary building block of probable cause. The affidavit must bring all of these pieces together.

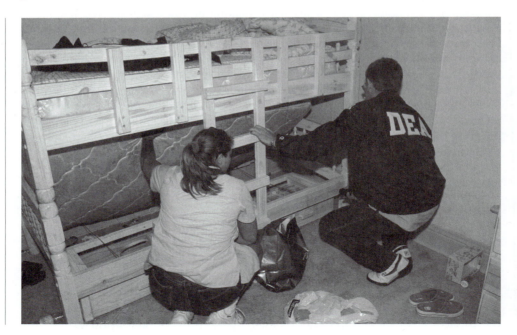

Officers must thoroughly describe the places to be searched and the items to be seized in the search warrant affidavit.
Source: © Mikael Karlsson

Describing Places to Be Searched

As you describe the places to be searched on the face page of the warrant, you should do so with the idea that an officer who had no knowledge of the investigation could serve the warrant at the correct location whether that be a house, a business, a vehicle, or a person.

In Southern California, a local police department's investigators attempted to serve a search warrant for narcotics at a residence. The investigator who wrote the warrant was at a different location serving another search warrant simultaneously. As officers checked the interior of the first location for hostile people, the entry team came to a closed bedroom door. They forced entry to the bedroom and were confronted with a man and woman in a bed. The man had retrieved a handgun from under the bed. When the man pointed the gun at the officers as they burst into the room, the officers shot and killed the resident. Later it was determined that officers were at the wrong address. The man they shot was only trying to defend his home from what he believed to be intruders.

This tragic incident underscores the need for great care in serving warrants. It is suggested that all officers involved in the search read the warrant and verify that the location being entered is the proper location. Additionally, officers should know what items are listed on the warrant as those to be seized. This can prevent errors in the search that can cause problems in court (e.g., looking in a pillbox in a search authorized for a rifle). This does not mean that officers serving a warrant must read the affidavit. Only the fact that the warrant has been signed by a judge, the location that has been authorized to search, and what the judge wants to be seized need to verified by everyone on the search team. This will prevent mistakes by the team in the service of the warrant.

Describing Buildings

Although a simple address meets the constitutional requirements of particularity, it is suggested that a description of the residence or building to be searched, beyond the address, be included. A brief description of the location gives those who are serving the warrant more information to ensure the correct location is being searched. The description of a building should include any identifying features such as color, type of construction, type of dwelling (apartment, single-family residence, or condominium), and any unusual permanent features. Also include the entire address, including *North, South, East,* or *West* and *Street, Boulevard,* or *Circle.* Providing more information than is required is better than risking the wrong location being entered and the potential for injury to innocent parties. Following is an example of the description of a single-family residence. Remember that this is just an example, and not intended to be a template for the description of all residences.

> The premises to be searched are located at 13772 West Trestle Boulevard, North Ludwig Bay, Massachusetts. The location is further described as a single-story, single-family residence with a brown wood roof and a tan exterior. The garage for this location is detached from the house and located on the west side of the residence. The numbers 13772 are attached to the area adjacent to the front door. The residence is located between Wilshire Street and Haven Road on the north side of West Trestle Boulevard. The areas to be searched include all rooms, attics, basements, and other areas

of the interior of the residence as well as the surrounding grounds, garages, storage areas, trash containers, and all outbuildings that may be found on the premises.

As you can see, this is a very thorough description. Any officer who is attempting to serve a search warrant at this location can take this description and reasonably find the correct house. Not all structures that will be searched are single-family residences. Apartment buildings, condominiums, commercial buildings with multiple occupants, and office buildings are some examples. These locations warrant just as thorough of a description; however, when describing these structures it is very important that the unit or office to be searched is also described. An easy way to be sure that the proper apartment or office is described is to use the number of the location (e.g., *Suite 213*) if it is located on the door or in an adjacent area. If there is no number present, then describe its exact location within the building or structure.

Describing Vehicles

Vehicles can be described using standard identifiers such as year, make, model, color, and license plate number. These will meet constitutional requirements for a search warrant description. An example would be *a gold 1974 Ford Pinto station wagon with an Ohio license plate BAC 0080.*

When the license number is unknown, a thorough description is required. In some instances it is wise to include the possible location of the vehicle, as shown in the following example.

> The vehicle is described as a 2007 to 2010 Mercedes-Benz E Class, silver in color with chrome wheels and a sunroof and minor traffic collision damage to the right front fender. The license plate is not known. The vehicle is believed to be parked at or near 239 Eighth Street, New York, New York.

Describing People

People are often the object of a search, either on their own or in conjunction with a vehicle or location. The constitutional requirement of particularity requires a thorough description of people to be searched as well.

When these people are not connected with a place to be searched, their probable location should be included in the description. A good example would be a person who sells drugs to an undercover officer in the course of a narcotics operation and an arrest is not made at the time of the transaction. The drug buy could take place in a residence, business, or on the street. Officers may not have the ability to locate a driver's license for a person or even obtain a full name. Nonetheless, the person must be named in the warrant for the police to do a search of his or her person for more drugs.

When a person has not been identified by name the description should be as complete as possible, including unusual physical characteristics and nickname or monikers, if known. A typical description might be:

> The person known as "Shorty," a white male, approximately 20 to 30 years of age, 6'7" and 270 lbs. with a short trimmed beard believed to residing at 43400 Riverside Drive, Palm Springs, California.

If the police are fortunate enough to discover the true name of the suspect, the description is then fairly easy. Many times the police will have the ability to identify someone to this extent from prior investigations or investigations by other agencies that are being conducted concurrently to the one producing the search. The usual name, physical information, and government identification number is a sufficient description. It might look like this:

> The person known as Nicklaus Trent, black male, 6'4" and 225 lbs. with black hair, brown eyes, and a date of birth of March 16, 1989.

Describing Property to Be Seized

Since the list of items a search warrant may target is quite long and beyond the scope of this book, we will cover only a couple of areas. Descriptions of property must be as thorough as possible. An example of a description that is not sufficient would be *all stolen property* or *any illegal drugs*. The goal of the particularity requirement is to restrict the police from seizing any object they find in the course of the search of an authorized location. The previous property descriptions would be seen in constitutionally prohibited general warrants. A description that would satisfy the particularity requirement would be *A Glock 9 mm pistol serial number 12345* or a description that identifies the type of drug to be seized, such as heroin, methamphetamine, or marijuana.

In the case of a robbery investigation, the victim may describe the clothing worn by the suspect. Once a suspect is identified, the police may want to search the suspect's residence for this clothing. The description of the clothing need not be exact but the affidavit should closely reflect the description given by the victim.

The course of the investigation will dictate what type of property is to be seized. It is not necessary to list any additional property that the police speculate might be found during the course of a search. This property will likely fall under the *plain view rule*, if the officer is in a place where he or she has a lawful right to be and the illegal nature of the property is immediately apparent. If the police search a residence as a result of an investigation into residential burglary, the list of property stolen in the crime should give the search warrant applicant the description needed. This is another reason it is essential to provide good stolen property descriptions in crime reports.

When preparing this list, you should also include indicia of ownership of the residence or building in addition to items that would prove who lives or operates a business or structure. These items will include bills for telephone, electricity, and other utilities as well as personal mail that may have been received at the residence.

Describing Illegal Drugs

In an investigation into illegal drugs and their sale, many items should be added to the list of items to be seized. These should include the type of drug that is likely to be found. Items such as packaging material; ledgers, also known as pay/owe sheets; paraphernalia for ingesting the substance; and cash proceeds from the sale are commonly found in a location selling illegal drugs. Additional items would include information on storage spaces and storage containers. This is where the training and experience of the officer becomes important. Officers who are expert in the field of narcotics investigation will be able to testify to the likelihood that these and other items will be found in a location.

Describing Stolen property

In the prior example, where the item being described was a Glock firearm, the identifying feature of the gun being described is the serial number. Other items of property may have distinct markings, or may be distinct by their construction, such as jewelry. Often the description of this type of property is difficult because the owner does not have description from the jeweler (or an appraisal) and no pictures that clearly show the items. The list of property in these cases should be as specific as possible.

Drafting an Affidavit

As previously discussed, the affidavit has two parts. First, is the statement of expertise by the officer preparing the search warrant? Second, is the statement establishing probable cause? The statement of expertise is only a few paragraphs long; the statement of probable cause is the predominate part of the affidavit. Both are discussed in detail in the following text.

Many states require writing in the third person in the affidavit. In these states or counties the writer of the warrant affidavit will be referred to as "your affiant." Officers should check with the local DA's office and comply with **local rules of the court**—rules regarding procedures for civil and criminal proceedings for specific courts of law.

Writing the Statement of Training and Experience

The statement of training and experience is usually the first paragraph of the affidavit. It is also known as the hero sheet, as mentioned earlier. The purpose of the first few paragraphs is to identify the officer and establish his or her expertise. Take a moment and think about the classes you have taken in criminal justice. Try to list the courses and the lectures you have heard on the possession of heroin for sale or entry techniques for residential burglars as they force their way into a house. You will see that this is a daunting task. It is compounded if you haven't kept records of this training.

Officers should keep exhaustive records detailing all of their training and experience. Unfortunately, few officers are vigilant in maintaining these records. With the advent of personal computers, both desktops and laptops, nearly everyone has access to a spreadsheet or database program. Each night (or morning) at the end of shift the officer should enter a list of the arrests made along with some notes of circumstances surrounding the arrest into the database. The types of reports that are taken and investigations assisted are also an important piece of information. Each in-service training class an officer attends, including police academy and traditional academic coursework, should have a place in the spreadsheet. Included should be instructor names and hours spent in each class.

This information will be invaluable in three different scenarios. The first is when an officer goes to court. Let's say you are required to testify in a traffic collision case. The night before trial, you should review the spreadsheet and determine the precise number of traffic collision investigations you have been involved in, noting the **primary collision factor** (actual cause of a traffic collision) of each. You can use this information to establish expertise in the investigation and bolster and add credibility to your testimony.

This type of preparation pertains to any court testimony. If you make an arrest for being under the influence of a narcotic substance you will certainly be asked to qualify as an expert in heroin intoxication. Time spent on the witness stand can be much more pleasant and much shorter in duration if you have the information regarding your prior arrests, training, and prior expert testimony on this subject immediately available.

The second time this information can be used is during a promotional examination. While taking a competitive examination for detective, the ability to accurately tell an interview panel the types of investigations you have been involved in, the numbers and types of arrests you have made, and the search warrants you have written can put you ahead of other candidates that don't arrive for the interview as well prepared. Keeping this information at hand is a habit that you will have to force yourself to acquire, but it will pay solid dividends in the future.

A statement of training and experience should be prewritten and available at any time. If your spreadsheet is immediately available you can use the information for search warrants in the field. Many officers keep this on a USB flash drive where it can be accessed and edited to fit any search warrant where he or she has special expertise. You do not have to return to the station to prepare your warrant application. You can access your statement of training and experience right in the field.

The statement first should identify you and then state your tenure in law enforcement including both civilian and sworn experience. Most statements of training and experience outline education as well. Next is training and experience, including academy classes and continuing education. Many people overlook in-service training, briefing training, and informal training sessions with more experienced officers that have a level of expertise in a topic. This is where the spreadsheet comes in handy. The statement of training and experience should be updated frequently because the need to write a search warrant may occur at any time. Having a prewritten statement of training and experience can save quite a bit of time. Following is sample statement of training and experience for a search warrant prepared in the course of narcotics investigation.

> My name is Larry Cherney. I am currently employed by the San Diego (CA) Police Department working in the patrol division. I have been employed as a police officer for more than five years. I possess a bachelor's of science degree in criminal justice and a master's of science degree in criminology. I have been assigned to the patrol division for the past five years. While in the police academy I received 24 hours of training in the recognition of controlled substances. I have received more than 80 hours of additional training in the investigation of illegal controlled substances. I have conducted 130 investigations into the possession and sale of controlled substances. I have assisted in the investigation of controlled on 95 occasions. I have interviewed 23 individuals regarding their experiences using, producing, and selling controlled substances. I have testified as an expert in symptoms of stimulant, heroin, and alcohol influence 11 times in the Superior Court of the State of California in San Diego County.

As you can see, this person has only five years' experience as a police officer and all of it is in patrol. Yet, when you read his statement of experience he certainly possesses a significant level of knowledge. In fact, the officer has qualified as an expert and has testified in state court on issues similar to those that will be the subject of the search warrant. By keeping good records the officer is able to recall this information and demonstrate that he can come to informed expert opinions.

Writing the Statement of Probable Cause

The next part of the affidavit is the statement of probable cause. The U.S. Constitution requires a warrant to be based on probable cause (U.S. Const., amend. IV). Upon reading an affidavit the judge should be able to come to the decision that it is more likely than not that the items to be seized will be in the places to be searched. The affidavit should be clear, logical, factual, and concise. Simply stated, the affidavit is not much more than a police report. The affidavit establishes that a crime has occurred or is occurring and that the items that can be seized under state law will be found in the location a judge authorizes you to search. An affidavit cannot support a search with rumor or supposition; the proof must be factual and logical.

The statement of probable cause must establish a few things. Earlier we discussed the requirement by some states that certain conduct must be present before a search warrant may be sought. However, it is safe to say that all states require that a crime has occurred. The statement of probable cause must clearly establish a crime. Once the crime is established it must be shown that the suspect was somehow involved in the crime. The next step is to connect the suspect to the premises or persons or vehicles that the officer wants to search. Finally, the affidavit should state the officer's opinion on why the items that are sought will be in the locations to be searched. While these steps will vary based on the facts of the investigation, they should help organize an affidavit.

Establishing Probable Cause

It is important to note that the sections of an affidavit are not separated with headings; the sections are important to establishing probable cause. The affiant cannot state opinion in an affidavit without establishing his or her level of expertise on the topic. The expertise of the affiant must support the conclusions that the facts lead to in the statement of probable cause.

Like a police report, the affidavit must logically lead to a conclusion that will result in the issuance of the search warrant. The affidavit should be objective in tone, and the facts should lead the judge to agree with the writer.

Showing That a Crime Has Occurred

This is a very important piece of the affidavit. A search warrant will not be issued without a crime having occurred. Earlier in the chapter we discussed the requirement of some type of conduct that will allow a judge to authorize a search. The grounds that will lead to a search vary from state to state based on state statute—for instance, California Penal Code Section 1524(a), which shows that a crime has occurred, will satisfy most requirements.

This can be accomplished by reciting the basic facts from other related crime reports or from information that the officer has developed that will rise to a new crime. In the sample affidavit on page 177, the officer establishes that a crime has occurred by attaching the police report of another agency. The crime of receiving stolen property is also established by the officer's investigation at the scene of the traffic stop.

The crime can also be established by the information supplied by a member of the community. This information can be as simple as a tip received from a neighbor to paid information from an informant. The use of informants is an expansive part of the law beyond the scope of this chapter. Some of the issues regarding informants are discussed in a separate section.

All elements of the crime should be established and supported in the affidavit just as in a crime report. While a member of the community may tell the police about a crime, it is up to the officer to prove the elements of the crime.

Showing That the Suspect Is Involved

The next section in an affidavit should show how the suspect is involved in the commission of the crime, selling or distributing the product of the crime, or concealing evidence of the crime in some fashion. This can be as simple as the suspect selling narcotics to an undercover officer or being in possession of property that has been stolen, or as complex as a person who is a member of large conspiracy that steals and then sells weapons or other contraband.

Establishing the suspect's involvement is an important link in the warrant that must show that the person is in possession of—or the property under his control contains—the property to be sought. This may be accomplished by the officer's observations, the investigation, or precise verifiable information from an informant. In the sample affidavit on page 177, the suspect implicated himself in a statement that would be admissible in court as proper Miranda warnings were given before he was interviewed.

In other circumstances an informant who is "reliable" might tell an officer that within the past few hours he saw contraband at a specific location. The officer then must corroborate the information from the informant. This might include past information on the location or residents, observations from surveillance, or by conducting a "controlled buy" with the informant. The controlled buy is an operation in which the informant purchases drugs from the suspect after being thoroughly searched by the investigator for drugs, contraband, or money.

These are not the only ways to demonstrate the suspect's culpability. The investigation will reveal how to structure this portion of the affidavit. Officers writing the affidavit must be careful to avoid conclusory statements in the affidavit just as those statements are improper in police reports. Making the statement that Patrick has violated *California Penal Code Section 496 because he has received stolen property* does not make this a true statement. The statement must be supported with facts that show Patrick's involvement. Below Patrick admits that he has additional property that he knows is stolen. With this statement and the expertise of the officer it would be reasonable for the investigating officer to come to the belief that a crime is occurring.

Tying the Suspect to the Places to Be Searched and Showing That Contraband Is Present

Now the suspect must be linked to the location to be searched. This can be accomplished in several ways. Surveillance is a popular method of establishing a connection between the suspect and the location.

In the late 1980s several task force teams combined officers from federal agencies and local law enforcement who identified and conducted surveillance on people involved in the Colombian cocaine trade. Confidential informants were used to establish criminal conduct and cases were "put together" by watching money transactions. Suspects would pick up money from locations or others involved in the cocaine trade and then deliver it to people who would illegally send the money out of the country. Many search warrants on locations were issued based on the expertise and knowledge gained by detectives working with interagency cooperation. These warrant affidavits combined information from confidential informants, surveillance by officers, and the expertise of highly experienced officers.

In the following example the suspect was connected to the location using another method. The officer used the suspect's identifying information and computer databases to establish the location where additional stolen property would be found. The use of state and federal databases and state identification cards can easily link someone to a location. Another way might be through the use of Internet social networking sites. Many police departments have officers who actively use these resources to locate people. It is amazing what people will "post" on these sites thinking that the information is confidential when in actuality the information is available for all to access and see.

In the sample affidavit on page 177, the difficult part is linking the stolen property to the location. In the example, the suspect did it by his statements. Many officers neglect to link each part of the affidavit by not relying on logical steps. They will believe a connection exists because it seems logical. The affidavit must link each part to others.

This linkage is illustrated in another case from California. During the course of a narcotics investigation, officers learned that a suspect would meet with the potential purchaser of illegal drugs only at one of several different shopping centers near his home. Officers contacted the suspect by phone requesting to buy cocaine. The undercover officer had earned the suspect's trust from other buys of drugs in parking lots in the area. The suspect met the officer and made the sale. Although you would think the link was complete, the officers could only speculate where the drugs were actually coming from. What the suspect did not know was that officers had identified his residence through department of motor vehicle information developed from his license plate and were watching him as he left the residence. The suspect drove directly to the "meet" from his house and made the sale with several officers watching. This information was put into an affidavit and the judge issued a search warrant for the house, the vehicle, and the suspect where significant evidence and contraband was found.

Stating the Officer's Opinion

Finally, in the affidavit the officer will state his or her opinion and why he or she believes the information leads to the conclusion that the items listed in the warrant will be found. This section can also be looked at as a summary. The information should state what was discovered during the course of the investigation and why it leads the officer to the conclusion he or she holds.

WHEN OFFICERS SEEK SEARCH WARRANTS

Generally, police officers seek search warrants in three types of circumstances: (1) when an officer (or officers) observes that a possible crime is taking, or has taken, place; (2) when a combination of citizen informants and the follow-up investigation of officers lead the officer to believe that a crime has taken place; and (3) when information from confidential informants and the subsequent follow-up investigation of officers lead the officer to believe that a crime has taken place. Each provides different challenges in the writing of a search warrant affidavit.

Officer's Observations

When the search warrant is the result of the observations of officers, then the affidavit may well use a format or sequence of information similar to the police report. This affidavit would start with the statement of experience and then state how the investigation began. If the warrant is written by a patrol officer based on a call for service or observation, it might also begin in a similar fashion:

> On 03-16-10 at approximately 1645 hours I saw a dark blue Jeep SUV California
>
> license 5000AAA fail to stop at a stop sign in violation of California Vehicle Code
>
> Section 22450.

The affidavit would continue from this point documenting the investigation, which leads up to a belief that property to be seized would be in a location to be searched. Just as the first sentence of the statement of probable cause reads like a police report, the rest of the affidavit would read like a police report. Great care must be taken to draw the lines between the suspect, the crime, and the location (or persons) to be searched.

As officers write affidavits it is important for them to remember that the conclusions they reach must be logical and supported with logical inference or their expert opinion supported by training and experience. A police officer is believed to be credible by a judge reading an affidavit. All officers have training and experience beyond the average person due to their training at the police academy. Following is an example of an affidavit requesting a search of a residence for stolen property. This is continuation of the facts from the previous example.

> Your affiant initiated a car stop on the vehicle and contacted the driver, Jeffrey Patrick, DOB 09-04-84. A warrant check revealed that Patrick had an outstanding warrant for driving on a suspended license. Patrick was placed under arrest and your affiant searched the vehicle Patrick was driving prior to towing the vehicle pursuant to California Vehicle Code Section 14602.6. During the search a loaded Ruger Blackhawk handgun (serial number 124274) was located under the driver's seat. Your affiant advised Patrick of his Miranda rights which he said he understood and would waive. Patrick stated that the gun was stolen in a burglary that occurred in the City of Irvine on 03-14-10. A check of the gun's serial number through the state computer system revealed that the gun had been reported stolen on 03-15-10 in a burglary in Irvine, which occurred on 03-14-10. When your affiant asked Patrick if he had additional property stolen from the burglary, Patrick said, "yeah, at home, but I want an attorney." No more questions were asked. The interview with Patrick was videotaped with the mobile video system in the police vehicle; a transcript of the interview is attached.
>
> Your affiant contacted the Irvine Police Department and utilizing the report number listed in the stolen gun computer "hit," a clerk in the records division told your affiant that jewelry, a laptop computer, a wallet with a California Driver's License N900933, and a Sony

PlayStation were also taken (see list of property to be seized for a detailed list). A copy of the original Irvine Police Department (DR 10-450) crime detailing the theft is attached.

The vehicle that Patrick was driving was registered to Jeffery Patrick of 31287 Woodhollow, Irvine, California. The address matched the address showing on Patrick's driver's license and the same address Patrick gave when he was booked into the Orange County Jail.

Based on my training and experience and the facts and circumstances of the contact with Patrick, his arrest, and subsequent statements, your affiant is of the belief that the property stolen in the March 14 burglary in Irvine will be found at 31287 Woodhollow, Irvine, California.

This is an example of a simple affidavit establishing probable cause that particular stolen property will be found in a particular location. Notice how it follows a logical sequence. The affidavit details the facts that explain to the judge that the contact with the suspect was legal, that a crime has been committed, and that the suspect has additional property in his possession at his residence. This incident involves initial contact by the officer with the suspect. Many search warrants are based on information from others where the officer has had no contact with the suspect and the officer's expert opinion.

Information Provided by Citizens

The second way an investigation and search warrant application might begin is with information supplied by a citizen informant. The citizen informant can be distinguished from the informer as the citizen informant. An informer, often called a confidential informant, usually has some interest in the case. Whether it be a **pecuniary** (monetary) interest or a case pending against him or her, the confidential informant (CI) has some reason for informing. The citizen informant is innocent of criminal involvement and volunteers information wanting to help law enforcement. The officer should look to state law regarding the need to disclose the name of a citizen informant in an affidavit. Even if it is not required, the affidavit should describe the citizen with facts that would lead the judge to determine that this is, in fact, a citizen informant.

Your affiant received a phone call on 04-12-2010 from a person who described himself as a neighbor of suspect Keith. He said he has met Keith on several occasions and described Keith as "rough looking, like he gets into trouble." The person told me that he has seen several people approach the front door of 1342 Alhambra Road, Peyton, New Mexico. Suspect Keith answers the door and takes a small object from the person at the door and then gives something in return. On one occasion he saw a M/W approach the door and drop the item he had in his hand. Although the informant was across the street, the caller could plainly see it was U.S. currency. Keith took the currency (an unknown amount) and gave the person a small object. The person left the house and walked to a red Nissan Sentra, New Mexico license AAA 000. He then saw the subject take a glass pipe, place the item he had just received from

Keith, and light the contents. He inhaled deeply and drove away. I have never spoken with the informant before and he told me that he has no pending cases with the court and the caller was not currently under arrest or wanted for any crimes. He said "he wanted to help keep the streets clean."

In this example the citizen's background and reason for providing the information are set out in the last two sentences. This information must be included in the affidavit.

Information Provided by Informants

The third way an affidavit might begin is based on information supplied by a **confidential informant** (**CI**). The confidential informant often has been arrested and is asking for consideration in the pending case or is attempting to get paid for the information supplied. This *interest* makes the *veracity* of the information suspect.

A long line of cases deal with the use of confidential informants. This is an area that an officer should utilize local resources, receiving formalized training and by conferring with the local DA before attempting to write a search warrant based on information supplied by an informant. We will cover only a couple of basic rules when dealing with informants.

The first rule in dealing with confidential informants is that an officer should not try to "cloak" the CI in the clothes of a citizen informant. This will backfire and cost the officer not only the case but his or her reputation as well. Officers sometimes forget that the courts will not support omissions from affidavits they consider material. The information in an affidavit should be truthful and accurate, including information about the motivation of the informant. The key factor is that the affidavit shows that the information from the informant is reliable.

There are several ways that the information from a CI can be found to be reliable. The test for reliability was established by the U.S. Supreme Court in *Illinois v. Gates* (1983). The court held that reliability is based on the totality of the circumstances. In the *Gates* case, an anonymous informant sent the police a letter accusing the Gates family of selling drugs. The letter outlined the way in which the drugs were being obtained. The police began a surveillance of the Gates residence and Mr. and Mrs. Gates and each of the actions that the letter writer alleged would happen occurred. The judge issued a search warrant and drugs were found in the Gateses' home. Both Mr. and Mrs. Gates had participated in obtaining drugs for sale and both were prosecuted. After their conviction they appealed, arguing that the information in the affidavit did not rise to the level of probable cause and that the informant, who was not identified, was unreliable based on prior case law. Based on the totality of the circumstances of the information in the letter and the conduct of Mr. and Mrs. Gates, the court agreed with the lower court and upheld the search. When police prepare an affidavit, the reliability of informants and probable cause must stand up to this test.

Reliability on a current case can be inferred when the CI has given information in the past. This is simply noted by stating, for example, *the CI has given me accurate information on at least four prior occasions involving the sale of heroin*. The use of informants is a complex part of the investigation process. Officers should seek training from other experienced officers, prosecutors, and courses on their use.

SPECIAL CONSIDERATIONS FOR SEARCH WARRANT AFFIDAVITS

A few special considerations continue to arise in the area of search warrants. A search warrant cannot be based on information that is considered to be old or stale. Officers must also comply with knock and notice and certain times for service. While this is not a comprehensive list of such issues, these two are recurring themes in appellate cases on search warrants.

Requirement of Freshness

The information in a search warrant affidavit that establishes probable cause must be recent. If a police officer arrests a person with stolen property in January it will be unlikely that a search warrant will be issued on that information in March. This is an example of *stale information* for an affidavit.

The information may be "refreshed" by further investigation, but that information must pertain to the information that is stale. The updated information must show that the items to be seized are still in the places to be searched. In the example in the previous paragragh, a new, more recent arrest for a similar charge might refresh the affidavit. Another possibility would be a reliable informant supplying information indicating that the stolen property was still present within the past few days.

These are not the only ways to refresh a warrant affidavit; they are merely examples. When preparing an affidavit the officer must provide information that shows that items are present. The issue of staleness is an important issue. Questions on this and a particular set of circumstances can be discussed with the local DA before the affidavit is presented to a judge.

No Knock and Night Service

The service of search warrants is usually limited to certain hours of the day. Officers must also comply with **knock and notice** requirements. Generally, warrants may be served between 6 a.m. and 10 p.m. Officers must also knock, demand entry, and announce the reason for the demand. Both of these knock and notice requirements are intended for the safety of anyone in a location. The police breaking down a door and rushing into a location especially at night is likely to cause a violent reaction from the occupants.

There are times when safety may require just such an entry. The destruction of certain types of evidence may also justify a late-night or rapid entry. Because a "no knock" or night entry can be very dangerous for all involved, including the police and all inside, only on rare occasions will a judge authorize night service and no-knock entries. If an officer believes that it is necessary to serve the warrant in this fashion the request may be made to a judge. The affidavit must outline the reasons why an entry that is contrary to general rules is preferred.

1. Most police searches are performed without a warrant. A warrant provides judicial authorization for a search. The U.S. Supreme Court has repeatedly stated that the preferred method for a search is the search warrant.

2. Prior to the U.S. Constitution and the Fourth Amendment, officers of the king could ask for authority to conduct a search based on mere suspicion that contraband was present at a location. While this was true in England as well as the colonies, in England the purpose was to suppress sedition—written statements criticizing the king and his government. The colonials had developed a significant smuggling trade to avoid the king's taxes. Searches in the colonies were based more on preventing smuggling than on seditious pamphlets.

3. The Fourth Amendment consists of two requirements: reasonableness and the search warrant. No warrant can be issued unless a police officer (or federal officer) swears to its veracity and the information in the warrant rises to the level of probable cause.

4. Only a law enforcement officer can apply for a warrant and only a judge can approve a warrant. The warrant consists of the affidavit and the actual warrant. The affidavit explains to the judge why probable cause exists.

5. Once the officer completes the affidavit and the warrant, the documents are taken to a judge for review. In many jurisdictions a representative of the local prosecuting agency must first review the documents. This is often the district or city attorney. Alternatively, the affidavit can be read to a judge over the telephone. The judge can then authorize a search.

6. Great care should be taken in the various descriptions on the search warrant. These include the places to be searched, buildings, vehicles, and persons, and the property to be seized. Mistakes in serving warrants in the wrong location can be lead to tragedy.

7. How property, locations, and people are described in the affidavit is important. Careful descriptions will help meet the constitutional requirement of particularity. If property or locations are poorly described, judges will not sign the warrant or the warrant may be successfully challenged in court.

8. The statement of training and experience is an important part of the affidavit. An officer who demonstrates expertise in the area of the investigation that the warrant is related to will be able to support his or her opinion at the end of the affidavit. Officers should keep extensive records of their training and experience.

9. The best approach to the statement of probable cause is a logical step-by-step approach. First, establish that a crime has occurred. Here the suspect or location to be searched is tied to that crime. Next, establish that there is some evidence or fruits of the crime. Finally, link the location or person to be searched to that evidence.

10. Officers usually seek search warrants in three general circumstances. The first is a need that arises from an officer's independent observations or investigation. The second is the need based on information provided by citizen, and the third is from information from confidential informants. Each of these circumstances will affect the affidavit.

11. The reason the Constitution required that search warrants be written was to protect a person's home and effects. The peace of the home was not to be destroyed by the government without a good reason based on fact and only after an independent person reviewed that information. Today, the courts have required that a search warrant be based on information that has recently been uncovered, or that is fresh. Information that is found to be stale may cause the warrant to be invalidated.

12. The peace of the home is further protected by the requirement that the government agents serving a search warrant must first knock, announce the reason for their presence, and demand entry. Only after waiting a reasonable period of time for someone to respond to the door may entry be forced in the location. This is known as knock and notice. The times of day that a search warrant can be served are also limited. While freshness of information is an absolute requirement, a judge can allow night service and no-knock warrants with a proper showing by the police in the affidavit.

Exercises—Preparing Information for a Search Warrant

DESCRIBING PLACES TO BE SEARCHED (PRIVATE RESIDENCES)

INSTRUCTIONS: Prepare a description of your residence, as it would appear on a search warrant.

exercise 1

DESCRIBING PLACES TO BE SEARCHED (COMMERCIAL BUILDINGS)

INSTRUCTIONS: Describe a room in your school building. Remember that the goal of a description as you complete this assignment is to create a description for a search warrant.

WRITING A SEARCH WARRANT AFFIDAVIT NARRATIVE

INSTRUCTIONS: Assume that you are conducting an investigation of a terrorist cell. Your affidavit establishes probable cause that you will find images of locations that are to be blown up with explosives. These include pictures of a school, a shopping mall, and a post office. Describe the things you might seize containing or displaying these images.

exercise 4

WRITING A STATEMENT OF OFFICER'S EXPERIENCE (HERO SHEET) FOR A SEARCH WARRANT AFFIDAVIT

INSTRUCTIONS: Using the following information, prepare a hero sheet for the officer. Use current dates and your name.

1999–2001 Nordstrom Department Store retail security: investigating retail theft, shoplifting, employee theft, and commercial burglary; more than 100 arrests for these crimes

2001–2005 Buena Park Police Department, Community Service Officer: investigating cold crime reports including theft and burglaries

2006 State Police Academy: 40 hours of burglary investigation training

2006–2010 patrol officer, Buena Park Police Department: general patrol duties

03-09-11 to 03-10-11 temporary assignment, narcotics investigation

Investigated more than 300 burglaries; 150 shoplifting arrests

Pleasanton Community College Advanced Officer Training: 80-hour burglary investigation course, 40-hour substance abuse course, 80-hour general investigation course

Currently assigned to detectives as a burglary investigator

_____

_____

_____

_____

_____

_____

_____

_____

_____

_____

_____

_____

_____

_____

_____

_____

_____

_____

_____

_____

_____

_____

_____

_____

_____

_____

_____

_____

_____

_____

WRITING A COMPLETE SEARCH WARRANT AFFIDAVIT

INSTRUCTIONS: Using the information from Exercises 1–4, prepare a logical and complete affidavit for a search warrant. Use current dates.

_____

_____

_____

_____

_____

_____

_____

_____

_____

_____

_____

_____

_____

_____

_____

_____

_____

_____

_____

_____

_____

_____

_____

_____

_____

_____

_____

_____

_____

_____

_____

_____

_____

_____

exercise 5

glossary terms

Confidential informant (CI)   179

General warrant   164

Hero sheet   166

Indicia   165

Internet service provider (ISP)   165

Knock and notice   180

Local rules of the court   172

Pecuniary   178

Per se   163

Primary collision factor   172

Reasonable expectation of privacy   164

Scope   163

Telephonic warrant   167

9

Writing for Correctional Officers

INTRODUCTION

The fundamental elements of report writing do not change whether the writer is a police officer, detective, or correctional officer. In previous chapters we discussed in detail the fundamentals of effective investigative and administrative report writing. In this chapter we will focus exclusively on report writing for correctional officers. Correctional officers face some specific challenges that are unique to their field. The nature of their work, while similar in many respects to traditional police work, differs in some key areas. Correctional officers are tasked with the supervision, transportation, and care of incarcerated inmates. Depending on the type of correctional facility, these inmates can be convicted felons, delinquent juveniles, or adult defendants awaiting arraignment or trial for misdemeanor offenses. This extreme variety of correctional clients creates an environment that is unique in the criminal justice system.

Due to the unpredictable nature of inmate behavior, correctional officers must be constantly attentive to the behavior and demeanor of inmates. They must rapidly detect actions or situations that might cause injury to the inmates or put staff members at risk. Once a potentially hazardous situation is observed, officers must act quickly but appropriately to intervene and control the incident before it becomes dangerous or disruptive. The nature of the correctional environment creates a high degree of civil liability for correctional officers and institutions. Inmates frequently *act out* in irrational, unpredictable, or violent ways. Many inmates in correctional facilities suffer from mental illness or addiction to controlled substances (Schmalleger & Smykla, 2011). Supervising and monitoring these individuals is a primary task for correctional officers. When officers must take action to subdue or control an inmate, these events must be properly documented, particularly when the action involves use of force. This written documentation becomes the official record of the officer's actions and will frequently be crucial evidence in civil or criminal proceedings. It is extremely important that this documentation be clear, accurate, and well written. We will discuss several specific types of incidents and reports in this chapter.

INCIDENT REPORTS AND REPORT FORMS

Correctional officers regularly complete several types of **incident reports** and **report forms**. Each report is designed to address specific types of incidents or occurrences (Guffey, 2005). Some of these reports are very basic and document routine work activities or tasks. Other reports are required when more serious incidents such as injuries, assaults, or use of force incidents occur. Whether the report is being written for a routine task or for a more significant event or action, it should be accurate and well written.

The actions of officers are frequently reviewed and judged based on the written account of the incident. The time-honored criminal justice adage applies here: "If it is not written down it did not happen!" Failure to accurately document your actions can adversely affect your career and your professional reputation. When in doubt about whether or not to write a report, go ahead and document your actions completely and accurately.

Reports on Felonies Committed by Inmates

The investigation of felony crimes is one of the primary tasks of law enforcement officers. The serious nature of these incidents requires that they be thoroughly and proficiently investigated. Officers are tasked with investigating the incident, collecting evidence, apprehending and interviewing the suspect(s), and preparing the case for successful prosecution. This is true whether the crime occurs on a city street or inside a correctional facility. The unpredictable and sometimes violent nature of the correctional environment ensures that serious crimes such as assaults, rapes, and homicides are a reality of correctional life. Even with the best efforts of correctional staff, crimes by inmates against other inmates or institutional staff occur frequently.

The fundamental principles of criminal investigation apply wherever the crime occurs and should always be followed. The focus of this chapter is on report writing and not criminal investigation, but it is impossible to complete a thorough report if proper investigative procedures are not followed. For this reason a short outline of investigative steps is provided. This list is only a guideline and is not all inclusive.

1. Respond and render aid to any injured victims.
2. Identify, apprehend, and secure any perpetrators.
3. Protect and preserve the crime scene. This includes physically securing the scene and controlling who has access.
4. Locate and interview witnesses to the incident. If there are multiple witnesses they should be separated so that their testimony is untainted by discussion of the event with other witnesses.
5. Process the crime scene for evidence including diagramming or photographing the scene, collecting physical evidence, and packaging evidence for other processing.
6. Follow up on all investigative leads. This can include interviewing witnesses who may have not been present but could provide background information about the incident.
7. Document the findings once the investigation has been completed. Take the time to think about the steps you have taken and in what order (chronology) they occurred before you begin writing.
8. Once the report is written, turn over the incident to another agency for further investigation or to the district attorney for prosecution.

Properly documenting the investigation is essential because the quality of the investigation relies on a well-written report that documents the actions of the investigator and establishes the facts of the incident. The written report should end with a logical conclusion, incident resolution, or investigative findings. It will contribute significantly to a successful prosecution or resolution of the incident.

Log Books

The completion of log book entries is an essential task of correctional officers. A **log book** is the official record of the correctional officer's daily actions. Many of the tasks that these officers perform on a daily basis can become routine, mundane, and ordinary and it would be easy for them to become complacent or take shortcuts when completing the tasks. This would be a mistake because officers never know which incidents are routine and unimportant and which might become more significant or important in the future.

Log book entries are typically required whenever an inmate moves within the facility, meets with a visitor, or leaves the facility for medical or court appearances. Log book entries take the form of a running journal or narrative. They are the written record of the activities or tasks performed by officers throughout their shift or assignment, thus these entries should be completed with the same level of diligence as any other type of report. Officers should also document any notifications made to superiors. Most significant incidents in a correctional facility require that notification be made to supervisors or administrators. Recording the name of the person contacted and time of notification provides documentation that it took place should questions arise at a later time.

Frequently log books are the only record of events and actions within the facility. Events that might seem routine and mundane can take on a sense of urgency when significant or high-liability incidents occur within the facility. For example, recording the time that an inmate on suicide watch was last observed or when a door was last secured can become critical should that information become part of a criminal investigation or administrative review. Documenting when injuries were *first* observed on an inmate might become important if an allegation of abuse was being investigated. A lack of care or due diligence in recording facts or observations can come back to haunt officers. It could be days, weeks, or years later that a written log book entry might be scrutinized or questioned; shortcuts taken today can have long-term consequences. Take the time to do it correctly the first time.

Reports on General or Partial Lockdowns

Lockdowns are used in jails and prisons to secure specific areas of the facility. **General lockdowns** typically include the entire facility wherea **partial lockdowns** can include a single cell block or specific part of a facility. During a lockdown inmates are secured in their cells or bays and restricted from moving throughout the facility. This allows staff members to quickly and safely access various parts of the facility without interference from inmates. Correctional facilities frequently use facility lockdowns to maintain control of inmates during a disturbance or if there is the potential for a security threat. Lockdowns are also used whenever staff members must gain access to an area for patdowns of inmates or contraband searches of cells. It is important to accurately document the actions that lead up to a lockdown as well as the actual lockdown itself. Inmates frequently file grievances and internal complaints about the conduct of correctional staff. By documenting the actions of staff members during a lockdown these accusations can be successfully defended. If an incident or injury does occur during a lockdown and civil litigation results, this documentation can be vital evidence in court. The notification of the lockdown to supervisors or administrators should be documented as with any other significant event.

Disciplinary Reports

One of the primary responsibilities of correctional officers is maintaining order and inmate discipline in the correctional facility. The fair and consistent application of rules and the instigation of discipline against inmates for infractions are essential for the efficient operation of a correctional facility. Any disciplinary action taken against an inmate must be accurately and completely documented. Correctional officers must be diligent and timely in recording the details and observations of violations of institutional rules. This documentation should include:

1. The time, date, and location of the infraction or incident.
2. The name and identification number(s) of the inmate(s) involved.

3. The disciplinary regulation or rule that was violated.
4. A detailed description of the specific prohibited conduct.
5. Any supporting witnesses to the infraction or incident.
6. Any physical evidence to support the allegation.

Most correctional facilities provide a grievance process for inmates to appeal discipline or sanctions imposed against them. A well-written **disciplinary report** will support any punitive action that might be taken by a disciplinary board or correctional administrator.

Memoranda

Another form of writing in the correctional environment is the **memorandum,** or *memo*. This is the most widely used form of communication in most correctional departments or facilities. Memos are a less formal form of writing used for routine communication within the correctional facility or between levels of command. They can be typed or handwritten. Most memos follow a standard format or structure such as the following:

To:

From:

Date:

Subject:

Memos can be written for a wide variety of routine functions or requests. They can be used by administrators or supervisors to communicate information throughout the workforce on significant events, policy changes, or personnel matters. Individual officers can generate memos to make personnel requests such as transfer requests, training requests, or shift assignment changes. Memos can also be written to respond to requests for information from supervisors. While memos are considered a less formal means of communication, they should always be accurate, complete, and well written. Memos are frequently the official written record of significant events or officer actions and are regularly used in disciplinary and administrative matters within the correctional facility. Criminal trials, civil lawsuits, and other forms of litigation often incorporate memoranda as evidence. A poorly written or inaccurate memo reflects negatively on the writer and can adversely affect careers or reputations. Officers should take the time to properly write and edit all written correspondence. This is the best practice in any vocation, but is extremely important in the correctional environment where officer actions are frequently reviewed and scrutinized both internally by administrators and externally by the courts.

In today's world of ever-changing technologies, it is appropriate to discuss the use of electronic mail (e-mail) in the correctional environment. Today's correctional agencies frequently use e-mail systems to communicate within the facility and to outside agencies. The very casual nature of electronic communication might lull writers into a false sense of security. E-mail communications should be treated the same as an official report or memoranda. Any communication authored on an agency-owned computer or system is a *public record* and as such can be obtained easily through a freedom of information request by the public. Officers should *never* write anything in an e-mail that they do not want to be viewed by the general public.

MAJOR INSTITUTIONAL PROBLEMS

We define **major institutional problems** as significant incidents such as fires and fire alarms, contraband seizures, staff or inmate injuries, and deaths that must be investigated and documented by correctional officers. Correctional officers must respond to a wide variety of these incidents as part of their assigned duties. The unpredictable nature of the corrections environment requires that officers be very adaptable to changing circumstances and situations and respond quickly but appropriately. These incidents can affect the efficient operation of the facility and must be handled competently and professionally. When injuries or damage to the facility occur during major events or problems civil liability can be incurred by the correctional agency or individual officers. The actions of officers in these situations will frequently be reviewed and evaluated by supervisory and administrative personnel or internal affairs investigators to determine if policies were followed or if the actions taken were justified. These reviews rely heavily on the officer's written documentation of an incident and the quality of the narrative descriptions of the actions of the officer. A well-written and professional report reflects favorably on the writer and will withstand any scrutiny or review.

Fires and Fire Alarms

One of the more significant dangers in a correctional facility is fire and smoke inhalation. The design of most correctional facilities makes rapid detection and suppression of fire extremely important. The confined areas of inmate cells and the lack of open space increase the danger from smoke inhalation and fire. The limited number of exits and ways to exhaust smoke from the facility only contribute to these risks. Serious injury or death from smoke inhalation can occur within minutes in a confined area such as a cell or corridor. Most modern correctional facilities incorporate technologies to detect fire quickly and initiate fire suppression with automated water sprinkler systems and emergency exhaust ventilation.

Correctional staff must remain alert to the early detection of fire. Many items such as toiletry, paper products, and bedding that are readily available to inmates are potentially combustible. Inmates frequently activate fire suppression systems to flood cells. This can disrupt the orderly functioning of the facility or create a diversion to distract or occupy correctional staff. Any activation of fire suppression apparatus or suspicious fires should be investigated and thoroughly documented in a **fire and fire alarm report**. The time, location, and specific details of any alarm activation should be recorded. If the activation of a fire alarm is the result of an intentional act or results in property damage, injuries, or loss of life the incident may rise to the level of an arson investigation.

Contraband Seizures

The detection and interdiction of illegal substances or unauthorized contraband into the correctional facility is a primary task of correctional officers. Possession of illegal drugs and weapons can pose a serious threat to inmates and staff and impede the safe and efficient operation of a correctional facility. Inmates have unlimited time and energy to devise unusual and creative ways to conceal and transport illegal contraband. Controlling the flow of contraband into and within the facility requires a high level of diligence and investigative skill from officers. Frequent patdowns

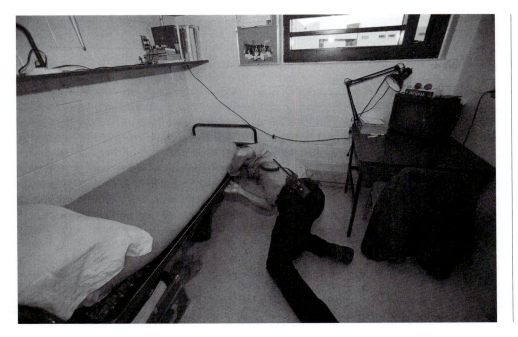

Correctional officers are tasked with the detection and seizure of contraband.
Source: © Mikael Karlsson/ Arresting Images

and searches of inmates, random searches of inmate cells, and physical sweeps of common areas frequented by inmates are routine but essential tasks of correctional officers.

Whenever contraband is discovered a **contraband seizure report** must be written documenting the circumstances that led to the seizure. Typically a contraband seizure will result in either disciplinary action or additional criminal charges being pursued against an inmate. A well-written and accurate report of the seizure will ensure a successful criminal prosecution or the imposition of disciplinary sanctions. Contraband seizure reports are also used for institutional intelligence gathering and ongoing training for correctional staff. Keeping a record of inmate patterns and methods for hiding and transporting contraband ensures that staff will be able to detect and deter future incidents of smuggling or concealing contraband.

Staff or Inmate Injuries

Whenever staff members or inmates are injured in a correctional facility documentation must be completed. The cause of these injuries can range from simple workplace accidents to serious or life-threatening injuries from physical assaults. Any injury to an inmate or staff member should be thoroughly investigated and documented in a **staff or inmate injuries report.** If the injury is the result of a criminal act by an inmate it must be documented as part of a criminal investigation and for future prosecution.

Accidental injuries to inmates or staff must also be investigated and documented to protect the correctional agency from potential civil liability. Reports on injuries to staff members may also be used to identify training needs, the need for policy changes or equipment, or facility deficiencies. It is just as important to use proper investigative procedures in an accident investigation as it is for a criminal investigation. Incidents that initially appear to be accidents can turn out to be something much more serious or criminal in nature. A thorough investigation and a well-written report of the facts relating to the injury can protect the correctional facility from civil liability.

Death Investigations

Deaths in correctional facilities, while rare, are always significant events. Suicide is a leading cause of unnatural death in prisons and jails (Bureau of Justice Statistics, 2010). The unanticipated death of an inmate in a correctional facility always requires a complete and thorough investigation and must be documented in a **death investigation report**. If the death is unattended by a physician, then it must be treated as a homicide investigation until foul play is ruled out. This will require strict adherence to crime scene procedures, protection of evidence at the scene, and a thorough investigation by qualified investigators.

Initial responding officers should secure the scene once the death is confirmed and begin the investigative process. Documentation should begin immediately. The initial observations of the scene will be very important as the investigation proceeds. Exact times of discovery of the deceased and any medical response should be noted and recorded. A detailed description of the deceased body and the area around the body should be documented and photographed. A contamination list of anyone who entered the crime scene during the investigation should also be made. Any witnesses should be identified and segregated prior to being interviewed, and any physical evidence should be preserved and processed by trained crime scene personnel.

The death of an inmate is always a significant event that will be scrutinized both internally by correctional or law enforcement staff and externally by the media and the public. Inmate deaths frequently trigger a review of officer actions and facility procedures. The death of an inmate that is the result of officer negligence or misconduct will most likely result in civil litigation or potentially criminal prosecution. Proper investigation and documentation of investigative findings can exonerate an officer from wrongdoing or can be used to improve staff training in high-liability areas.

Detection and prevention of escapes and escape attempts are the primary responsibility of correctional officers.
Source: David R. Frazier Photolibrary, Inc.

Escapes and Attempted Escapes

One of the primary tasks of correctional officers is the prevention of escape from the facility. The proper monitoring and supervision of inmates is the most effective way of preventing escapes or detecting a planned escape. Inmates can be ingenious and ruthless in planning and executing escapes. Correctional officers must be vigilant to detect evidence of escape plans or inmates attempting to hide contraband or the implements needed to orchestrate an escape. Routine inspections and random searches of inmate cells and common areas must be done to prevent inmates from concealing tools or weapons that could be used to facilitate an escape. Even ordinary items such as bed sheets, grooming implements, eating utensils, or workshop tools can be used as weapons or tools to facilitate an escape. Officers must constantly be vigilant to observe inmates who might be attempting to conceal or inappropriately use these items.

If an escape is attempted correctional officers must act quickly to prevent the escape or quickly respond to recapture the missing inmate(s) once it is discovered. The documentation of escape attempts must be complete and accurate in an **escape and attempted escape report**. Escapes or attempted escapes from a correctional facility are criminal offenses and must be thoroughly investigated just like any other criminal investigation. The scene should be preserved and any evidence processed, photographed, and collected. Witnesses should be identified and interviewed and written or recorded statements obtained. The written report of an escape or attempted escape can have a multitude of uses. It can be used in court to prosecute the inmate for additional criminal charges; it also can be used to train officers on detection or prevention of future attempts.

USE OF FORCE OR DISCHARGE OF WEAPONS

Anytime a correctional officer uses force it is a significant event. Correctional officers, like their counterparts in law enforcement, are among the few governmental agents authorized by law to use force. However, officers are justified in using force only in certain situations. These situations could include to protect themselves or other staff members from assault; to protect inmates from assault or injury by another inmate; to prevent the escape of an inmate; to compel compliance with lawful orders; or to control inmate actions in a potentially hazardous situation. Levels of use of force by correctional officers are limited to specific situations and should be used *only* in compliance with established agency rules or state laws. The amount of force that a correctional officer can use ranges from an arm bar or mild pain compliance technique to using deadly force

Correctional officers frequently must use force to compel compliance from inmates or protect life. These incidents must be properly documented.
Source: © Mikael Karlsson

with a firearm. The amount of force used by officers must always be reasonable based on the amount of physical resistance or violence they encounter. The use of too much force in a use of force situation can be deemed excessive and can expose the officer to discipline or criminal culpability.

Officers can also employ a wide variety of less-than-lethal weapons to control inmates. These can include batons, chemical sprays, electronic control belts, Tasers, and impact munitions. Officers can also use a variety of defensive tactics or empty-handed techniques for their own protection from assault or to respond to inmate resistance. Each of these measures must be used in a reasonable manner to counter inmate resistance. Excessive use of force by officers is a serious matter that can expose the officer to administrative punishment, civil liability, or criminal prosecution.

Due to the very serious consequences of use of force by correctional officers, complete documentation of the incident is required in a **discharge of weapons report.** Correctional officers are held accountable for the amount of force used against an inmate. Failure to document a use of force is cause for disciplinary action in most correctional facilities. Officers receive considerable training on the proper amount of force to be used to control or subdue an inmate. If the amount of force used by the officer is determined to be excessive, then the officer could face administrative discipline or criminal prosecution. It is vitally important to accurately document any use of force against an inmate. The quality of documentation in the **use of force report** is frequently the deciding factor in any review of the officer's actions in a use of force incident.

A completely justified use of force by an officer that is improperly documented may cause a supervisor or administrator to misinterpret or question the actions of the writer. For example, when documenting a use of force incident involving an inmate by simply stating *The inmate came at me and I hit him with my expandable baton*, this statement leaves a lot to be desired. The reader is left to interpret what *came at me* really means and where the officer *hit* the inmate can make the difference between a lawful use of force and one that is a criminal act. A better statement might read: *While moving the inmate through a narrow corridor he lunged at me with a clenched fist. To protect myself I struck him once on the forearm with my expandable baton to block his punch and bring him under control.* This statement is more detailed and gives the reader a clearer picture of the incident and some justification for the use of force.

The most common mistake in writing a use of force report is lack of detail or descriptions of the inmate's actions that precipitated the use of force. Leaving out pertinent facts or observations may lead the reader to *fill in the gaps* or misunderstand the nature of the incident. Any injuries that result from the use of force should be documented and photographed. A report narrative that chronologically describes the actions of the inmate and the resulting use of force by the officer in accurate and complete detail with "no gaps" or factual errors is most effective. The reader should feel as though they were at the scene of the incident and can visualize the actions of the inmate as well as the officer.

1. Correctional officers are tasked with reporting a wide variety of incidents that occur inside the correctional environment. Each of these incidents requires a thorough investigation and proper documentation.

2. Violence in correctional facilities is a reality of the correctional environment. The investigation of felony crimes that occur within correctional facilities is one of the essential tasks of correctional officers. It is important to properly investigate and document these incidents so that they can be successfully prosecuted.

3. Reports on general and partial lockdowns, log books, and disciplinary reports are some of the report types used by correctional officers routinely. They are used to document the actions of correctional officers when dealing with daily activities within the institution. These can include investigating inmate infractions, incidents, or disturbances and violations of institutional rules.

4. Memoranda are the most common form of written communication in most correctional faculties or departments. They are used for a wide variety of routine requests and documentation of events. Even though they are a less formal form of communication, their importance should not be underestimated. They often become the official written record in external and internal reviews and court proceedings.

5. Fire detection and suppression are major concerns in correctional facilities. Inmates frequently activate alarms and water sprinkler systems to disrupt facility functions. Any fire alarms or activation of fire suppression apparatus should be thoroughly investigated and properly documented.

6. Deaths in correctional facilities are a rare occurrence but must be thoroughly investigated. When the death occurs in a custody setting, every aspect of the circumstances should be explored and verified. A well-written report should answer any questions or concerns related to the death.

7. One of the primary tasks of the correctional officer is the prevention or detection of escapes from the facility. Any escape or attempted escape must be completely investigated and thoroughly documented. Reports documenting escapes can be used to file additional criminal charges against the involved inmate or to provide intelligence on the methods used to facilitate the escape for training.

8. Completing reports documenting the use of force by officers against inmates is one of the most important tasks of correctional officers. Correctional officers should use only the level of force that is reasonable to protect themselves, other staff, or inmates, or to compel compliance from inmates who act in a resistive or threatening manner. Often the officer's written documentation is the primary deciding factor in any review of officer use of force. For this reason officers should be thorough and diligent in documenting their actions in a use of force incident.

Exercises—Writing Correctional Reports

exercise 1

WRITING A REPORT OF A FELONY CRIME

INSTRUCTIONS: Draft the narrative portion of a correctional incident report using the following facts:

Inmates involved (name and numbers): Marcus Smith #34570, and John Brown #45124

Date and time of incident: 08-08-11 1400 hours

Nature of incident: Aggravated assault by inmate

Location: Exercise yard outside Building 3

Others present: 10 other inmates; two guards C/O Jones and C/O Martin, and Sergeant Finch

Facts of the event:
Inmates Smith #34570 and Brown #45124 were in the exercise yard along with several other inmates and guards. A physical altercation ensued between Smith and Brown, with blows being struck by both inmates. Smith produced a weapon from his pocket and stabbed Brown repeatedly. Brown was stabbed repeatedly with a sharpened 4-inch metal spike. The spike was recovered on the ground.

Injuries:
Inmate Brown suffered six superficial stab wounds to his lower back and shoulder. Inmate Smith received a split lip and a cut on his cheek 1 inch below his left eye. Both inmates had bloody knuckles. C/O Jones sustained a sprained wrist while breaking up the altercation.

WRITING UP A DISCIPLINARY ACTION

INSTRUCTIONS: Draft the narrative portion of a correctional incident report using the following facts:

Inmates involved (name and numbers): Barbara Crystal #26090
Date and time of incident: 08-23-11, 2100 hours
Nature of incident: Inmate out of place
Location: A Pod, cell 6
Others present: C/O Franco

Facts of the event:
Inmate Crystal was observed coming down the stairs from A Pod near cell 6. Inmate Crystal is assigned to B Pod cell 4B and has been previously warned by me not to be found in this area. C/O Franco alerted me to Crystal's location from his station in the control booth.

---

exercise 3

WRITING A MEMORANDUM FOR TRAINING REQUEST

INSTRUCTIONS: Draft the narrative portion of a memorandum using the following information:

To:	Sergeant Mark Price, "A" shift supervisor
From:	C/O John Jones, "A" shift
Date:	10-08-11
Subject:	Training Request

Facts of the event:

You are requesting authorization to attend advanced defensive tactics training for correctional officers at another correctional facility (Northeastern Regional Correctional Facility). This training is being held November 4–9 from 8 A.M. to 5 P.M. This type of training is not offered at your facility and would help you meet the requirements for advanced certifications and make you eligible for promotion to assistant shift supervisor.

e x e r c i s e 4

DOCUMENTING A CONTRABAND SEIZURE

INSTRUCTIONS: Draft the narrative portion of a correctional incident report using the following facts:

Inmates involved (name and numbers): Inmate Fisher #00789 and
Inmate Harrison #11988

Date and time of incident: 08-18-11, 0900 hours
Nature of incident: Contraband seizure (marijuana)
Location: D Pod, cell 8
Others present: C/O Gordon and C/O James

Facts of the event:
A search of the cell occupied by the listed inmates revealed approximately 5 grams of suspected marijuana concealed in a piece of toilet paper stuffed under the lower bunk of inmate Fisher.

WRITING A PRELIMINARY REPORT ON A DEATH INVESTIGATION

INSTRUCTIONS: Draft the narrative portion of a correctional incident report using the following facts:

Inmates involved (name and numbers): Inmate Robert Fraley #99846
Date and time of incident: 10-18-11, 0100 hours
Nature of incident: Death Investigation
Location: B Pod, cell 12
Others present: C/O Berry and C/O Adams

Facts of the event:
The listed inmate was found unresponsive and not breathing. He was lying face down in his cell and was cold and stiff to the touch. EMS was called and CPR was administered by C/O Berry. Fraley was pronounced dead at 0115 hours. Fraley was last seen sitting on the side of his bunk at 2430 hours by C/O Adams. There were no obvious signs of trauma or foul play. Fraley was the single occupant of cell 12.

glossary terms

Commonly Used Homophones, Commonly Misspelled Words Used in Reports, and Commonly Misused Homonyms

Commonly Used Homophones

Ad: A listing of goods and services for sale.
Add: Combining two or more numbers to create a sum.

Ail: Problems of health and somatic pain.
Ale: An alcoholic spirit similar to beer.

Aisle: A pathway between chairs or pews.
Isle: A reference to an island, as in *British Isles*.
I'll: Contraction of *I* and *will*.

All: Inclusive of everyone.
Awl: A tool used for making holes.

Aloud: A reference to sound, as in *to read aloud*.
Allowed: To offer permission.

Altar: The lectern at the front of a church.
Alter: To change, as in tailoring clothes.

Ate: To have consumed food.
Eight: A numeral following seven and preceding nine.

Bale: A bundle of something.
Bail: A sum of money paid to ensure one's appearance in court.

Ball: A round toy.
Bawl: To cry.

Bear: Large furry mammal.
Bare: Absence of covering or clothing; naked.

Beech: A type of tree.
Beach: A sandy place near the ocean

Bean: A type of legume.
Been: A verb of being indicating past tense.

Bury: To place in a hole and cover.
Berry: A type of fruit.

Bite: To close one's teeth around an item.
Byte: A measure of computer space on a disk or hard drive.

Bolder: To be demonstrative and/or challenging.
Boulder: A large rock.

Bough: A large tree branch.
Bow: To bend at the waist in a show of respect.

By: Near to something, or the author of something.
Bye: A statement as one leaves.
Buy: To make a purchase of something.

Cannon: A type of weapon.
Canon: A rule or law.

Cereal: A breakfast food.
Serial: A series of events.

Clause: An element in a contract.
Claws: The talons of a bird, or nails of an animal.

Current: Timely; at present.
Currant: A dried fruit similar to a raisin.

Dear: A term of endearment.
Deer: A short-haired mammal known for its antlers.

Die: To cease living.
Dye: Coloring used in clothing and other objects.

Dough: Raw materials for making bread; slang for *money*.
Doe: Female deer.

Commonly Used Homophones

Do: Verb indicating intended action.
Due: Something that is owed.
Dew: Moisture left on surfaces early in the morning.

Earn: To achieve through work or effort.
Urn: A vaselike container.

Fair: Equitable or just; or a carnival-type location.
Fare: The fee paid for some service such as a bus ride.

Flour: Ground wheat or grain used for baking.
Flower: Any of a variety of plants, shrubs, or herbs.

Great: An interjection of well-being.
Grate: To rub against an abrasive.

Groan: To moan and complain.
Grown: To have gotten larger or taller.

Hare: A wild rabbit.
Hair: Material found on the top of most heads.

Hall: A passageway.
Haul: To take away.

Hear: A reference to auditory ability.
Here: Verb of being indicating placement.

Heard: Past tense of *to hear*.
Herd: A collection of cows.

Heel: The back portion on the bottom of a foot or shoe.
Heal: To repair or mend.

Higher: Above something else.
Hire: To offer employment to someone.

Hole: A dug-up area in the ground; a tear in a garment.
Whole: A measure of completeness.

Horse: A four-legged beast of burden.
Hoarse: A soreness of the throat causing speech difficulty; a
    raspy voice.

Hour: A measure of time.
Our: An indication of possession.

Knew: Having knowledge.
New: Novel, or innovative.

Knot: A means of securing twine, cord, or rope.
Not: A denial.

Know: Possession of information or knowledge.
No: Negative response to a question.

Laps: A number of routine circuits of something.
Lapse: To skip something or allow it to miss occurring.

Led: Past tense of *to lead*.
Lead: To be the head of a line or direct others.
Lead: A soft, malleable metal.

Loan: To permit the use of something temporarily.
Lone: Singular, alone.

Mail: Letters sent through the post office.
Male: The opposite gender to *female*.

Mane: The fringed hair of a horse along its neck.
Main: The central item or issue.

Mist: Moisture in the air; light rain.
Missed: To not have seen or captured something or someone.

Muscles: Tissue in the body that is associated with strength.
Mussels: A type of shelled mollusk.

Pane: A sheet of glass in a window.
Pain: A somatic discomfort.

Prey: The weaker object of an attack.
Pray: Uttering of promises or requests to an omnipotent being.

Peace: A state of calm.
Piece: A segment of something.

Principal: The head of a school.
Principle: A noble point or stance.

Read: The ability to understand written words.
Reed: A strawlike material or grasslike vegetation.

Rain: Precipitation that falls from the sky.
Reign: To maintain a sovereign leadership.

Road: A cleared, sometimes paved area for vehicles to travel.
Rowed: Using paddles to power a boat's movement.

Commonly Used Homophones

Root: Portion of a plant, shrub, or tree.	Tale: A story.
Route: The path one may take to or from something.	Tail: The wagging end of a dog or cat.
Sale: An offer for purchase at a discount.	Tied: To secure.
Sail: A means of moving a boat.	Tide: The ebb and flow of the ocean.
Sea: The ocean.	Toe: The digits on a foot.
See: Visual ability.	Tow: To haul or pull something.
Sight: The ability to have vision; ability *to see*; to locate.	Veil: Material worn over a person's face or head; a covering.
Site: A specific location.	Vail: To yield or recede.
Steal: To take something that is not yours.	Waste: To misuse or have unnecessary surplus.
Steel: A metal composed of iron and coal.	Waist: The section on the body around the hips.
Suite: A fancy hotel room.	Weather: Indication of climatic conditions.
Sweet: A pleasant taste; opposite of *sour*.	Whether: Refers to *if* or *should* some action be taken.
Tact: The ability to use diplomacy.	Which: Indicates what particular one or ones.
Tacked: Secure something to a wall or board.	Witch: A member of the Wicket religion.
There: Indication of location or direction.	Wood: Fibrous material from a tree.
Their: Indefinite pronoun of possession.	Would: Willingness to do something.
They're: Contraction meaning *they are*.	
	Write: Draft words into sentences.
Threw: Tossed something.	Right: Correct; or indication or directions opposite to left.
Through: Indication of position passing between something.	

Commonly Misspelled Words Used in Reports

allot	abandon	abate	abdomen	abduction
abetting	abortion	abrasion	abrogate	abscond
abutment	accelerant	accelerate	accelerator	acceptable
accidental	accommodate	accessible	accomplice	accosted
accumulate	accused	accustomed	acquaintance	acquit
addict	adjacent	adjoining	admission	admonishment
adultery	adversary	affidavit	aggravated	aggressive
alcohol	alias	alibi	all right	allegation
alleged	allusion	alongside	already	alternate
although	amateur	ambulance	ammunition	amnesia
among	animosity	announce	anonymous	antenna
apoplexy	apparent	appearance	appointment	apprehend
apprise	argument	arraignment	artery	ascertain
athlete	athletic	attorney	attributed	authoritative
autopsy	available	backward	bail	ballistics
barricade	battery	bazaar	beginning	believe
belligerent	berserk	bicycle	billiard	bizarre
blackmail	brevity	bribery	bruises	bureau
burglary	bystander	cache	cafeteria	cajole
calendar	caliber	campaign	canister	capricious
carburetor	cardiac	carefully	carnal	cartridge
cashier	cassette	casualty	catastrophe	Caucasian
cemetery	certificate	changeable	chauffeur	chief
choose	chose	chronological	circumstances	circumstantial
coarse	cocaine	coerce	coercion	cognizant
cohabitation	collaborator	collateral	collision	collusion
column	comatose	combustible	comfortable	commission
communicate	communication	committed	compel	complacent
complainant	complement	compliance	complicit	complying
compulsory	concealed	conciliatory	concurrent	confusion
connive	conscience	conscious	conscientious	conspiracy
conspiratorial	construe	consensus	contempt	convenience
conviction	congregate	cooperate	cooperative	copulation
corner	coroner	corpse	correlate	corroborate
corrugated	cough	counsel	council	counterfeit
courteous	credible	criticism	crotch	cruelty
cruising	culminated	curfew	cursory	customary
dangerous	debris	decedent	deceptive	decision
decomposition	degradation	defamation	defamatory	defecated
defendant	definitely	defraud	deleterious	demeanor

Commonly Misspelled Words Used in Reports

demented	denied	denominational	dependent	deployed
deposition	derogatory	derringer	desecrate	desperate
despondent	detainer	developed	diagnosis	diagonal
diaphragm	dilapidated	dining	diner	dinner
disappearance	disastrous	discipline	discotheque	discreet
discrepancy	discrepant	discrimination	disease	disguise
disinfectant	disinterested	dispatched	dispensary	disposition
disqualified	distinction	divergent	divorce	divorcee
divulge	dormitory	drawer	drunkard	drunkenness
dual	dubious	duplex	duress	dynamite
earring	eccentric	eclectic	eighth	electricity
elevator	elicit	eliminate	embarrass	embedded
embezzle	emergency	emphysema	employee	employer
employment	endemic	ensuing	entice	entrusted
epileptic	equipment	equipped	equivalent	erection
erotica	erratic	eviction	evidence	exceeded
except	excited	excused	executed	exercise
exhaust	exhilarate	exigent	exonerate	expedite
explosion	extinguish	extortion	extradition	extremities
facetious	facsimile	familiar	fatigued	feces
fellatio	feminine	fictitious	filthy	fisticuffs
Flammable	flippant	fondling	forcible	forearm
forehead	foreign	foreigner	forfeit	fornication
forth	fortitude	fourteen	fourth	fraud
fraudulent	fugitive	fulfill	gagged	garage
garbage	gassed	gauged	genuine	government
graffiti	gratification	greased	grenade	grievance
guarantee	guilty	habitually	Halloween	hallucinogen
hallucinate	harassment	hazardous	headache	hemorrhage
heroin	hiccup	hierarchy	hijacked	Hispanic
hitchhiker	homicide	hoping	horizontal	humane
humorous	humiliate	hurried	hypochondriac	hypodermic
hysterical	identified	identity	idiosyncrasy	ignorance
illicit	illiterate	imaginary	imitation	immature
immediately	immigrant	immigration	impatiently	impeccable
impervious	implicit	impromptu	impugn	incapacitate
incest	incoherent	inconsequential	incidentally	incinerate
incoherent	inconsistent	incorrigible	incredible	independent
indict	indigent	indignant	indiscriminant	indispensible
induce	ineptitude	inevitable	inflammable	informant
infringement	ingenious	inhabited	inhibition	initial

Commonly Misspelled Words Used in Reports

innocence	innocent	inoculate	inquire	inquiry
inquisitive	insinuated	insolence	insolent	insufficiency
intelligent	intercept	intercourse	interdiction	interference
interior	interpret	interrogation	interrupted	interstate
intimidate	intoxicated	intractable	intruder	invasion
irrelevant	irresistible	insolate	insulation	issuance
it's	its	jalousies	jealousies	jeopardize
jeopardy	jewelry	joyriding	judgment	justifiable
jurisdiction	justification	juvenile	Kava Kava	kerosene
khaki	kidnapping	kleptomaniac	knots	knowledge
knuckles	labeling	laboratory	laceration	ladder
lascivious	latent	later	latter	lattice
Laundromat	lawyer	lavatory	legible	legitimate
leisure	length	lessee	lessor	lewd
liable	liability	library	lien	lieutenant
lightning	likely	liquor	litigate	lividity
livor mortis	loiter	loiterer	longer	loose
lose	losing	louvers	luggage	machete
magazine	maintain	maintenance	majority	malice
malicious	malign	management	mandatory	maneuver
manslaughter	manual	manufacturing	marginal	materiality
marijuana	marital	matinee	maturity	mayhem
meant	medal	medevac	medical	megapixel
memorandum	memorize	menace	menstrual	menstruation
merely	metal	microphone	midriff	mileage
minimal	minimum	minor	Miranda warning	miscellaneous
mischievous	misdemeanor	misspelled	mitigate	modus operandi
moisture	molest	monogrammed	moped	moral
morale	morgue	morphine	mortgage	motorcycle
mountainous	multiple	municipal	murderer	muscle
museum	mustache	mutilated	narcotics	narrow
naturally	necessary	necessity	necklace	nefarious
negligent	neighborhood	nephew	nervous	neutral
niece	nineteen	ninety	noisy	nosey
noticeable	notify	nuisance	numerous	obedience
obligation	obnoxious	obscene	obscure	obsolete
obstacle	obstinate	obstruction	occasion	occurred
occurrence	offender	offense	official	opiate
operator	opinion	opium	opponent	opportunistic
opposite	oppositional	ordinance	oscillate	pandering
panicked	parallel	paramedic	paraphernalia	parolee

Commonly Misspelled Words Used in Reports

pastime	pathology	patience	patient	pedestrian
pejorative	penalty	pendant	penis	penitentiary
perimeter	perishable	perjury	permanent	permeate
permissible	perpetrator	persecute	personal	personnel
perspiration	persuade	persuasion	petulant	picnicking
placid	planning	plausible	plea	poisonous
polygamy	possession	preceding	precipitate	predicament
pregnancy	prejudice	preliminary	premeditation	premises
prerogative	prescription	presence	presentence	pretrial
previous	principal	principle	prisoner	privilege
probable	probably	proceeds	proceedings	procuring
profane	profanity	projectile	promiscuous	pronounced
pronunciation	proposition	prosecute	prosecutorial	prostitution
protective	provocation	psychologist	publicity	punctured
pungent	pursuit	qualifications	quality	quantity
quarrel	quiet	quite	quotient	racial
radial fracture	railing	rapport	rapture	readily
reagent	reality	really	receding	receive
recidivism	recidivist	reciprocal	reckless	recognizance
recognize	recommend	recreation	rectify	redness
referred	relevancy	relevant	remanded	remedial
renewal	repetition	reprieve	reprisal	repugnant
reputation	reputed	residence	resident	residential
resistance	resolution	respiration	restaurant	restitution
resuscitation	revived	revoke	revolver	ridiculous
rigor mortis	rummaging	ruptured	ruse	sacrifice
salient	sawed-off	scarcely	scene	schedule
scissor	scrutinize	scuffle	secretary	sedative
semiautomatic	semiconscious	separate	separation	sergeant
shill	shining	shoplifting	shrubbery	silhouette
similar	similarly	simultaneously	Sinsemilla	skeleton
skeptical	slapped	sleigh	sleight	slight
snub-nosed	sodomy	solely	solicitation	son-in-law
specimen	spherical	spiral	spontaneous	squalid
squalor	statistics	statue	status	statute
stomach	strangulation	striped	subdued	subjugate
submitting	subpoena	substantial	subterfuge	subtle
subversion	subversive	succeed	successful	sued
suffocation	suicide	sullen	sulky	summons
sundry	sundries	superintendant	supersede	supervisor
supplement	surrender	surreptitious	surveillance	suspended

Commonly Misspelled Words Used in Reports

suspicion	suspicious	swerve	sympathy	symptom
taboo	tacit	tamper	tattoo	taunt
taut	temperament	temperamental	temperature	tendency
terrorism	testimony	tetanus	theater	their
there	they're	thieves	thorough	throat
through	tongue	towel	toxic	toxicological
tractor	trafficking	tranquil	transferred	traverse
treacherous	trespassing	tries	truancy	Tuesday
turbulent	turpitude	turquoise	twelfth	twelve
typewriter	umbrella	unconscious	undoubtedly	uniform
unnatural	unnecessarily	unregistered	unsanitary	unusually
urgent	vacancy	vaccination	vacuum	vagina
vagrant	valuable	vehement	vehicle	velocity
venereal	veracity	versatile	vertical	veterinary
vicinity	vicious	Vietnamese	vindictive	violation
viscous	visible	vitamin	volunteer	waist
visceral	waitress	warehouse	warrant	warrantless
waste	weapon	wear	weather	Wednesday
weight	weighty	weird	where	whether
whole	wholly	whore	wily	wiry
witnessed	witnesses	wreck	written	yield
you're	your	zealous	zealot	zigzag

Commonly Misused Homonyms

acts	ax	
accept	except	
access	excess	
ad	add	
advice	advise	
aid	aide	
aides	ades	AIDS
allusion	illusion	
ant	aunt	
ate	eight	
bail	bale	
bald	bawled	
bare	bear	
base	bass	
be	bee	
beach	beech	

Commonly Misused Homonyms

beat	beet	
billed	build	
bazaar	bizarre	
blew	blue	
brake	break	
bread	bred	
but	butt	
by	buy	bye
capital	capitol	
cell	sell	
cent	sent	
cents	scents	sense
cheap	cheep	
clause	claws	
chews	choose	
counsel	council	
close	clothes	
course	coarse	
creak	creek	
crews	cruise	
dam	damn	
days	daze	
decent	descent	dissent
desert	dessert	
dew	do	due
die	dye	
discreet	discrete	
doe	dough	
dual	duel	
elicit	illicit	
eye	I	
fair	fare	
feat	feet	
find	fined	
fir	fur	
flea	flee	
flew	flu	flue
for	four	
forth	fourth	
foul	fowl	
gait	gate	

Commonly Misused Homonyms

gored	gourd	
grate	great	
grill	grille	
groan	grown	
hail	hale	
hair	hare	
hall	haul	
halve	have	
hay	hey	
heal	heel	
hear	here	
heard	herd	
hi	high	
him	hymn	
hoard	horde	
hole	whole	
hoarse	horse	
hoes	hose	
hour	our	
in	inn	
its	it's	
knew	new	
knight	night	
knot	not	
know	no	
lain	lane	
lead	led	
loan	lone	
lose	loose	
made	maid	
main	mane	Maine
meat	meet	
minor	miner	
none	nun	
oar	or	ore
oh	owe	
one	won	
pail	pale	
pain	pane	
pair	pare	
past	passed	

Commonly Misused Homonyms

pause	paws	
peace	piece	
peak	peek	
personal	personnel	
plain	plane	
prince	prints	
principle	principal	
quiet	quite	
rain	reign	rein
rap	wrap	
rapped	wrapped	
read	red	
read	reed	
real	reel	
right	write	rite
ring	wring	
rode	road	rowed
role	roll	
root	route	
rose	rows	
rung	wrung	
sail	sale	
scene	seen	
sea	see	
sew	so	sow
shone	shown	
side	sighed	
sighs	size	
site	cite	sight
slay	sleigh	
soar	sore	
soared	sword	
sole	soul	
steal	steel	
tail	tale	
teas	tease	
their	there	they're
threw	through	
throne	thrown	
tide	tied	
to	too	two

Commonly Misused Homonyms

toad	towed	
toe	tow	
tray	trey	
wade	weighed	
waist	waste	
wait	weight	
war	wore	
way	weigh	
wear	where	
weather	whether	
week	weak	
which	witch	
whose	who's	
wood	would	
your	you're	

Chapter 1

Associated Press. (2004, March 15). *New police cars have voice recognition*. Retrieved from PoliceOne.com: http://www.orpc.unh.edu/Project54PoliceOne.PDF

Astington, J., & Baird, J. (2005). Why *language matters for theory of mind*. New York: Oxford University Press.

Brewer, B. (2007). ABCs of mobile reporting. *Law and Order, 55*(11), 36–44.

Dees, T. (1999). Dictating reports and preparing for disasters. *Law and Order, 47*(7), 15–17.

Dees, T. (2005). New technologies at IACP 2004. *Law and Order, 53*(2), 308–314.

Department of Justice, Bureau of Justice Statistics. (2003). *State and local law enforcement statistics, computers and information systems*. Retrieved October 21, 2009, from www.ojp.usdoj.gov/bjs/sandle.htm

Foster, R. (2005). *Police technology*. Upper Saddle River, NJ: Pearson Prentice Hall.

Frazee, B., & Davis, J. (2004). *Painless police report writing* (3rd ed.). Upper Saddle River, NJ: Pearson Prentice Hall.

Gavigan, J. (2008). The state-of-the-art police agency software. *Law and Order, 56*(11), 32–42.

Geoghegan, S. (2009). Laptops and handheld computers. *Law and Order, 57*(3), 38–45.

Groff, E., & McEwen, T. (2008). *Identifying and measuring the effectiveness of information sharing technologies for law enforcement agencies: The making officer redeployment program effective*. Retrieved October 21, 2009, from www.cops.usdoj.gov/files/RIC/Publications/e08084156-IT.pdf

Manning, M. (2000, February). $150,000 dictation system lets police call in reports. *St. Louis Business Journal*, p. 14.

Rutledge, D. (2000). *The new police report manual* (2nd ed.). Cincinnati, OH: Copperhouse/Atomic Dog.

Simon, S. (2005). Reducing redundancy in report writing. *Law Enforcement Technology, 32*(4), 94–99.

Straus, J. (2008). *The blue book of grammar and punctuation* (9th ed.). San Francisco: Jossey-Bass.

Wallace, H., & Roberson, C. (2004). *Written & interpersonal communications*. Upper Saddle River, NJ: Pearson Prentice Hall.

Chapter 2

Fawcett, S. (2004). *Evergreen: A guide to writings with readings* (7th ed.). Boston: Houghton Mifflin.

Glenn, C., & Gray, L. (2007). *Hodges' Harbrace handbook* (17th ed.). Boston: Thomson Wadsworth.

Chapter 3

American Psychological Association. (2009). *Publication manual of the American Psychological Association* (6th ed.). Washington, DC: Author.

Berg, B. (2007). *Criminal investigation*. Boston: McGraw-Hill.

Glenn, C., & Gray, L. (2007). *Hodges' Harbrace handbook* (17th ed.). Boston: Thomson Wadsworth.

Chapter 4

Berg, B. (2008). Criminal investigation (3rd ed.). New York: McGraw-Hill.

Boyd, S., Melis, A., & Myers, R. (2004). Preparing for the challenges ahead: Practical applications of future research. *The FBI Law Enforcement Bulletin*, 73(1), 2–6.

California v. Trombetta, 467 U.S. 479 (1984).

Foster, R. (2004). *Police technology*. Upper Saddle River, NJ: Prentice Hall.

Palmiotto, M. (2004). *Criminal investigation* (3rd ed.). Lanham, MD: University Press of America.

Chapter 5

Bennett, W., & Hess, K. (2007). *Criminal investigation* (8th ed.). Boston: Thomson Wadsworth.

Biggs, M. (2008). *Just the facts: Investigative report writing* (3rd ed.). Upper Saddle River, NJ: Prentice Hall.

Frazee, B., & Davis, J. (2004). *Painless police report writing: An English guide for criminal justice* (3rd ed.). Upper Saddle River, NJ: Prentice Hall.

Glenn, C., & Gray, L. (2007). *Hodges' Harbrace handbook* (16th ed.). Boston: Thomson Wadsworth.

Chapter 6

Brady v. Maryland, 373 U.S. 83 (1963).

Hess, K., & Orthmann, C. (2009). *Criminal investigation* (9th ed.). Belmont, CA: Delmar Cengage Learning.

Ramirez, D., McDevitt, J., & Farrell, A. (2000). *A resource guide on racial profiling data collection systems: Promising practices and lessons learned*. Washington, DC: U.S. Department of Justice.

Terry v. Ohio, 392 U.S. 1 (1968).

Chapter 7

Brady v. Maryland, 373 U.S. 83 (1963).

Graham v. Connor, 490 U.S. 386 (1989).

Miranda v. Arizona, 384 U.S. 436 (1966).

Samaha, J. (2007). *Criminal procedure* (7th ed.). Belmont,
CA: Wadsworth.
Terry v. Ohio, 392 U.S. 1 (1968).

Chapter 8

California Penal Code, Section 1524.
Illinois v. Gates, 462 U.S. 213 (1985).
Katz v. United States, 389 U.S. 347 (1967).
Mapp v. Ohio, 367 U.S. 643 (1961).
Mincey v. Arizona, 437 U.S. 385 (1978).
Samaha, J. (2011). *Criminal law* (10th ed.). Belmont, CA: Wadsworth.

United States Constitution, amend. IV.
U.S. v. Leon, 468 U.S. 897 (1984).

Chapter 9

Bureau of Justice Statistics. (2010). *Deaths in custody reporting program, mortality in jails* 2000–2007. Retrieved September 27, 2010, from http://bjs.ojp.usdoj.gov/index
Guffey, J. (2005). *Report writing fundamentals for police and correctional officers*. Upper Saddle River, NJ: Pearson Prentice Hall.
Schmalleger F., & Smykla, J. (2011). *Corrections in the 21st century* (5th ed.). New York: McGraw-Hill.

A

Abbreviation   A shortened form of a word or phrase.

Abstract word   A word that could have multiple meanings.

Active voice   A style of writing that allows the reader to understand who did what to whom. When the subject of a sentence is in action (acts or performs some activity) the verb is in active voice.

Adjective   A word that modifies or describes a noun or pronoun.

Adverb   A word that modifies or changes a verb or an adjective.

Apostrophe   Form of punctuation used to mark omissions and possessives of nouns and pronouns.

Arrest report   Report specifically used to document facts and evidence to support probable cause when a suspect is arrested.

Automated field reporting system (AFRS)   Report writing system that allows officers in the field to input incident and crime data using computers.

C

Capitalization   Writing a word with its first letter as an uppercase and the remaining letters in lowercase.

Chain of custody   Establishing and documenting the possession of evidence from the point of seizure until the evidence is introduced at trial or final disposition

Chronology   The use of time sequences in a report narrative to document the order of occurrences in an event.

Civil damages   The amount a person or entity has to pay a person who is harmed and then sues the culpable party.

Cold crime scene   A crime scene where a crime has already occurred and no suspects are present.

Colon   Form of punctuation that signals that something will follow; part of the standard format in most memoranda in businesses and in most police and correctional agencies; can be used inside a sentence to join one complete sentence to another complete sentence; used to lead into a vertical list.

Comma   Form of punctuation used to set off separate elements within a sentence.

Computer-aided dispatch (CAD)   System that incorporates software that assists in managing and dispatching police calls for service.

Conclusory   Consisting of or relating to a conclusion or assertion for which no supporting evidence is offered.

Concrete word   A word that conveys a clear meaning.

Confidential informant (CI)   A person who often has been arrested and is asking for consideration in a pending case or is attempting to get paid for the information supplied to law enforcement agencies.

Conjunction   A word that links or conjoins other words in a sentence.

Conjunctive adverb   An adverb that joins independent clauses together to form a single sentence; sometimes referred to as a transitional word or phrase.

Contraband seizure report   The detection and interdiction of illegal substances or unauthorized contraband into the correctional facility must be documented in this written report.

Contraction   The shortening of a word, syllable, or word group by omission of internal letters.

Coordinating conjunction   A word that can be used to connect two independent clauses; for example, *for, and, nor, but, or, yet, so*.

Corpus delicti   The body or elements of the crime.

Correlative conjunctions   Pairs of conjunctions that appear in two places in a sentence; for example, *both/and, either/or, neither/nor, not only/also, not only/but also, and whether/or*.

Crime analysis unit   Unit within a law enforcement agency tasked with the analysis and reporting of information relating to crime trends and patterns.

D

Death investigation report   Deaths in correctional facilities are always significant events and require a complete and thorough investigation and documenting in this report.

Demonstrative pronoun   A pronoun that demonstrates or indicates a particular person or thing; for example, *this, that, these, those*.

Direct quote   When you write exactly what someone else has said or written; denoted with quotation marks.

Discharge of weapons report   Report used to document the discharge of weapons by correctional officers.

Disciplinary report   Report used to document the violation of institutional rules by inmates.

Division of records (DR)   Division of a police department responsible for maintaining the originals of police reports in a filing system.

E

Elements of the crime   The necessary components of a criminal statute that establish a violation of law and subject the perpetrator to criminal liability.

Ellipsis   A series of three periods at the end of a sentence, used to indicate an omission of quoted material.

Escape and attempted escape report   Report used to document an escape or attempted escape by an inmate or inmates of a correctional facility.

Excessive verbiage A style of writing that uses too many words; writing in a confusing or verbose manner.

Exculpatory Tending to show innocence.

F

Face page The first part of a crime report that identifies the incident type and the date, time, and location of the occurrence; also includes demographic information on the victim and witnesses.

Fair market value An estimate as to the actual value of an item.

Filing The formal filing of criminal charges against a defendant by a prosecutor.

Fire and fire alarm report Report used to document any fires or fire alarm activations in a correctional facility.

First-person writing A style of writing where the writer uses *I* to describe what he or she observed, did, or said and what was told to him or her by others.

G

Gender agreement Agreement in grammatical gender between words in the same construction.

Gender neutrality A style of writing that uses language that neither stereotypes either sex nor appears to be referring to only one sex when that is not the writer's intention.

General lockdown The securing of inmates in their cells or housing units throughout a correctional facility for security measures.

General warrant Warrant that allowed the king's officers to search a premises. No showing of probable cause was necessary.

H

Hero sheet A statement of the officer's experience that establishes the officer's identity, training, and experience.

Homonym A word that is identical in form with another word, either in sound (as a homophone) or in spelling (as a homograph), or in both, but differs from it in meaning.

Homophone A word that sounds like another word but has a different meaning and spelling.

Hot crime scene A crime scene where a crime is in progress or has just occurred and suspects may still be in the area.

I

Incident report Report used to document any significant event or occurrence in a correctional facility.

Incident/complaint report Standard report used by most police and correctional agencies to document the full range of criminal and administrative incidents that warrant the attention of police and correctional officers.

Indefinite pronoun A pronoun that replaces a noun without specifying which noun it replaces.

Indicia Things that tend to show a relationship.

Intelligence-led policing (ILP) A crime-fighting strategy that uses real-time crime information and analysis to detect crime trends and patterns.

Internet service provider (ISP) The company that provides Internet access services.

Interjection A word that begins a sentence indicating some sort of emotion.

Interrogative pronoun A pronoun used to ask a question or interrogate in the course of the sentence; for example, *who, whom, which, whose, what*.

Introductory paragraph A beginning paragraph used to orient the reader to the activities of the officer and how the officer arrived at the scene to begin his or her investigation.

Intuitive pen A device that captures data as the officer writes on any surface and then downloads the data into the computer via a docking station.

Italics A font style that can be used to emphasize the importance of a word or phrase, or for publication titles.

J

Jargon Specialized terms with specific meanings associated with a particular occupation or profession.

Judicial authority A judge will grant the police the power to conduct a search or make an arrest after probable cause is established. This authority is symbolized with an arrest or search warrant.

K

Knock and notice Requirements as to when and how officers must execute the service of search warrants.

L

Legalese A style of writing that uses legal-sounding or associated terms.

Local rules of the court Each court of law has rules regarding procedures in both civil and criminal proceedings. Courts are very strict in the application of these rules. Anyone who is presenting official documents in these courts should know the local rules.

Log books The official record of the daily actions of correctional officers in a correctional facility.

M

Major institutional problems Significant incidents in correctional facilities such as fires and fire alarms, contraband seizures, staff or inmate injuries, and deaths must be investigated and documented by correctional officers.

Memorandum A form of writing that is the primary method for administrative communication in the correctional facility.

Mobile data computer (MDC) A microcomputer, usually a laptop computer, that is installed in a patrol vehicle to allow for input and access to data and software.

Mobile data terminal (MDT)   "Dumb" terminals, with keyboards and screens, that allow officers to receive calls for service information and make queries from computers housed at a central headquarters.

Modus operandi (MO)   The method of operation used by a suspect to commit crimes.

N

Noun   A word used to name a person, animal, place, thing, or abstract idea.

Number agreement   A noun and the words that modify that noun must agree in number.

O

Objective narrative writing   A style of writing that prescribes that writers "let the facts speak for themselves" and avoid opinions or bias in their writing.

Objective reasonableness   The legal standard used to judge an officer's actions. Courts will consider whether a reasonable police officer in that position use that amount of force.

Owner-applied number (OAN)   A number applied to a piece of property by the victim, typically a social security number or driver's license number.

P

Paragraphing   A way of providing a framework for conveying information and ideas in writing.

Partial lockdown   A procedure used to secure inmates in their cells or housing units in a specific part of a correctional facility for security measures.

Passive voice   A style of writing used when the writer wants to emphasize the recipient of the action rather than the actor.

Pecuniary   Monetary payment.

Per se   A Latin term meaning "in itself." *Per se illegal* would mean that an act is illegal in itself.

Period   Form of punctuation used at the end of a complete sentence, or after an abbreviation; for example, *e.g., i.e., vs., etc.*

Personal digital assistant (PDA)   Small, portable computing device with the capability to input, access, and store data.

Personal pronoun   A pronoun that represents people or things; for example, *I, me, you, he, him, she, her, it, we, us, they, them.*

Plural possessive   An apostrophe should be used when showing possession by more than one person, or for nouns ending in *–s.*

Plural pronoun   A pronoun that is used in place of another pronoun that must also be plural.

Possessive pronoun   A pronoun that indicates possession or ownership; for example, *mine, yours, hers, his, theirs, ours, its.*

Preposition   A word that connects or links a noun and a pronoun to some other word in the sentence.

Primary collision factor   The actual cause of a traffic collision on a traffic collision report. Usually noted in terms of a state vehicle code section that has been violated by the party most at fault.

Private person's arrest   The right of a private person to make an arrest for a criminal offense.

Probable cause   Whether a reasonable person would believe that a person had committed the crime to be charged based on the facts and circumstances known to the officer at the time of the arrest.

Pronoun   A word that can be used to replace a noun or another pronoun.

Pronoun agreement   Pronouns are words that are used to take the place of, or to refer back to, a noun or some other pronoun. The pronoun used should agree with the noun it is being used to replace.

Punctuation   Symbols used to indicate the structure and organization of written language.

Q

Quotation marks   Form of punctuation that is used to set off and represent exact language (either spoken or written) that has come from somebody else.

R

Racial profiling   "[A]ny police-initiated action that relies on the race, ethnicity, or national origin rather than the behavior of an individual or information that leads the police to a particular individual who has been identified as being, or having been, engaged in criminal activity" (Ramirez et al., 2000).

Reasonable expectation of privacy   The legal standard to judge when a person can be free from government interference. An example would be the interior of a person's residence.

Recalcitrant   Stubborn or defiant resistance to authority.

Record-keeping system   System, process, or technology used to capture and maintain official records in criminal justice agencies.

Records management system (RMS)   Computer software and system used to automate the processes of data entry, storage, retrieval, and sharing of information about persons, vehicles, wanted persons, and other records.

Reflexive pronoun   A word that reflects or refers to someone or something else in a sentence in a possessive manner: for example, *myself, yourself, himself, herself, itself, ourselves, yourselves, themselves.* Also referred to as an intensive pronoun.

Relative pronoun   A word that relates one part of a sentence to another, or refers to some other element of the sentence; for example, *who, whom, which, that, whose.*

Report forms   A variety of report forms are used in correctional facilities to document significant events and the routine activities of correctional staff.

Report writing software   Computer software that allows officers to input information and narrative summaries into a standard template or format.

Retail value   The price that an item of merchandise is offered for sale.

Run-on sentence   A sentence that runs together two independent clauses without a conjunction or punctuation.

S

Scope   The extent or range; used to define the legal limits of a search. The scope of the emergency will limit the areas the police can search and the items they can seize.

Secondary crime broadcast   Basic information obtained from a witness that establishes what crime has occurred to assist officers in locating possible suspects.

Semicolon   Form of punctuation that separates independent clauses when they are *not* joined by a comma and a coordinating conjunction.

Sentence fragment   An incomplete sentence. To be complete, a sentence must contain a subject and a verb, and convey a complete idea.

Singular possessive   An apostrophe can be used to show possession or ownership.

Singular pronoun   A pronoun that is used in place of another indefinite pronoun.

Staff or inmate injuries report   Any injury to staff or inmates is a significant event in a correctional facility and should be documented in this report for liability and training purposes.

Statement from a witness   The written or verbal account of what a witness saw or heard.

Subject identification   It is important to properly identify the subject in a sentence. This makes the writing clearer and easier to understand.

Subordinating conjunction   A word used to join a subordinating clause with a main clause.

Supplemental crime broadcast   A radio broadcast that tells officers involved in an incident whether or not a crime has occurred, suspect and vehicle descriptions, and other valuable information that may have been unavailable when dispatch or call takers talked to the reporting person.

Supplemental report   Report used to document individual observations and actions separately or to add additional information to a complaint or arrest report.

Suppression   The remedy for evidence that is illegally seized by the police before it can be used in court by the government in a prosecution.

T

Telephonic warrant   A search warrant that is issued by a judge after hearing the affidavit over the telephone.

Third-person narrative   A style of writing that uses proper names (nouns) or uses pronouns such as *he, she*, and I when referring to people in the narrative.

Topic sentence   A sentence that states the main idea of the paragraph.

U

Uniform Crime Report (UCR)   An annual report maintained by the FBI that is a compilation of nationwide crime statistics containing information on reported losses and range of property and persons' crimes.

Use of force report   Report used to document the use of force by correctional officers.

V

Verb   A word that asserts something about the subject of the sentence and expresses an action, event, or state of being.

Verb tense   The use of verb constructions to describe past, present, and future time frames when writing.

W

Warrant arrest   An order from a judge that certifies probable cause exists to make an arrest and commands any officer to do so.

Warrantless arrest   An arrest made based on probable cause that does not require an arrest warrant or that was committed in the view of a law enforcement officer.